ENCOUNTERS

ENCOUNTERS

Extraordinary Accounts of
Angelic Intervention and What the Bible Actually
Says about God's Messengers

ALLIE ANDERSON-HENSON
& DONNA HOWELL

DEFENDER

CRANE, MO

ENCOUNTERS: Extraordinary Accounts of Angelic Intervention and What the Bible Actually Says about God's Messengers
By Allie Anderson-Henson and Donna Howell

Defender Publishing Crane, MO 65633 ©2019

ISBN: 9781948014281
A CIP catalog record of this book is available from the Library of Congress.

Cover design by Jeffrey Mardis.

Unless otherwise noted, all Scripture from KJV

We would like to thank Jesus Christ, our Lord and Savior, without whom nothing would be possible. We would like to thank Tom and Nita Horn, Joe and Katherine Horn, and all the wonderful people at Defender Publishing/Skywatch TV for their love and support.

To James, my wonderful husband,
and to my children, Joe E and Althia.
—Donna Howell

To Randy, John, Karol, Gwyneth, Kat, Reagan, and Ian.
—Allie Anderson-Henson

CONTENTS

1

True Stories of Angelic Intervention

*I*magine you're driving alone on a deserted road, late at night. There is nobody else traveling along this quiet trafficway, there are no streetlights, and you're miles from the nearest town when a tire blows out and your vehicle begins to veer erratically. Is the car *completely* out of control, or is it only out of *your control*?

Picture yourself homeless, destitute, alone. You've exhausted the last of your resources, and the hunger pains tearing through your abdomen serve only as a reminder of the desperation and hopelessness yielded by life's failures. You're at the end of your means—then a mysterious visitor materializes, seemingly from out of nowhere, and offers precisely what you need as if he could read your mind. As you turn to thank him, he's gone. Was another *person* ever really there?

Envision around you, day and night, a valiant, thriving battle between good and evil raging within a shrouded jurisdiction. This army surrounds you each step you take, intervenes on your behalf, and wages spiritual warfare when the human soul is at stake.

These beings are the narrow escape when you *think* you have a situation under control.

They are the delay causing you to sidestep danger.

They are the invisible door that slams shut, barricading the malevolence that follows closely behind.

They are the silent guardians, keeping watch, even when you *think* you're alone.

They are strong, decisive, fearsome, and mission-minded, and these militant entities stand continually at the ready, awaiting command from the Almighty God.

They are angels, and following are the stories of God-ordained, miraculous intervention.

Bruce Van Natta

(As told to the author)

Thursday, November 16, 2006, began like any ordinary day for Bruce Van Natta, a married father of four small children who was active in his local Christian church. Despite the morning chill over the Lakes area of Wisconsin, Bruce left his house early and drove to work in the utility vehicle that housed his diesel repair tools. The job he would be finishing that day was rectifying a coolant leak on a Peterbilt logging truck, a project he had started earlier in the week. He had already disassembled the engine and done most of the work; all that remained was reassembling the parts and reinstalling the engine.

Little did Bruce know that before this day would end, he would face off with the grave, make a life-or-death decision, and experience magnificent, supernatural, angelic intervention.

Once at work, Bruce located some parts that had been delivered and spent the majority of the day working with another mechanic to wrap up the project. All went smoothly, and soon the only thing left to do was run a test to make sure the issue was resolved before he would be free to leave. His coworker would then finish some other fixes that the

Peterbilt was undergoing. Checking the time just after 6 p.m., Bruce happily made a note to himself that, at this rate, he'd be home for dinner.

Bruce started the engine to make sure the problem had been fixed. While he waited for the engine to reach the proper temperature, he began to pack up his tools, until the mechanic he had been working with asked one last favor: Would Bruce try to pinpoint the source of an oil drip that had been puzzling him for some time? Bruce agreed, and his coworker pointed out a vague area near the front, bottom vicinity of the grill. To get a better look, Bruce would need to slide beneath the vehicle on a creeper—a flat, gurney-type platform on wheels. Because Bruce's own heavy-duty steel one was already packed away with his other tools, he quickly borrowed the assistant's plastic creeper and rolled himself into position on his back.

This Peterbilt was of a conventional style, sometimes known as a "long-nose" body type, with a hood and fenders and a tall, forward-facing chrome bumper. From beneath, the front axle was the part of the vehicle that was lowest to the ground, carrying between five and six tons of weight without a load, as it was now. To make that side of the engine more accessible and to get the hoist underneath, the front, passenger-side wheel had been removed and a round bottle jack had been placed to support the weight of the vehicle on this side. No further safety equipment had been put into place.

As Bruce began to assess the underside of the motor, he asked the assistant mechanic to climb inside the rig and read the temperature gauge on the dashboard. At this time, the front axle was stationed over Bruce's abdomen. As his coworker proceeded to enter the cab in order to read the needle on the dash, the weight of the truck shifted, momentarily releasing the downward pressure that had been holding the bottle jack in place. The lift device's angle budged, but the vehicle returned to its original position. At this, the change in weight placement caused the tool to fly from its location, which allowed the Peterbilt to drop to the concrete floor, crushing Bruce's torso beneath more than five tons of blunt metal.

"Lord, help me!" Bruce called out. His diaphragm had been shoved up into his chest, instantly restricting his breath to short intakes, and he began coughing up blood.

He pressed against the truck in an attempt to lift it off his body, but to no avail. Again, he pleaded, "Lord, help me!"

Looking down, Bruce could see that the gap between the lowest point of the steel and the ground was about an inch on the left side and about two on the right, so he quickly realized that his midsection had been crushed to those dimensions. Likewise, he was aware that the metal was approximately six inches thick, thus his injury filled a similar span across his body, comprising the entire area between his ribs and the top of his pelvic bone.

(In a later interview, Bruce reflected that, despite the severity of the injury, the shape of the damage was so defined that it reminded him of cartoons he had seen as a child, wherein the shape of the indention in an injury was exaggerated for the sake of comedy. For example, when Wiley Coyote, the misfortunate villain in the vintage *Road Runner* cartoons, was hit by a train, his body literally folded into the shape of the track. On a more serious note, Bruce also recalled that he surely would have been cut in half had he used his own steel-reinforced creeper instead of borrowing his coworker's plastic one, which had crumbled beneath Bruce on impact.)

Immediately in a panic, the assistant mechanic called 911. He didn't know how to get the vehicle up and off of Bruce because the area beneath it was far too narrow for any hoist to be inserted. In desperation, the man collected the jack that had flown from its previous position and placed it below the leaf spring of the front passenger side. Bruce tried to ask the assistant not to do that, for fear that the flexibility of the suspension system would cause the device to fly from its position a second time, this time, with fatal consequences. The subordinate, however, was determined to get the load off of Bruce and proceeded, despite argument. Soon, the Peterbilt was up and off of Bruce's body, hovering just above the wounded man. (Bruce later learned that the initial impact had severed major arteries in five places, and while the metal was still on top of him, it had blocked those injuries, minimizing the bleeding.) Once the pressure was lifted off Bruce's body, the blood was allowed to flow freely onto the garage floor.

Still worried that the rig would fall on him a second time, Bruce begged the assistant mechanic to get him out from beneath the truck, but by now, the flatness of his body was apparent to the comrade, and the man refused to move him. By now, both were convinced that Bruce's spine, as well as his internal organs, must have been damaged. The coworker refused to take any action for fear of causing further injury. In desperation, Bruce reached above his head, gripping the bumper of the Peterbilt (much as a gymnast performing a chin-up would reach for the bar with an upward motion), and pulled himself toward it. This shifted his body enough that his head was now protruding from beneath the front grill. Although Bruce wanted to move himself farther, the effort took all of his strength; he simply couldn't do it. At this point, the effect of the blood loss began to kick in, causing his lucidity to fade. Succumbing to the sleepiness closing in, Bruce's eyelids grew increasingly heavy and finally shut.

At that moment, Bruce felt himself somehow eject from his body and hover above it, near the ceiling of the garage. He looked down on the scene, strangely distant from the happenings, even unaware that *he* was that the one who lay there, dying. It was as though he were watching strangers.

All the man felt was perfect peace: no sorrow, no regret, and none of the physical pain that his broken body below had been subjected to. The colors in the scene below were more richly intense and vibrant than human eyes ever see in the physical realm. He observed as one man (himself) lay broken, bleeding on the ground, while the other knelt nearby, repeating apologetic phrases to the lifeless body as he cried and cradled the man's head. The wounded one didn't respond, but remained silently still, eyes shut.

Suddenly, a panoramic observation widened for Bruce, as if a camera lens had zoomed out. As his view broadened, Bruce noticed two more beings in the picture. But these weren't human, as the first ones Bruce had seen. Each was stationed on either side of the incapacitated man. It was immediately apparent that they were separate but identical. Light emanated from them; golden, ringlet-curled hair flowed from their heads, cascading down their backs to about their waistline. Thick, woven fabric—armor-like, seemingly made of intertwined rope—covered their masculine bodies in what could only be described as shining, white robes. Each wore a golden belt cinched tightly, exposing the bulging shape of his muscular build. Although identifiable as angels, they didn't have wings, as many images depict. The assistant mechanic maintained his position at the victim's head, apologizing for the accident. The beings' height, even from their kneeling position, reached at least two feet beyond that of Bruce's coworker. (Bruce later estimated that, were the heavenly creatures standing rather than kneeling, they would be about eight feet tall.) The figures were distinctive to look at, and piercing illumination was perceptible throughout their bodies, although they weren't transparent.

Their hands were placed beneath the truck on the injured man's abdomen, upon either side of his injury. From his position above, Bruce could see only the angels' backs as they looked down, intent on the man on the floor. They remained very still, with somber, statuesque focus. They did not speak to one another, nor did they look up to interact with Bruce as he lingered overhead, watching.

From his viewpoint, Bruce could see emergency personnel beginning to arrive. Paramedics entered through the front door and to bustle about the garage, talking busily with each other and gesturing toward the incapacitated man. The angels were undistracted by the activity around them. Despite the panicked bustle, not one person stepped through or over either of the angels at any point. It was as though the responders worked around the heavenly creatures without even realizing it.

The last two of the ten or so medics to arrive came in through a different door (Bruce's knowledge of this fact later became one of many elements that confirmed his out-of-body experience to skeptics). He could see that one of them, a young woman, had long, flowing, vibrant-red hair. By this time, the first responders had stopped life-saving attempts, because CPR would only have pushed more blood from his body. The redheaded woman walked up to the man on the floor and kneeled beside him, oblivious to the fact that she had positioned herself directly between two massive angels. Hesitating only briefly, she began to pat the cheek of the man, commanding him to open his eyes. Despite his lack of a pulse, his ashen skin, and his blue lips, she ordered him to wake up. The spiritual visitors remained undistracted. The injured man lay unresponsive. The persistent woman began to ask the other people in the room for the victim's name. When a fellow responder answered her question, she tapped the man's face again.

"Bruce Van Natta, open your eyes!" the woman instructed more than once. Each time he didn't react, she repeated the words, her voice escalating.

From his vantage point, Bruce couldn't understand why, but the command within the woman's voice gripped his attention. Suddenly, he felt a momentum sweep him from his position, forcefully pulling him downward and back into his body. Despite the fact that no CPR or other life-saving measures were being administered, the woman's words had carried the authority to usher him back. Instantly, Bruce found himself stretched out below the redhead, looking up at her. She continued slapping his cheek and telling him to open his eyes.

The physical pain that suddenly enveloped Bruce was indescribable. Only now was he aware that *he himself* was the man beneath the truck. With this realization, Bruce remembered what he had seen moments before from above. Quickly, he glanced around to see if the angels were still at their posts on either side of him. He couldn't see them.

He closed his eyes, and when he did, the peaceful painlessness returned. As this bliss surrounded him, he felt himself leave his body again, this time floating past the ceiling of the garage and into a sort of vacuum-forced tunnel filled with light. He felt himself moving farther away from his body more rapidly with each passing instant, and he somehow knew that heaven was at the other end of this indescribable pathway. But each time he began to succumb to the momentum's draw, he heard the words: "Bruce Van Natta, open your eyes!"

Each time the woman gave that order, he obeyed. And each time he did, the horrible, searing pain of his dying, crushed body returned.

A battle began to rage inside Bruce's mind. It was as though he could hear two voices arguing for his fate. One was gruff and negative, encouraging him to give up and die—after all, he would go to heaven, so what reason was there to remain here on earth, anyway? Yet something in Bruce's discernment told him that this advice came from someone with a malevolent agenda. The second expression was quiet and firm, offering Bruce a choice. Bruce knew that in order to live, he would have to return to his body and endure unspeakable physical pain. He was aware that if he chose to remain in this life, the road ahead of him would be a rough one.

The voice that gave Bruce the decision told him, "If you want to live, you're going to have to fight, and it will be a hard fight."

Why fight? The pain was excruciating. It would be so much easier to drift off into this vortex filled with light, into eternal bliss and peace...

As the argument continued in Bruce's mind, he kept drifting in and out of his body. He would open his eyes briefly, only to close them again, unable to withstand the agony. Then he would withdraw, floating upward toward the light again.

Suddenly, something occurred that pulled Bruce out of the volley that he had been engaged in. The redhead's words shifted and echoed the quieter voice he had heard in his thoughts. She ordered him to switch into a full-on combat mode. Bruce recognized the authority of these words and knew that God was speaking through her.

"Do you have a wife?" the woman demanded of the injured man.

"Do you have kids? What do you have in this world to fight for?" This was the first time that elements of Bruce's earthly life had crossed his mind since the accident. The suggestion of his responsibilities turned Bruce's mind to his obligations.

The answer was yes. He *did* have something to fight for!

Bruce had a wife and four young children who needed him. Up to this point, he hadn't recalled a factor compelling enough to motivate him to return to his body and undergo the unbearable hurt. Thinking about his family changed everything.

Bruce returned to his body and chose to stay there, regardless of the agony.

By the time he was taken by a life-flight helicopter to one of the most prominent trauma centers in the area, more than two hours had passed since the accident. During this time, Bruce found it essential to keep his eyes open. He didn't know how many more times he would be able to reopen them, should he allow them to close. For Bruce, the key to staying here on earth was his stubborn refusal to shut them again.

His strategy became finding something to focus his vision on in each new setting he was moved to. In the helicopter, he stared at the vent on the back of a responder's helmet. Medics continued to ask for his name and birthdate; he knew the answers, but since he was unable to speak, he remained silent, his sight fixated on that vent.

Later, at the hospital, one of the doctors became the focus of Bruce's vision. Too weak by now to move his head around, he followed the man with his eyes as he moved about, bustling among the nurses and other medical personnel. At one point, Bruce noticed the doctor was in a heated discussion with another physician. (When Bruce later asked what it was about, he was informed that a CT scan had provided no technical explanation for how Bruce was even alive. The anomalous results appeared like that of a "dead person," while his "heart was pounding as if…running a marathon."[1] The men had been exchanging opposing opinions about how Bruce survived.)

By any medical explanation, his severed arteries and veins *should have* caused him to bleed out within three to five minutes. Bruce had been given eighteen units of blood, but his wrecked body was unable to retain it. Finally, as he lay on the CT scanning equipment watching this exchange between the doctors, darkness closed in, and his ability to will his eyes open faded.

Summoning the last of his strength, Bruce finally spoke: "If you don't do something to help me, I'm going to die!"

Bruce's blood pressure, which had miraculously maintained life-sustaining levels up to this point, quickly plummeted to 0. Immediately, medical personnel moved him in preparation for emergency surgery. The doctors abandoned their discussion and engaged in arranging the operation.

Bruce later identified this moment as a turning point. Everything grew darker, but he somehow knew that the medical intervention that was about to take place would be effective. As the pre-anesthetic mask descended toward his face, he finally allowed his exhausted eyes to close. He believes this is the moment when the angels departed and God dispatched them elsewhere.

While Bruce was in the operating room that night, the doctor informed Bruce's wife that it was doubtful that he would live through the night because the injuries were just too extensive. Family, along with friends from church, gathered in the waiting room, and this group of prayer warriors decided that they would praise God for every thirty minutes Bruce remained alive. Over the following hours, these individuals, twice per hour, would join hands and form a circle, exalting and praising God for another half-hour of life.

Bruce surprised the doctors by surviving the night. The next morning, he was placed in an induced coma to allow his body time to heal from his extended injuries, particularly the major arteries that had been severed. (A later study by the University of Southern California on the mortality rate versus number of arteries severed indicates that Bruce not only should have bled to death within minutes of impact, but that he is also the only known survivor of injuries of this magnitude.) He is convinced that the prayers of his wife and fellow believers are what carried him through those first, difficult months following his accident. But, little did he know, there were more miracles to be seen in the upcoming future...

Four months after his accident, a segment of Bruce's small intestine that doctors had attempted to save began to die. Most adults have somewhere near twenty feet of this organ, while Bruce's remaining one hundred centimeters or so had been salvaged from several pieces patched together by surgeons. Because his small intestine still wasn't functioning properly, he was fed intravenously. Unfortunately, the human body isn't designed to take in nutrients this way for the long term. Bruce's pre-accident weight of 180 pounds dropped by more than one-third, and he was approaching danger of starvation. The doctor estimated that at this rate, the interceptive feeding would likely only keep Bruce alive for a year to eighteen months.

Upon receiving this news, Bruce lay in his hospital bed, prayerfully pondering this development. His solitude was interrupted by a visitor who, having met Bruce Van Natta in person only one time before, reintroduced himself as Bruce Carlson.

But Bruce Van Natta remembered Carlson immediately from another encounter...

About a year earlier, long before the life-changing incident with the Peterbilt logging truck, Van Natta had awakened during the night with a strange dream—one he immediately recognized as some sort of message from God. In this vision, he and a man he had never seen before were sitting together, eating sweetbread. When he awoke, Van Natta prayed for wisdom regarding the meaning of the dream. The only answer he received was that he needed to discuss it with the former pastor of his church, Ryan Clark. He had done so, but Clark was equally baffled. Two weeks after the reverie, Van Natta had traveled to visit his former pastor in person, and had also attended church with him, where he had been introduced to Bruce Carlson, the man who had shared the sweetbread in Van Natta's dream! At that time, Van Natta had talked Carlson about these strange events, but neither could make sense of its significance.

Yet, one year after the prophetic revelation and four months after Van Natta's terrible accident, Carlson stood in the dying man's hospital room. Carlson revealed that earlier in the same week, God had awakened him abruptly at 5 a.m., instructing him to fly to Wisconsin to pray for Bruce, who had been on the prayer chain at Carlson's church. The man had initially looked up the price of a plane ticket, which proved to be more than $900—more money than he believed he needed to spend at this time. So, shrugging off the incident as simply strange, he went about his business. The next morning, the same thing happened: God prompted him early in the morning with the same compulsion. This time, God added to the instruction: If Carlson would obey, God would perform a creative miracle.

Obediently, Bruce Carlson purchased the expensive airfare, expecting God to do great things.

Carlson began to pray for healing for the patient, specifying that his own plea was merely added to the countless others already being raised by many other saints. Carlson placed his right hand on Van Natta's forehead and petitioned with authority unlike any Van Natta had ever heard spoken in supplication.

"Small intestine, I command you to supernaturally grow in length right now, in the name of Jesus!" Carlson ordered.

At once, Van Natta's forehead began to burn as though electricity were coming from the man's hand, and a surging feeling spread throughout his entire body until it found its destination: the lower abdomen. Immediately, Van Natta felt a sensation in the afflicted region that he would later describe as feeling like "something cylindrical moving around inside of my stomach."[2]

Although doctors couldn't understand it (a response Van Natta was becoming accustomed to by now), Bruce was miraculously bestowed with what doctors estimate to be nine to eleven feet of small intestine. The medically salvaged, dying piece of this organ had grown nearly four times its previous, postsurgical length.

Bruce was able to eat again and soon began regaining weight. In an effort to obtain more insight, doctors conducted additional CT scans, X-rays, and an upper gastrointestinal series. The only knowledge these tests yielded was that Bruce Van Natta had experienced a miraculous healing that could not be explained by science.

Over the course of the year following his accident, Bruce spent much of his time in the hospital. He underwent myriad surgeries, transfusions, and other procedures. Experts have said that he *should* have bled out and died three to five minutes after the truck was lifted from his body, and early speculation was that he would never again walk without assistance. Other injuries that Bruce sustained included broken ribs, fractured vertebrae, and damage to his pancreas, stomach, and spleen. He was told that he would be on prescription pain patches and monthly medication shots for the rest of his life, and that he would have intestinal troubles forever. But what a mighty God we serve: Bruce is thankful to report that, other than the occasional stomach upset, he has made a full recovery!

Bruce later learned that in some Middle Eastern cultures, sweetbread is made of the cooked intestines and pancreas of a lamb. He felt that his dream of eating sweetbread with Bruce Carlson was prophetic, because after sharing the delicacy in his dream, the two later shared the miracle of healing.

Bruce Van Natta resides in Wisconsin with his wife, Lori, and their four children. He is a published author and speaker and the founder and president of Sweet Bread Ministries.

Bruce believes that angelic intervention happens around us much more often than we realize. Because we don't see these beings, we often take their protection and involvement for granted.

A final thought that Bruce leaves us with is this: God gives us all both the prerogative and the power to choose what we will do with our existence. "The Holy Spirit said *if I wanted to live, then I was going to have to fight....* In the same way He still gives people freewill choices today. We get to choose if we are going to believe in Him or not as our Lord and Savior...[and] if we are going to be warriors and fight the fight of faith or not."[3]

Mary Alawa

(As told to the author)

On February 28–29, 2012, a tempest erupted across several regions of the US, during which twisters tore through the Tri-Lakes, Missouri, area, wreaking destruction across Stone and Taney counties. A storm of this magnitude had never before hit the Branson area and hasn't since. This was only one of many regions ravaged by EF2–EF4-level cyclones during the storm that became known as the Leap Day Tornado Outbreak.

Recently widowed Mary Alawa had moved into her home near Branson several months earlier. It was a small, site-built house that she was renting with the intention to purchase. With the move, she had inherited the majority of the previous owner's abandoned belongings and was given authority by the new owner to dispose of the items as she saw fit. After months of storing them, Mary decided to have a garage sale.

It was a beautiful, balmy, February day. The temperature was in the mid-70s, the sky was clear, and—despite the early calendar date—spring seemed to be in the air. Mary had the articles priced and set up in the garage, and she planned to hold the event the following day. By evening, moving the heavy furniture and large objects had taken its toll on her back, so she stopped working.

She went inside the house to lie down on the couch with a heating pad. Aware of the thunderstorms predicted for the late evening, she thought nothing of it; that wasn't an unusual forecast for the area during the early spring.

Exhausted from her long day, she fell asleep almost immediately and snoozed soundly until around 1:15 a.m., when a strange static coming across the television set woke her. Through her large living-room window, Mary saw that the sky had turned to a strange shade of green.

The appearance of the atmosphere seemed ominous to Mary, but before she had time to process this thought, her cell phone rang in a back bedroom, where she had plugged the phone into its charger before her nap.

"Who in the world is calling me at 1:15 in the morning?" she thought, walking to her bedroom to answer the call. The caller turned out to be a young man who lived down the street attempting to warn Mary that she needed to take cover: A tornado was on its way. Immediately, the ominous, greenish glow Mary had noticed in the firmament moments earlier made sense.

A severe storm was about to strike.

Mary, still cradling her small phone between her left shoulder and her left ear, quickly stepped into the hallway, her mind racing to figure out where to take shelter.

What happened next was completely undeniable to Mary: She felt the distinct impression of a hand placed across the top of her shoulder, fingers toward the front of her body and thumb toward the back. Powerfully, the hand pressed downward, moving her to a crouching position on the floor directly beside the frame of her bathroom door, and it held her in place. The wind howled loudly, as though a freight train were driving through the building. Mary could no longer make out the words of the man on the phone, but she kept the device to her ear regardless. Everything around her began to shake and volley forcefully, and she was compelled to hold on to the doorframe beside her to keep from being thrown about.

"It's hitting me now! Lord Jesus, help me!" Mary called out, unsure whether it was furious wind or the actual tornado that had hit her home. She only knew that at this moment she was smack in the middle of a disastrous storm—with no opportunity of taking shelter. Mary clung to the doorframe with all her strength. Still wedging the small phone between her left shoulder and her left ear, Mary could hear static and fragmented sounds coming through the instrument, but could neither decipher nor reply to them. She later found out that her neighbor had heard her declaration that the tornado had hit her, and he had immediately headed her direction, rallying help. The house tossed and jostled, threatening to send Mary flying. Using all her strength, she prayerfully maintained her crouched position on the floor. A large, wooden-block calendar hanging on the wall above her was thrown from its place, bombarding Mary's head and shoulders.

Suddenly, the storm was over. Mary observed that the sky was an impermeable shade of black. Finally dropping the phone, which had long since died, Mary crawled down the hallway in total darkness. When she reached the living room, her eyes began to adjust to the lack of lighting. She discovered that as furniture had shifted during the tempest, it had piled across the wall where her front door was located, barricading her inside the house. Behind the shifted fixtures, she could see that her solid oak door had been ripped open by the storm and was hanging loosely from the outside frame of the home. In the kitchen, the refrigerator had slid from its station, smacking the wall opposite where it normally sat. The freezer had likewise been relocated, and its door had opened, spilling food into the room. Pulling herself up by a nearby recliner, she made her way through the labyrinth of strewn items and peered outside through the open entrance.

At first glance, Mary thought the storm had ripped the porch off of her house, but she soon realized that the very opposite had happened: It had torn the *house* off of the *porch*, and had thrown the structure thirty feet from its foundation!

The neighbor who had called to warn Mary of the tornado quickly arrived, offering help. Although she was shaken and sore from the jostling she had suffered while hanging on to the bathroom doorframe, Mary was able to move. With some help and encouragement from the young man, she made the four-foot jump out of her now-porchless house to the muddy ground below. Paramedics arrived on the scene and checked her medical condition; although her back was injured, she had received no life-threatening injuries and her condition was stable.

"I'm so glad you're alive!" the young man said.

"Of course I am," Mary replied incredulously, initially wondering why her neighbor would say something so dramatic. As she began to look around, however, the ruthlessness of the situation began to dawn on her. An enormous sycamore tree had fallen sideways on the ground, its massive root system torn loose from the earth and exposed. The same was true of a century-old oak that had previously stood proudly in the backyard. The garage that had been attached to the house was collapsed and in ruin. Windows were broken all across the home. The back of the structure was crushed, and the furnace and laundry appliances had been tossed outside in the mud. Power lines were down all around her, and the water pipe that was once connected to Mary's kitchen sink protruded from the ground, broken and spewing in geyser form. Mentally assessing the damage, Mary began to understand why those who witnessed the event had been worried that she may have been killed.

Additional emergency personnel began to arrive in greater numbers to evaluate the destruction. Upon seeing the house, each newcomer asked if everybody was alive. Other neighbors appeared from out of their homes to check on Mary's well-being. She recalls sitting on the giant sycamore, spanning the now-barricaded road, while she called the owner of the home to report what had happened.

Mary has no doubt that it had been an angel who pushed her to the floor and kept her safe during the tornado. In addition to God's protective intervention for her own well-being, Mary's cat—dear to her heart because it was a pet that had been brought out of her late husband's hospice days—was found alive in a kitchen cabinet.

Once they heard the news, Mary's friends showed up and insisted that she stay with them for the time being. Before the remnants of the home were demolished, Mary was allowed to reenter the scene to consider whether any of her belongings could be salvaged. She recovered her late husband's ashes, a few items of clothing, and some trinkets. What delighted her most on that day, however, was what she considers to be another miracle: When the building had shifted, the area rug had lifted and her sentimental photographs had slid perfectly into place beneath it. When she found the photos, they were dry and undamaged, safely tucked under the shield of the heavy carpet material.

The only window on the house that didn't break during the storm was one over which she had hung the small cross that had been kept near her husband during his time in hospice just before his death. Mary reflects on how God showed His love to her through this trying period of time as she remembers loved ones and complete strangers who helped her recover from the loss—both financially *and* materially. Through this catastrophic event, Mary maintains that God's protection is the reason that she remained safe, and that He used this experience to show her that He cares for her.

Mike Kerr

(As told to the author)

It was a rainy day, six years before the Lord spoke to Mike Kerr, giving him the distinct message: "Gather my people," thus inspiring the conferences ministry Hear the Watchmen. Up to that point, Mike had been a successful commercial real estate developer, and had worked on Wall Street, enjoying the money, property, prestige, and status that came with unrestrained financial success. He had even dated Hollywood movie stars and famous musicians. But in a fateful accident, Mike sustained injuries that caused him to become addicted to pain medications. After a time, he was unable to continue to obtain the prescriptions his body had come to need in order to function. So, soon, street drugs and alcohol became the substitutes necessary to manage the suffering. In what Mike describes as a period that was "seemingly overnight," he lost everything and found himself down and out on the streets of Los Angeles.

After about a year of living homeless in Southern California, Mike recalls a particular night when he had wandered for hours looking for a place to sleep. Exhausted, he roamed into the alcove of a Korean church. He slept for some of the night, and when he woke up in the small hours of the morning, he discovered that someone had stolen the shoes and socks off of his feet. Overcome by the blow of this loss and feeling as though he had hit a new, all-time low, Mike walked barefoot as far as he could on the streets of LA. He searched for something that might help him out of his impoverished state, but was unsure of exactly what that "something" could even be. Rain fell, adding a balmy element to what was already becoming a hot day. Now a vagrant, he looked down to realize that he had walked for so many hours that his feet were bleeding from the long, bare interlude with the concrete.

Weary, he sat down on the sidewalk, seeking relief for his sore and bloodied feet. As he watched the sunrise, he realized that he had inadvertently seated himself across from Union Station in LA, right next to a restaurant called Phillipe's. Ironically, this very restaurant was the place where Mike's father had taken him for meals when he was young. Memories of his teen years came flooding back. He recalled the days when his dad had worked in the downtown Los Angeles area and the two of them would meet at this very establishment for lunch in the middle of his father's busy workday. And now, he sat outside the place—homeless, barefoot, cold, hungry, and bleeding—face to face with memories of what used to be in the cold reality of what now was. The wind shifted, and a terrible, pungent smell hit Mike's nostrils. He looked around for the source of the odor, when sadly he realized that he, himself, was causing the offensive stench. Tears gathered at the corners of his eyes, but as quickly as they came, he blinked them back. The streets are a tough place, and Mike knew that there was no room for weakness or vulnerability, lest he open himself up to attack or exploitation.

—*Not to mention,* Mike thought, *I still have my pride.*

Mike had been raised in and out of church. It wasn't unusual for his family to attend worship services, but church selection criteria for the family was often based more upon appearance than on scriptural standards. A church's denomination or stance on foundational biblical issues was less important than the size of the church or availability of flashy youth programs. Thus, Mike was familiar with the concept that there was a God, but he hadn't yet personally and wholeheartedly devoted his life to Him.

Over the course of his past year on the streets, Mike had, several times, stood on freeway bridges, peering over the edge, trying to muster the courage to jump. On other occasions, he had sat by the train tracks waiting for a commuter and vowing that the next one that approached would be the one he would finally have the nerve to leap in front of at the last possible moment, leaving the vehicle no time to slow down before hitting him. Unsure of what had stopped him from following through with those self-destructive plans, Mike now sat staring at the harsh reality of his present life while gazing at Phillipe's, with its taunting, happy childhood memories. It seemed to Mike that, although he hadn't yet followed through with any plan of suicide, his life was still, in fact, over.

As he pondered, Mike recalled stories he had heard in church about God. He reminisced, remembering Sunday school teachers' and youth pastors' claims about God's love and kindness—and he even remembered the "salvation plan."

If God was up there, Mike decided, it was time for Him to act.

"God, either kill me or save me!" Mike cried out. It wasn't a flippant request. This petition for God to do one or the other of these extremes came from the innermost place in his being.

As it would happen in some people's testimonies, we might expect this to be the moment when a bright light shines through a cloud, beaming a ray of hope down onto Mike. Or perhaps, we might anticipate this to be the instant when an audible voice comes from the heavens, confirming love and destiny to him. Neither of these scenarios happened for Mike. He recounts feeling nothing change, seeing no rays of light, and hearing no audible voices. In fact, he simply remembers sitting there alone, with no modification to his situation of any kind.

Before long, a young man wearing khaki pants and a T-shirt approached Mike, holding in his hands a pair of sandals. He had long, medium-blond hair and a beard. He smiled kindly as he spoke.

"You know," the man said, offering the shoes to Mike, "I have no idea why I put these in my car today. I normally wouldn't have them with me, but you look like you need these more than I do."

Mike received the sandals gratefully, quickly putting them on his feet. But when he looked up to thank the man, but the stranger was gone. Mike's eyes darted up and down the street to see where his benefactor had gone, but he found no trace. Mike tried to stand, hoping to walk a bit to see if he could spot the man from a distance, but it had been so long since he had eaten that he was weak and it was difficult to stand. Resigned to his position, he sat, thankfully gazing at his sandals.

After about another fifteen minutes passed, a second gentleman approached. He had a manner similar to Mike's father: businesslike, well-groomed, and dressed in a suit. However, the stranger's bold, nearly harsh demeanor caught the homeless man off-guard. Mike later described the visitor's words as feeling like a "knife in the heart."

"I don't ever give money to bums like you," the stranger said, offering Mike a ten-dollar bill. The man acted as though his actions were as surprising to himself as they were to Mike. "For some reason I'm giving you this ten dollars. And I have also been told that this money will change your life."

Wordlessly, Mike accepted the currency, briefly turning it over in his fingers and staring at it with awe. He looked up to thank the man, and saw that he, like his earlier guest, had completely vanished.

Glancing up and down the street, Mike continued to try to spot the man somewhere on the sidewalk, perhaps walking away, but just as it had been with the guy who had given him the sandals, he could not locate him.

Overcoming his shock at the transaction, Mike's mind began to shift into the next process: what to do with his newly acquired cash. Mike was keenly aware that there was a liquor store just down the street. He also knew that street drugs were available all around him. Unlike this morning, there were now shoes on his aching feet. If he could muster the strength to get to the source of one of these quick fixes, he could buy himself a few hours of reprieve from the pain his life had become.

But the words that the man had spoken when he handed the bill to Mike lingered, burning deep within his soul. On top of this, somehow, the ultimatum he had presented to God earlier that day remained on his mind. There was something about the way the stern fellow's severe words seared, daring Mike to prove to the man, *or to himself*, that he was more, that *he could be more*, than the "bum" the business man had seen when he looked at Mike.

Mike had told God, just a short time earlier, to either kill him or save him. Now, he realized, God had put the ball back in his court. Somehow, Mike knew this was his last chance.

With no plan on his mind, Mike found the strength to cross the street to Union Station and there he sat on a bench, uncertain whether he should purchase a bus ticket with this precious newfound resource. The words he had spoken that morning to God repeatedly drilled his mind.

God, either kill me or save me… Either kill me or save me…

Somehow, he couldn't write off the visitation of the two mysterious men as coincidence. He knew their intervention had to be a turning point in his life. Mike also knew that he had to get out of downtown, where the temptation of drugs and booze would eventually overtake him, devouring his ten-dollar bill and leaving him lifeless. With this knowledge guiding him, Mike purchased a ticket, boarded the bus, and sat down, glad to be out of the muggy heat of the day. He was certain that he looked and smelled as awful as he felt, and confirmation came in the form of every passenger's unwillingness to sit near him. Mike remained in his seat, watching as other people boarded, then disembarked. Uncertain of where he was going, he rode the bus to the very end of its route, where he got off and began to walk aimlessly down the street.

Immediately ahead of him was a large building that had once been a grocery store with a tavern directly adjoined to its side. These two establishments had long since closed down, but the conjoined building had subsequently been converted to a transition ministry that operated—free of charge—a shelter for homeless people. This ministry, in addition to providing shelter and food for people in need, also offered services such as vocational training, addiction rehabilitation, case management, group therapy and individual counseling, and even employment assistance to help destitute individuals leave their impoverished lives behind once and for all and secure a brighter future.

Mike walked into the building and found himself standing in front of an old desk in a very small office. A musty smell permeated the room, and the disrepair reflected the need for a good handyman. A single vending machine stood in the corner, and an older woman with a cigarette in her hand stood at the door.

Mike regarded the woman, stating with candor, "I don't know why I'm here, but I am supposed to be here, and I need help." The woman returned his even gaze, and in what seemed to Mike to be a moment of providence, said, "We have been waiting for you."

The night before, Mike's shoes and socks had been stolen off his body while he slept on the streets of downtown Los Angeles. That was the last night he spent on the streets. Mike believes, without doubt, that the two men who had given him sandals and money had been angels in human form sent by God to answer to his desperate petition: *God, either kill me or save me.* The following months were filled with life-changing intervention provided by those involved in this ministry. Mike's life was redirected, rededicated to the Lord, and eventually set on a track for ministry.

In a later chapter of Mike's life, he returned to the area of downtown LA where he had received the two gifts. He inquired everywhere he could think of, describing the men and trying to locate them. He ran ads in local papers asking for anybody with information about either man to respond. He even spent a considerable amount of time driving around the area in hopes of spotting one of them. But the matter of not finding them was never any surprise to Mike. He knew all along that they were not of this earth.

An Encounter Later in Life

In 2016, Mike Kerr was riding his four-wheeler near his home tucked away in the mountains of Idaho. While tracking bear far into the mountains at seven thousand-foot elevation to photograph them, Mike had another, very different, experience with an angelic being.

It was a sunny, clear day. The weather was cool and breezy, and rumors of an early winter were circulating. Mike peered through his binoculars, spotting a bear about a mile away. Following a game trail (the path forged by deer during their migrating season), Mike persisted on his four-wheeler in pursuit of the animal. As the track curved near the edge of the mountain, he began to notice that it was becoming increasingly narrow, no wider than the deer had left it during their last voyage for this time of year.

Miles from civilization, he was aware that he was on a route probably never traveled by human beings—certainly not with any consistency. Having been, up to now, absorbed in getting closer to the bear, Mike now realized that he had managed to drive his four-wheeler down a trail that wasn't wide enough to facilitate such a vehicle, and one that was certainly too steep and too narrow to turn around on. To his right was a vertical incline that reached toward the mountain's peak, and on the left side was an abrupt cliff that overlooked an embankment where the remnants of a dry creek could be seen. Realizing that he was in a precarious situation, he decided to back the four-wheeler out of the area and give up the pursuit.

As he began reversing the ATV up the trail, he edged along the side of the mountain, intending to turn around once the track was wide enough. He kept watching sharply to his left to ensure that he wouldn't come too close to the edge of the drop-off. Preoccupied with this view, he didn't see the large rock to the right side of the trail until he hit it with his rear, right tire, which threw the rig's center of balance to the left. The ATV tilted toward the steep decline, and he could see that it was about to roll down the embankment, taking him with it and possibly crushing him. He tried to catch his balance and somehow eject himself, but the shifting momentum—coupled with his heavy backpack—prevented him from gaining control of his direction. Mike was unable to recover his balance enough to jump to safety.

Just as the ATV began to flip and roll down the precipice, Mike felt the distinct sensation of a strong hand grabbing him and pulling him from his ride. He landed on the ground nearby and then trundled about a hundred yards, miraculously sustaining only one injury: a broken toe. He watched from that position as his four-wheeler continued to soar through the air, losing parts as it flew so high that it literally cleared the tops of small pine trees, then bounced with a crash, making its brutal, tumultuous descent down the edge of the mountain, and finally landing with a thud some five hundred yards below the game trail he had driven on. When he recovered enough from his shock to decide what to do next, Mike realized he was too far away from home to try to walk. He removed his phone from his backpack and called a friend to come and pick him up.

The next day, Mike and his pal went back to retrieve what was left of the smashed ATV. It took the two men nine hours and some skillful chainsaw maneuvering to get to the place where the vehicle had finally landed. Both were struck with the realization that if it hadn't been for the hand that pulled Mike off of the vehicle, he would likely be dead. Even if he had survived, beyond the severity of the wounds that Mike surely would have sustained, no one would have known where to look for him if his injuries had rendered him unable to retrieve his phone and call for help. They slowly and carefully recovered the four-wheeler, despite its damaged condition and flattened tires, then loaded it onto the flatbed trailer they had brought with them and returned home.

As Mike and his comrade were driving from the retrieval of the wreckage, a season-long snowfall began, launching the harshest winter the area had seen in nearly thirty years. Had Mike still been up on that lonely mountain trail, incapacitated and awaiting help, he surely would have frozen to death.

Mike has no doubt that all three of these encounters were heavenly beings who intervened in his life at the most critical moments. "Angels show up at the time you least expect them to, but when you most need them to," Mike says. "That's when God will send them. How God sends them to you is *never* up to you. They can appear in the form of a person, or simply a force like the one that pulled me off of that vehicle."

Dorothy Spaulding

(As told to the author)
One day recently, I (Allie) was at lunch with Dorothy Spaulding, presi-

dent and founder of Watchmen Broadcasting. She and her husband, Russell, spent eight years walking across America, carrying a wooden cross and preaching the gospel. During this period, the couple relied on God for everything they needed, and Dorothy has many miraculous stories of His love, protection, and providence. During our time together that day, when she learned that I was working on a book about angels, she readily shared the following two stories with me.

One day, years ago, after a long week of ministering in Florida, I ended up riding on a public transportation bus. It was late at night and I was exhausted, and had planned to sleep the entire trip.

Many of the other travelers taking this bus were of different ethnicity than myself and did not speak English. The vehicle began to maneuver down Interstate Highway 10 headed east, and after a bit, the driver spoke to me.

"You'd better talk to me and keep me awake tonight, I'm really tired," came his conversational tone.

What an opportunity to witness! I took my Bible out of my bag and began to read aloud to him. This went on for some time—I'm not exactly certain how much time passed—before I fell asleep while reading to him. During my slumber, I saw myself in a vision: I was in a wheelchair due to a bus accident. Promptly, I woke up and prayed.

"In the name of Jesus, not one person on this bus will be hurt tonight. God, I ask that you would send your angels to watch over us," I prayed. I remained awake as long as I could, but soon sleep closed in again.

The next thing I knew, I woke up to the feeling of being jarred about. I looked around to realize that the bus driver had fallen asleep behind the wheel. The vehicle had drifted into the median of the highway, away from the eastbound lanes it had previously been traveling, and was now colliding with the decorative trees planted in the center divider. Impact with the small trees had awakened everybody on board. All riders panicked, as we would soon be headed into oncoming traffic!

Immediately wide awake, I sat up and shouted, "No, in the name of Jesus, no! Not one person on this bus will be harmed in the name of Jesus!" I began repeatedly restating the prayer I had spoken earlier that night. Others on the bus began to pray in their native tongues as well. While I didn't understand every word being spoken, I did recognize the Spanish pronunciation for *Jesus*, which was shouted by many around me.

In the twinkling of an eye, the bus was lifted from the center lane, placed on the far right shoulder of the road, and stopped.

"What just happened?!" the bus driver asked, shaking his head in disbelief. Quickly, the man pulled the vehicle over to the right shoulder. He got out to assess the damage done by the impact of all of the trees that had been hit. When he reboarded, his disbelief had escalated. Despite the fact that everyone had been a witness to the collision with multiple trees, it was announced that there was not one scratch on the bus.

The man made eye contact with me and said: "I'm so glad you were on this trip tonight."

On a separate occasion, I had been ministering down in New Orleans. I had borrowed a car from my friend who lived in Baton Rouge, and was on my way back to her house to return her vehicle. She had warned me that when the gas gauge reached the "E," there was very little grace period before it would be rendered immobilized. It was late at night, and I noticed the needle sinking closer to the "E," yet I was on a stretch of highway where stations were scarce at that time. As I began the trek across the eighteen-mile bridge that travels the interstate between Baton Rouge and Lafayette, the light alerting the need for more fuel came on, heightening my anxiety about the situation. I began to pray for God's help.

"Lord, please expand this gas. Please help me find a place to get more, and please keep me safe, in Jesus' name."

As I continued on, I saw an exit, but God prompted me to drive past it. I obeyed, despite the plummeting pointer on the dash. I approached another turn-off, but received the same warning, so I obediently passed it as well.

On the next off-ramp, I felt God directing me to pull off the highway. I took the junction, and parked on a small embankment beside the road, where several pickups were parked. I walked down to where the obvious owners of the vehicles were visiting near the water. I called down to them, asking if anyone had any fuel.

In response, a large, burly man approached me, and said he could help. I walked back to my car, which was conveniently near his truck. Retrieving a gas can and a large piece of cardboard from his rig, the man carried these items to my car and sat the container on the ground. He then pulled a very large knife off of his belt and used it to cut the cardboard into a triangle, which he then folded into a makeshift funnel, and used the device to fill the tank of my vehicle.

A bit startled by the knife, I began talking about Jesus. Every moment that he was pouring gas into the tank of that borrowed car, I was pouring as much of the gospel into his life as I could.

"Do you know Jesus?" I would ask. "Do you know that He loves you? That He cares for you?" The man didn't seem interested in talking about religion, so I continued on without a reply, preaching the gospel and the love of Jesus as he dispensed from the metal vessel.

As he finished his task, I gave him a five-dollar bill and thanked him. He told me to get into the car and make sure it would start. As I climbed into the driver's seat, he stunned me by sliding his hand up my dress.

I pulled away. Fear raced through my mind as I recalled the knife I knew he was carrying, instantly aware that he could easily kill me and throw both my body and the borrowed vehicle into the river nearby.

"I mean to have you, lady," he said in a gruff voice, attempting a second time to secure a grip on my thigh. My reaction was instinctive.

"No, in Jesus' name!" I yelled at him, kicking my legs away from his grasp.

Surprised, the man stepped back, but then approached a second time, once again placing his hands inside my skirt. Scrambling to escape, I shouted, "No, you cannot touch me, I'm a preacher! Let me go, in the name of Jesus!"

That moment, the man suddenly recoiled: He was instantly, supernaturally transported to the middle of the street nearby, frozen in place as if he were a statue. He stood there looking at me, seemingly unable to move. Astonished, I knew he was being held in place by an angel, although the force was invisible. I felt the Lord's firm urging, telling me to quickly circle the car around until it faced the road, and drive away. I hastily did this, and the man remained immobile, held by his unseen captor. I turned the car out onto the highway, watching his motionless frame fade in the rearview mirror's reflection as I made my escape.

The next morning, when I walked out of my friend's house and approached her car, there was a five-dollar bill laying across the seat, as if it were waiting for me.

Psalms 91:14–15 tells us that God delivers us in times of trouble because we know His name. If you call out to Jesus in your time of trouble, He will deliver you because He's a God that cannot lie. We are God's children and He loves us. He gives His angels charge over us, but it is our job to speak words of life over our circumstance. I have experienced God's providence and protection and I know that He takes care of me. In times of trouble, I have called out to God, and He has delivered me, just the way He will deliver you if you ask in His name.

Brian Duvall

(As told to the author)

Brian Duvall, a husband, father, and professional entertainer in Branson, Missouri, was in a reflective stage of life when he heard the song "Steal My Show" by Toby Mac. In 1996, Brian had cofounded and drummed for Johnny Q Public, a Christian band that toured and even performed with DC Talk, so the song performed by Toby Mac (former DC Talk band member and Christian vocal performer) not only stirred personal memories, but also inspired Brian to strive for a higher place with God. With the song's lyrics, Mac releases everything to God, telling Him to remove anything that stands in the way of His will and ultimate acclaim within his own life—hence the title. The piece so profoundly affected Brian that on this particular morning, his prayer became that God would move anything in his life necessary to ensure that his sincere, wholehearted devotion was sold out to God, first and foremost.

At the time, Brian was working as a professional drummer and operated a lawn-mowing service on the side. On this day, he had three yards to get done before his performance that evening. He dropped his daughter off at school, driving his pickup truck that carried his Scag Turf Tiger Zero Turn riding mower, then proceeded to the location of his first job. It was a property newly added to his workload by a previously established client. While Brian didn't know the street address, he had driven to the location before, so had no trouble finding it. As he arrived, he pulled into the driveway, which was situated on an uphill incline. Using trailer ramps placed at the distance between the mower's tires, he unloaded the machine and cut the grass. Nobody was home in the house on the property, and the job went quickly and without hindrance.

When he finished, he prepared to load the equipment back onto the truck bed. On this particular zero turn, a safety bar on each side pulls down toward the driver's thigh. To operate the vehicle, these bars must be pulled down over the lap, and in order for the driver to stand up, they must be lifted away. This feature engages and disengages the mower's ability to be used to keep it from being left unattended while the motor is running. Another feature of this model is that the engine rests on a plate behind the seat, causing the bulk of the weight to center on this one location. This plate is at the midpoint of the back of the rig, positioned at the middle of the wheelbase behind the operator. Because the incline of the driveway was steep to begin with, the added slope of the trailer ramps as Brian was reloading the mower caused the machine to become back heavy, and the equipment had no roll bar in place (a roll bar is a safety feature that would have stopped backward momentum and kept it from flipping, should the back end become unstable due to imbalance of weight). Adding to the steepness was the gap between the ramps; there was nothing to act as a blockade, should the mower roll backward. The uneven distribution of the mower's heaviness caused it to swing backward.

When this happened, the mower fell and landed upside down on Brian, pinning him to the ground on his middle and upper back, which emitted a loud, cracking sound. The zero turn was now inverted on top of Brian—the machine was still running and leaking warm gas all over him. While Brian's upper body was crunched forward under the weight of the load—his back abruptly folded at the point where the mower's seat made contact with the ground—his lower body was still trapped in the seated-rider position, due to the safety lap bars.

"Jesus, don't let me be alone!" Brian cried out.

At that moment, the glowing figure of what Brian instantly recognized as an angel appeared in his peripheral vision. He couldn't look directly at the being, but he could see the light emanating from its form. The ministering, nurturing presence brought immediate comfort, and it began to instruct him, telling him to remain calm.

Brian was convinced that his back was bleeding due to the sensation of warm liquid spilling across it, which he didn't learn until later was the leaking gasoline. Under normal circumstances, a safety feature in the seat would have caused the motor to shut off if the driver were to eject. However, this accident happened so quickly that Brian's weight wasn't displaced long enough to activate the safeguard.

Brian's mind raced.

The pain was excruciating, and the vibration of the vehicle, still running, was exacerbating the agony. Brian attempted to catch his breath, trying to think of what he should do next.

"We need to shut your motor off," directed a calm voice beside him. Feeling for the keys on the vehicle, Brian obeyed.

"We need to call your wife," the voice spoke again.

Brian's left arm was pinned against the mower and his phone was in his left pocket. Instinctively attempting to reach for the device only to realize this side was immobilized, a wave of panic washed over him.

"You need to use your other hand," the serene voice stated.

Brian reached for the correct pocket with his right hand, and the contents freely slid out onto the ground. Able to hit the icon that activated a voice call, Brian said, "Call my wife."

Unfortunately, his wife was picking up their youngest daughter from preschool and didn't receive the call. He tried again, with the same result. Brian recalls that as he lay beneath the machine, dialing his phone, the sky was a more intense blue than he had ever seen before, with the white of the clouds a beautiful and radiant white. He describes the experience as more than looking up at a stunning, vivid firmament; rather, it was like being somehow closer to the colors than a person can imagine. The atmosphere seemed more than three dimensional, and the clarity was breathtaking.

"We need to call someone else," the tranquil voice coached again.

"Call 911," Brian spoke into the receiver.

Below is a condensed segment of the transcript of Brian's call to Taney County 911:

911 operator: 911 dispatch, what is your emergency?

Brian: My lawnmower flipped over on me. I think I broke my back. (Brian attempts to tell his location).

911 operator: Okay…can you give me that… You said, first house on the left?

Brian: First house on the left.

911 operator: And the phone number you're calling me from, is that a cell phone?

Brian: That's my cell phone, no one is at the residence.

911 operator: Okay, and the lawnmower fell on top of you?

Brian: I'm sorry?

911 operator: You said the lawnmower fell on top of you?

Brian: Yes.

911 operator: Were you on top of it?

Brian: Yes.

911 operator: How old are you?

Brian: I'm 43.

911 operator: And this just happened?

Brian: Yes.

911 operator: Is there any serious bleeding?

Brian: I can't tell.

911 operator: Okay. We do have paramedics on the way. Do not move unless it's absolutely necessary, okay? I just need for you to be still, and not to move, okay?

Brian: I understand. Can you call my wife?

911 operator: Uh, yes, I can…just let me get a few more things for you. Is the lawnmower still on top of you?

Brian: Yeah. I shut it off, but it's still on top of me.

911 operator: Okay. And you don't know what the, uh…

Brian: I don't know what my injuries are, my legs are tingling.

911 operator: Okay, but you don't know what the house number is, correct? [A voice comes through dispatch radio in the background and confirms location with 911 dispatch operator.]

911 operator: You still there, sir?

Brian: Yes.

911 operator: We do have the ambulance and paramedics on the way, okay?

Brian: Yes, sir.

911 operator: Okay, again, do not move unless it is absolutely necessary, and if anything changes, I need you to call me back for further instructions, okay?

Brian: Yes, sir.

[The dispatch operator asks Brian for his wife's name and phone number.]

911 operator: Okay, is it okay if I give her [Brian's medical] information?

Brian: Yes.

911 operator: Okay, I will give her a call and let her know that you are being transported to a hospital, okay?

Brian: Thank you.

911 operator: Okay. Do you need me to stay on the phone with you until they get there?

Brian: I've got someone here with me.

911 operator: You've got somebody with you?

Brian: No, I'm by myself but…

911 operator: You should start hearing sirens any minute.

Throughout the phone call, Brian can be heard calling out to Jesus, asking for a divine touch to his body. Because this happened at a rural address, his position on the driveway was difficult for the first responders to see until they rounded a corner. Likewise, Brian couldn't see the ambulance, even after hearing it approach, until it arrived at his location—however, the radiant being remained beside him the entire time. When emergency personnel arrived, they didn't see or interact with the angel, but, as in Bruce Van Natta's story, they seemed to work around the entity without realizing it. Their first action was to begin by lifting the mower off of Brian's body. But, again, the angel advised him on what to do.

"We need to tell them to stop," the voice instructed calmly, "because you are pinned to the mower by the lap bars. If they pick this mower up and throw it, they will throw you with it."

So Brian told the medics that they needed to wait. When they asked Brian what they should try to do next, he was unsure, but the angel gave further instruction.

"They need to lift the machine up three feet, move the lap bars, and then carefully slide you out."

Brian relayed that instruction, which the emergency workers did not question; they simply did exactly as he directed. When he was free from the machine, the paramedics removed the gasoline-soaked clothing from his body and began checking vital signs and assessing his injuries before placing him on a stretcher and preparing for transport to a nearby hospital.

Once in the ambulance, Brian detected motion from the light-emanating angel who had remained by his side throughout the incident.

It was as though the being was passing near his head, and, for a brief moment, the light became blinding, then exited through the window of the truck. The angel spoke to Brian one last time: "You'll be fine."

Then, a paramedic reapproached Brian. "You're going to be all right," he encouraged.

"I know," Brian responded. "My angel just told me so."

The man surprised Brian by smiling. "Well, I've heard that before," He said. "And if that's the case, you *will* be!"

Interestingly, Brian's wife, after picking up their preschooler some distance away, saw that she had missed a call from him just before she heard an ambulance's siren. She knew something had happened. At the same time, her phone rang; Taney County emergency responders were calling to let her know that they had her husband en route to the hospital. She immediately headed that way and met the ambulance when it arrived at the emergency room. Brian's beloved was by his side, despite his inability to reach her by phone.

Inside the hospital, an exam indicated that he needed to be moved to another medical facility, where he underwent extensive surgery on his back. He received a bone graft to the crushed vertebrae and suffered ongoing, extensive swelling to the nerves in his spinal cord. After some time in intensive care, he was moved to a physical therapy facility. One evening, while he lay in his bed channel-surfing, he lingered on a Christian network program featuring a pianist playing southern gospel. The music was soothing and reminded him of the way his dad used to play. He listened as he drifted off to sleep.

During the night, with the TV still on, something awoke Brian. Without his glasses, he couldn't *see* who was speaking, but he remembers hearing a minister say, "If you're lying there broken, you're right where God wants you. Now he can move you, and He can use you to do different things. You can't build a house without breaking a tree into lumber. You can't plant a garden without breaking the ground. You can't make wine without smashing some grapes. So, if you're lying there broken, you're right where God wants you. Allow Him to mold and make you into what He wants you to be."

In that moment, Brian realized that God had answered his prayer on the day of the accident—He had been moving Brian into a place where God would *truly* be the top priority within his life. What God was working on all along was *him*. Brian confesses that he had made a habit of using the daily circumstances in his life as excuses not to step forward into what he was being called to do. Brian understood what God was saying to him: "Put Me in charge of everything. I will use you, if you will step into My complete will for your life."

While Brian doesn't believe that God *caused* his accident, he believes that God *allowed* it for the sake of bringing him closer to God Himself. Ultimately, Brian knows that when he cried out for Jesus not to leave him alone, God heard his prayer and answered it by sending the heavenly being to comfort and help him. The more Brian's body healed, the more he dedicated his all to God's service. He started volunteering at his church and soon was serving as a youth pastor there. The accident drove Brian's life into an entirely new direction of ministry.

Brian knows that it was an angel who helped him that day. The temperature on the date of the accident had soared to well over ninety degrees, and nobody had been at home at the rural property. Without intervention, Brian is certain that he would have remained pinned, his upper back folded in half under the seventeen-hundred-pound mower for many hours until one of the residents had arrived home later that evening. Aside from the intense and prolonged suffering he would have been forced to endure, the complications of his medical injuries would have surely been much worse, possibly even fatal combined with heat exposure and dehydration.

Doctors initially estimated that Brian had less than a 10 percent chance of walking again. His digestive system, due to the injuries sustained that day, stopped functioning properly. He developed a rare form of diabetes that occurs as a result of his nerves sending incorrect messages to his pancreas. His career as a drummer—his livelihood—appeared to be over. However, six years later, he continues to improve. He walks normally, plays the drums, and despite the fact that he still has no feeling in certain parts of his feet and legs, he has been seeing a Christian doctor who offers the encouragement that Brian's healing is imminent. Ironically, while most parts of his feet still suffer residual numbness and are irresponsive, the parts that operate normally are the ones necessary for working the foot pedals on his drum set.

"If you have a relationship with God," Brain says, "if you really love Jesus, then the way to profess your love for Him is by refusing to allow other things to take the place of what He has called you to do for Him. If God calls you to do something, don't allow anything to stop you from that thing you think God is telling you to do."

An Unexpected Friendship

After being off for six months after his accident, Brian returned to work during the spring of the following year, when his daughter and her fiancé came to watch him play drums. As Brian interacted with his daughter and future son-in-law during the show, a man sitting near the young couple commented jovially, "You must know each other."

His daughter told the man that the drummer was her father, and she let him know about her dad's recent accident and miraculous recovery. After the show, she introduced the gentleman to her dad—a divine appointment that initiated a friendship that will last their lifetime. Brian told the man that a heavenly being had been beside him, helping and protecting him. Strangely, Brian couldn't have guessed that the man, who introduced himself as Dick Lacey, would respond by telling him that he, too, had a story of angelic intervention...

Dick Lacey

(As told to author)

On May 31, 2013, sixty-six-year-old Dick Lacy had gone to help a friend replace the deck on his home. This structure hovered a dozen feet above the concrete ground. Unbeknownst to Dick, some of the supporting boards below the deck had been cut with a chainsaw in preparation for the lumber replacement. Before he could be warned about the stability of the now unsupported area, Dick stepped out onto the deck, it gave way beneath him, and he fell twelve feet to the pavement below.

Although he was positioned to land head first, an invisible force shifted him forward at the neck just before impact so that his shoulders took the brunt of the fall. He never saw the angel who "caught" him, but he has no question that the power that repositioned his body just before landing was angelic. As he lay on the ground below the disassembled deck, he turned his head to his right in attempt to see who was there, sitting beside him. Surely this must be the person who had protected him. But he saw no one, nor did he hear anything supernatural. The only evidence of his heavenly visitor's presence was the supernatural peace that washed over him as he attempted to wiggle his toes...

They moved.

Thank you, Jesus!

Next, he tried his fingers, which also moved.

Thank you, Jesus!

Despite the indescribable pain of broken shoulder blades and collarbone, punctured lung, three cracked discs, and multiple broken ribs, with each body part that responded in movement to his neural command, he praised and thanked Jesus for safety through the fall that doctors would later tell him should have paralyzed or even killed him.

Dick spent the next five days in intensive care and the next ten weeks in recovery. He credits an angel that he neither saw nor heard for protecting his head during that horrific fall, and he praises the Lord for keeping him from being paralyzed. In addition, Dick is thankful for a wonderful, loving, and compassionate wife who nurtured him selflessly once he was taken home. Without her amazing, kindhearted support, he surely would have spent months in a facility completing his recovery.

Dick is now seventy-one years old, and, although he lives with pain that he has to manage on a daily basis, he gives glory to God for the fact that his multiple injuries have stabilized after what doctors later told him should have been a fatal or at least crippling event. Further, two years after the fall, he survived cancer, which he also praises the Lord for.

Jimmy Jones

On April 27, 2011, United Parcel Service (UPS) employee Jimmy Jones was driving his delivery truck during what the National Weather Service confirmed as the "largest tornado outbreak in US history,"[4] wherein twenty-one states from Texas to New York were buffeted by 358 twisters over four days. When Jimmy saw the cyclone touch down, his first thought was to find an underpass for shelter, knowing that a mere ditch would never provide enough protection from what he later learned was an F4 tornado.

Jimmy quickly pulled his vehicle onto the shoulder under a nearby bridge and hurriedly climbed the steep, concrete walls to the crevice beneath the ninety-degree angle of the passageway. Furious wind slapped Jimmy's face and hurled debris at him as he frantically made the climb, all the while calling out to God for help and safety. Upon reaching the top, Jimmy saw a man calmly sitting on a blanket within the gap. Jimmy ran to the man, shouting, "Sir, we've got to take cover, there's a tornado!"[5] The man's only response was to stand up, stare at him, and say,

"Is that right?"[6] What resonated to Jimmy was the tranquil demeanor of the stranger; he didn't seem shaken at all.

Jimmy wedged himself as best as he could into the crack below the overpass, clinging to a small piece of exposed rebar protruding from the structure. The storm outside raged with such fury that items were thrown about, hitting Jimmy in the back something he later described as feeling as though he were being stabbed with an ice pick. After some time, the feel of the wind behind him shifted, and a vacuum force threatened to pull Jimmy out of his shelter. Holding as tightly as he could to his small, blunt anchor, Jimmy fought against the draw sucking him into the tempest. After what felt like an eternity, at last, the storm subsided. Finally releasing the rebar he had clung to for life, Jimmy turned and saw that the man was still nearby, sitting placidly on his blanket. As Jimmy faced him, the stranger peacefully stood up. Soon, emergency responders were scrambling on the highway below, rescuing the injured from vehicles that had been thrown about. Jimmy saw that his truck had been torn up, and multiple automobiles had been tossed and totaled. Paramedics were taking inventory of passengers and assessing fatalities.

When he saw emergency responders attempting to locate the driver of his UPS truck—now a mangled mass of metal—Jimmy quickly descended the steep wall of the underpass, emerging to let them know that he was safe by shouting, "Here I am, I'm up here with this fella!"[7] However, as he turned to gesture toward his companion during the storm, the man was gone, as was his blanket. The area was littered with debris and twisted metal, so much so that the only way for anyone to have left their shared hiding place would have been to descend alongside Jimmy. But instead of the man coming from the sheltered area by foot, as Jimmy did, he was merely gone without a trace.

Mystified, Jimmy quickly began to ask the people around him about the mysterious figure, but no one had seen anybody other than Jimmy materialize from the structure. Some responders speculated that perhaps the man had been drawn out into the tornado. But Jimmy had distinctly seen him stand up *after* the wind had died down.

Jimmy believes that this stranger had been an angel sent by God to soothe Jimmy with supernatural peace during this storm and to keep him safe. "God is and has been wonderful to me," Jimmy said. "He's a loving God, He's a caring God, He's my Lord and Savior. Here [on earth] we need to be doing things for Him, because when it's all said and done…nothing else is gonna matter."[8]

Tom Horn

Angelic beings engage daily in spiritual warfare, although much of it occurs without our even having knowledge of it. When I (Allie) was six years old, my dad pastored a church in an area heavily afflicted with occult activity. This region had been one of the earliest along the West Coast to host a large Satanic church. The building had since been purchased and burned down by a minister, but nonetheless, the residual occult activity remained. On many occasions, my dad responded to requests for help from people who were dealing with spiritual attack, often after dabbling in some kind of dark activity such as utilizing ouija boards or other occult paraphernalia.

One morning, our church service ended in the usual style after an altar call and a couple of songs. As the congregants prepared to go home, many of the church members' children were running playfully through the parking lot when a commotion in the corner of the lot caught our attention. I approached to see what the matter was, since my dad was seemingly at the center of the occurrence and voices were escalating. At that point, my mother grabbed me by the arm and took me into the house next door, which was the parsonage where we lived at the time. She sat my three-year-old brother on the living room floor beside me and moved toward the front door to step outside. I could see through the window that my mom stood right outside the house with the two of us children safely inside, and the ensuing commotion unfolding was only yards in front of her. With one hand on the doorknob, the other reaching for the sky in prayer, my mom began interceding for the situation developing in the parking lot.

I couldn't understand at the time the full implications of what was happening, but later in my life, the details were filled in for me. My dad has since written this story in his first book, *Spiritual Warfare: The Invisible Invasion,* and is abridged as follows:[9]

As I walked out of the front door of the church, the friendly chatter and usual handshaking was suddenly interrupted by a strange, young woman who seemed to come from out of nowhere [in the church parking lot] and began motioning for my attention…she ran up to me waving her hands muttering something about her boyfriend…. Suddenly, the young girl stopped and pointed toward an unknown vehicle sitting in the parking lot. She said, "He told me to turn in here and park." Unaware of the circumstances, and surrounded by dozens of believers [who were beginning to watch the scene as it unfolded]… I approached the automobile. As I did…I surprised myself by whispering, "Lord the battle is yours." I wasn't sure why I had said it, but somewhere deep down in my spirit, I knew that I had been prompted to do so.

I could see a mat of tangled hair as the young man sat hunched over in the passenger seat of the convertible. Consciously, I walked up and tapped on his shoulder, intending to ask how I could be of help. I didn't get the chance. Without warning, his head jerked upward to expose a wild and beastlike snarl…. "Man of God, I'm gonna kill you!" With that, the possessed young man jumped out of the vehicle and moved toward me, shouting, "You're gonna die! I'm gonna kill you, man of God!"

…A strange calm began to sweep over me, unlike anything I had experienced previously. "Lord, the battle is yours," is what I had whispered.… In an instant my thoughts were clearer than they had been earlier. I had more composure and was more certain of the power of the gospel than the circumstances should have allowed.… Later, it was evident to me that Christ with me, and Christ within me, had been in control of the entire situation.

As mature believers gathered around and began to pray, the next thing that happened was to become for most of us the single most supernatural event we had ever seen. Before I could move, the young man started toward me in a full run. Like some kind of ferocious animal, his eyes glaring and his teeth snarling, he leapt at me like a lion after its prey. But, he ran into something. It's hard to explain [and yet every time I have heard him tell this story, he has always described it as indubitable angelic intervention, as the man was lifted into the air and thrown backward several feet by an invisible force]. To the human eye there was nothing there. Yet something, invisible but very real, had moved into position between me and the young man… and had stopped his motion so completely that he propelled backward with a look of astonishment on his face. Falling to the ground, he began convulsing and thrashing wildly about. A moment later, he jumped to his feet again. This time he stood straight up, looking at me with piercing and unholy eyes. To this day I can still remember those hollow eyes, black as night. They were filled with such glaring hatred that it became immediately apparent that this was a conflict between supernatural forces—a battle for the status of a human soul.

The Saints bowed to their knees around the young man, not in fear, but in awe of what they had just seen. The young man stood frozen, his jaws gritting together so hard that I could hear his teeth cracking. His eyes rolled back into their sockets, and his body began to twist and contort. It reminded me of the special effects used in making the film, *The Exorcist*. His arms turned backwards; his legs, his fingers, his neck and his head, began to twist with the grinding sound. His body writhed and trembled as blood ran out of his mouth and out of his nose. It was just as if large invisible hands had taken hold of his body and were trying to tear them apart.

Again he fell to the ground. This time with help from others, we took the opportunity to grab him in an attempt to keep him calm. Since it was already evident that he could not injure any one of us, our concern was to keep him from doing any additional harm to himself. The problem was that he had the strength of several men. I watched as burly loggers joined their arms and weight together in an attempt to hold him down. Each time they were about to gain control, a snear would cross his lips and he would lift them off the ground. He grabbed a large, three–inch wide occult medallion that was hanging around his neck, pulling it with such force that he broke the thick metal chain. He shoved the medallion and the chain into his mouth, and was trying to swallow them both, but someone caught the chain and quickly pulled it out.

His hands beat and plucked at his head uncontrollably, tearing his face and eyes. I thought to myself, Jesus, do something, or this kid is going to die! I was reminded of the young demoniac in the ninth chapter of Mark.... In the Gospels there are several accounts of demonic possessions where the spirits, upon being exorcised, attempted to destroy their hosts. Suddenly it was clear.... A young man, possessed by evil, wanted deliverance.... We found out later that the girl had driven the car, while the possessed boy sat slouched down on the seat, giving directions without looking up at the road.

It seems the young man had decided that morning to give

up his occult activity and convert to Christianity. That's when it happened. He had suddenly lost all control over his body. No matter how he tried, he could not regain his composure. He could not stop an involuntary attack by his own hands. He had struggled with the ongoing assault all the way to the church, until at last he had lost all remaining mental discretion.... Somewhere during his lifetime, he had turned his will over to a sinister power, and now he was being torn unmercifully, flailing about the parking lot.

Sometime during the struggle, I thought I had heard an intelligible appeal. It was just a whisper, but I was sure I had heard the young man say, "Please, help me." I listened closely, and in the midst of the snarling and threatening curses, I heard it again, "Help me." It's hard to describe my emotions, but I knew the battle would be over soon. Thankfully, it was. Notwithstanding an energetic, demonic struggle, accompanied by the most visible evidence of demonic reality, a beautiful and full deliverance came through the name of Jesus Christ...the young man's eyes opened, and with his right mind he accepted Jesus and prayed the sinners' prayer. He went on to become a regular member of the youth activities in that church.

We glorified God that day and were amazed at the power of the gospel.

The Search for Truth Regarding Angels

While investigating stories of modern-day angelic visitations, I began to look for people who had personal encounters to speak of. What I found was astonishing. Many people claiming such interventions told tales that directly contradicted activity that would coincide with Scripture. Others gave accounts of these beings working miracles for their own glory (not for God's), while still another group asserted their involvement with entities who regularly engaged in acting as "their spirit guide." Worse, some people's experiences were laced with fear after attempting to communicate with spiritual beings through the use of modern, manmade tools such as angel cards (tarot cards created to help you communicate with "your angels") and angel boards (communication boards similar to ouija boards, made for contacting spirits under the guise of communicating with benevolent spirits[10]).

In addition to such rampant tales claiming to point toward heavenly beings, some recent teachings state that it's possible for individuals to discover that they're not human at all, but instead are "earth angels," defined as spiritual beings of light who dwell on earth to promote peace and tolerance for all. Still other self-proclaimed experts on the matter claim that it's possible for human beings to *become* angels under the right circumstances. In addition to these and other false beliefs, a common denominator seems to be that people enjoy referring to spiritual beings as *their own,* as though such entities belong to and answer to mankind.

A simple Google search of the phrase "guardian angels" renders thousands of stories and lessons from people claiming to have the truth about these beings. The subject is extremely popular in modern media, and theories regarding angelic beings abound without limitation—or accountability. But, what do we know to be *scripturally true* about such creatures? Where does the Bible stand on items like angel boards, angel cards, or similar paraphernalia? Where do we go to discern certainty from delusion concerning angels, and beyond this, how do we know whether claims of angelic visitation or intervention are credible? Additionally, where does the Bible stand on the concept of trying to communicate with these entities, and are we allowed to petition them with our requests?

Scripture describes angels as serving many functions. They are ministering spirits, warriors, protectors, messengers, prophetic participants, and more. Of such is an army of incredible power, made up of creatures who await God's orders, who have the ability to nurture, minister peace and strength to those who are hurting, and deliver vital messages. They engage in spiritual warfare, keep watch over and protect human beings, and even have a vital role to play in end-time prophecy.

Strangely, however, the modern portrayal of a heavenly being's nature and mission seems to be nothing like the Bible's descriptions of strong, commanding warriors who stand imbued with the authoritative supremacy of the Almighty God. In contrast, outside of Scripture, angels are often portrayed through images of soft, effeminate spirits fueled by emotion, or even, as modern cherub art often conveys, winged *babies*. Ironically, the same churches that recognize the forceful, militant qualities of such entities likely display "cute" or "decorative" art portraying them in their weakness in nurseries or ladies' restrooms. How is it, then, that our modern impression of angels is so polarized?

Furthermore, why has our view shifted from seeing these creatures as powerful attendants who await the orders of the Almighty God to seeing them as the soft, almost fairy-like beings that some humans believe await *our* command? These are questions that we must ask in order to preserve a healthy, *theologically balanced* understanding of the creatures who play such a vital role in God's plan.

To answer these queries, we must begin by rolling back the clock to examine where, in history, our definition and portrayal of heavenly beings began to divide.

2

Misconceptions from
the Old World

*E*very time a bell rings, an angel gets his wings.

Right?

Ha! No…

We can throw back our heads and enjoy a hearty laugh at the idea that anyone would be silly enough to adopt theology from some iconic Christmas movie. But would you be surprised to learn that most Christians' comprehension of angels is based on cultural nuggets every bit as meaningless as that?

Almost every book on the market featuring angels as the main topic depicts the beings as cute (but weak), naked toddlers with golden wings and a bow and arrow, or as partially (or wholly) nude blonde women with white, feathery wings—and they're all usually hanging out in the clouds. However, almost all (except for textbooks and encyclopedias) fail to explain what events in social, religious, and political history have helped create these artistic impressions, and they don't point out that many (if not most) of these iconic models originated from deeply warped, pagan legends frequently related to deviant sex amidst the deities of the Greek/Roman mythological pantheon. Additionally, many contemporary materials on the subject endorse the theologically unacceptable ideas that humans can or should give angels orders or worship them. These same sources conveniently avoid divulging any explanation for how this old-as-dirt, pagan-god worship has come to be redressed under societally acceptable, New Age ideologies represented in seemingly harmless terms like "spirituality" and "enlightenment."

Sadly, even Christians are vulnerable at times to misunderstanding what Yahweh designed His messengers to be…and that is dangerous on at least two fronts: 1) Believers can be misled in their own faith when biblical foundations are absent; 2) Believers might not be equipped to help the lost who have entrenched themselves in New Age mysticism. Considering the angelic ties to pop culture's spirituality trends—and with as harmless, flowery, floaty, and sparkly as that looks to the lost (*especially* to the youth)—it is crucial to understand the solid, biblical truth about angels lest we fall prey to *the enemy's own appearance* as the prettiest and shiniest of all angels (2 Corinthians 11:13–14).

The scriptural angel stands in such stark contrast to the "Christian angel" sold in the ornament aisle every Christmas season that no book daring to challenge that culturally time-honored image would be complete without explaining how it originated erroneously and extrabiblically. So, we *could* head straight to "what the Bible says" about angels and skip past important historical factors as many others have done, but doing so would ultimately render an incomplete study and leave gaping holes in our conclusions later on.

So in this book, we're going to reflect upon a few key events in history that have shaped modern beliefs about angels so that we can recognize unbiblical concepts for what they are (namely, artistic fabrications of human imagination, usually relating to mysticism), in order to open our minds that much more to what the Word of God says about these messengers, instead of clinging to the traditional concepts established by world's lenses we're normally programmed to peer through.

An important reminder: Your concepts of angels might be challenged by the following information. Heartbreakingly, not *every* angelic intervention story has such a happy ending as those featured earlier in the book. Let's step back in time to another era, another day, when such testimonies of angelic interaction/intervention were potentially fatal…

The Execution of a Heretic

On May 30, 1431, at 9 in the morning, in the center of the *Vieux-Marché* fish market in Rouen, France, eight hundred English guards stood alert with shields, swords, and lances, ready to intervene the moment the growing crowd displayed any signs of civil unrest. Some in the gathering were weeping sorrowfully for the teenager, committed to pray as they had been asked to the night before when the holy entourage carried the elements of the Eucharist to the prison chambers for the final communion. Others stood piously, eagerly imagining the moment when they would later toast to the heretic getting precisely the brand of smoke and flames on a stake that she deserved.

Voices quieted from an anxious buzz to gasps and whispers as a lonely cart clunked into view. A terrified face—framed by choppy, boyish, dirty hair—gazed back at the throng. Bystanders strained to catch a glimpse of the weak and trembling figure, but it was only those closest to the cart who heard the faint words uttered from within, "O Rouen, Rouen! must I then die *here*?"[11]

The prisoner's frame seemed to shrink increasingly as the cart was hauled to the three erected scaffolds, upon two of which were the territorial leaders of the English Church—the most noteworthy names in the region's judiciary system. The third scaffolding—the one built for and dedicated to the sole purpose of burning to the ground—was stationed higher than the other two…and this was a cruelty that had been specially arranged for this occasion: all the more to make an example of the heathen. On any other given day, as was the official procedure for burning at the stake, the executioner would light the base, wait until the flames reached the specified height, then approach the scaffold from the back and tighten a rope around the throat of the condemned with intent to suffocate. This process ensured a quicker death, humanely sparing the prisoner (and those assembled below) from a disturbing, lengthy, torturous public burning. But the scaffold constructed in Rouen's prized landmark of industry had, this day, been arranged to such a height and width that the peak of the stake was viewable from anywhere in the marketplace…and the chief executioner had access only to lighting the flames and leaving the rest to play out in the most dramatic fashion.

This heretic, the powers that be had decreed, was going to suffer for a long time where all could see.

A professor of good report, hailing from the University of Paris, stood and delivered a convincing presentation in the prisoner's last hour—a message loosely based upon 1 Corinthians 12:26: "When one limb of the Church is sick, the whole Church is sick."[12] It was therefore concluded that the Church was in need of surgery, a cutting off of the infected limb, and that the Body could have nothing further to do with this poor, doomed creature, who would now be burned alive and go on to be judged by the Lord. The professor lent the pedestal to Judge Pierre Cauchon, Bishop of Beauvais, for a reading of the listed offenses. Before he had been given the opportunity to carry out his duty, the desperate captive, in front of everyone, "had knelt down and invoked God, the Virgin, St. Michael, and St. Catharine, pardoning all and asking pardon, saying to the bystanders, 'Pray for me!'"[13]

How could it be that this once fierce champion of battle had come to this? Just months prior, every English soldier ran in fear at the mention of this war commander's very name, let alone the widespread panic that spread through the troops whenever they knew the commander was present. This deliverer, believed to have been sent by God, had let loose battle cries so passionate in the face of combat that they boomed above the piercing din of clashing swords and across the plains like a lion's roar.

This crusade victor charged a banner into the fray head-on, refusing to stop or flee—even after taking an arrow to the chest. It was a demonstration of willpower and internal strength unlike anything the English had ever witnessed in even the fiercest of opponents.

And now, the hero was reduced to pleading for a single peasant's merciful prayer mere minutes before the flames. Each of the holy men in robes stared back at the young soul so recently convicted of sacrilegious crimes against God and nature...and each felt just the smallest sensation of guilt.

After all, she might have fought like the bravest of men...but Joan of Arc was only a teenage girl, sentenced to the flames before she would see her twentieth birthday.

"Please," Joan's young, feminine voice croaked emotionally over the thick silence. "Please, every one of you, fathers, for *me*... A mass for my soul. For *me*. Please..."

Bishop Cauchon, the central religious figure over her case—in an attempt to keep his emotions reined in since several of his fellow bishops had now started to weep for the girl—read over the charges against Joan as she remained on her knees. He concluded with the Church's official position: "Therefore, we pronounce you to be a rotten limb, and, as such, to be lopped off from the Church. We deliver you over to the secular power, praying it at the same time to relax its sentence and to spare you death."[14]

The secular power, as we all know today, did no such thing. Joan of Arc was burned at the stake and faced worse executional methods than were even allowed at the time, just to draw it all out and prolong her torture. The only comfort afforded her were two crosses, crudely fashioned from two sticks and hurriedly delivered to her by an Englishman. one, she wedged into the front of her dress above her heart, where it remained with her until the end. The other was held at the level of her eyes so she might look upon the symbol of her Savior as she died.

As the fires were lit, she never accused the earthly king who had abandoned her or the Church who had done the same. She gave no words of revenge or spite, nor did she attempt to rebuke the people whose lives she saved and who later deserted her to die as a heretic. When the flames reached her, she called upon God, the saints, and the *angels*—of whose voices, Joan had famously sworn, had led her to unfathomable victory in the legendary battle of Orléans toward the close of the Hundred Years' War. Eyewitnesses at the time of her death have said that she confirmed the voices were with her in the end:

> She bore witness to them [as the flames reached her], "Yes, my voices were from God, my voices have not deceived me." The fact that all her doubts vanished at this trying moment must be taken as a proof that she accepted death as the promised deliverance; that she no longer understood her salvation in the Judaic and material sense, as until now she had done, that at length she saw clearly; and that, rising above all shadows, her gifts of illumination and of sanctity were at the final hour made perfect unto her.[15]

This clarity spoken of in the historical account likely refers to Joan's confusion as her days drew to a close. She believed that as her enemies were planning her demise, her voices had told her not to worry, she would be delivered—a promise she interpreted to mean an *earthly* deliverance from the English back into the warm and welcoming hands of the French. As described in this quote and others, many believed the voices were as accurate as they had ever been since the beginning. As the truth of her imminent death dawned upon her, so, too, did the spiritual implications of the promised deliverance, and Joan passed into the next world into glory…as "delivered from her enemies" as possible in this life and the next, and into arms more welcoming than even at her mother's cottage back home.

Many think they can guess, because of a movie they watched or what an elementary school teacher told them, what ultimately led to

Joan's execution: English political biases within the tribunal denying Joan the right to a legal advisor; trumped-up charges without sufficient evidence; and countless attempts to trap her with confusing rhetoric, etc. Then, when all of that failed, a grasping-at-straws cross-dressing charge held enough of a societal shock factor (especially in light of how Joan's aggressors were choosing to interpret Deuteronomy 22:5 in the interest of the trial) that her dark fate within such theocratic litigation became easier to seal, since it was being run by trusted theologians of the Catholic faith. (With their hero out of the way, the national spirit of France would be crushed and its people hopeless and suppressible, the English believed. History tells that it didn't quite happen the way they may have hoped.) And whereas *all* of these factors were at work, what condemned Joan in reality (politics) wasn't what condemned her on paper, which is a completely different animal. Sure, that comprised a "cross-dressing" charge—a heresy against God and nature—but when one truly examines the reaction both the French and the English had anytime she was around, it quickly becomes obvious that nobody really cared if she removed her braid and wore protective gear on the battle-field. The Church threw that "final straw" charge on top of the others just to get the trial over with more quickly and secure her death before someone had a chance to intervene on her behalf. The whole world at that time, including the Church, thanks to the Maid of Lorraine proph-ecies (discussed shortly), had been expecting a woman in battle armor for centuries. In all honesty, everyone had long since been prepared for her to wear exactly what she wore.

The angelic visitations, however…*those* were different. Whether or not leadership of the Church had expected her to utter those revela-tions, there's a vital historical element that many individuals overlook, one that might have driven the very last nail in Joan's coffin and played a key role in developing how we view angels today, both in art as well as in function.

Joan said she had repeatedly been visited by an angel since at least the age of thirteen, if not earlier.[16] Then she allowed herself to be pressured into *describing* the visitor…and *that* was ultimately her downfall.

In those days, it was not at all uncommon that a person of the Church would claim to have been visited by an angel; that claim alone typically wasn't grounds for a death sentence. Discerning a holy spirit from a wicked one—then determining what evil or righteous actions the individual took as a result of the encounter—*that* was the issue that most concerned the Church, and almost all accounts could be (and often were) found condemnable, no matter what they described.

What a delicate affair it was, and what a trap it became for countless victims interrogated by the Church in those days. The sin wasn't within the actual *claim* of a visitation. It was more complicated than that. Since any description of God by a human would fall short of His true, transcendental magnitude as Creator of the universe, the blasphemy was in the description, alone.

First, let's take a look at what few details Joan was willing to share during the trial, and then we'll visit the cultural and religious circumstances around that time that made such superficial descriptions so controversial:

Joan: The first time God sent a voice to help me and guide me, I was much afraid. The voice came towards noon, in summer, in my father's garden: and I had [not] fasted on the preceding day. I heard the voice on my right, in the direction of the church; and I seldom heard it without a light. This light came from the same side as the voice, and generally there was a great light. When I came to France I often heard the voice…. If I was in a wood, I easily heard the voice come to me. It seemed to me a worthy voice, and I believed it was sent from God; when I heard the voice a third time, I knew that it was the voice of an angel. This voice always protected me well, and I understood it well.

Judge: What instruction did this voice gave you for the salvation of your soul?

Joan: It taught me to be good and to go to church often; and it told me that I must go to France.... [Then, a little later in the trial:] The voice told me I could no longer stay where I was; that I should raise the siege of the city of Orleans; that I, Jeanne, should go to Robert de Baudricourt, in the town of Vaucouleurs of which he was captain, and he would provide an escort for me. I told the voice that I was a poor maid, knowing nothing of riding or fighting.... Then when I reached Vaucouleurs [this happened when Joan was sixteen years old], I easily recognized Robert de Baudricourt, although I had never seen him before; and I knew him through my voice, for the voice had told me it was he. I told Robert I must go to France. Robert twice refused to hear me and repulsed me; the third time he listened to me and gave me an escort. And the voice had told me that it would be so.[17]

This wasn't the only time that Joan's voices led her to instantly recognize a person of notable importance in light of what she believed the angel of God had told her to do. One notorious and celebrated scene of her life is the first meeting between Joan and King Charles VII. Having been informed that she was coming to meet him, King Charles, in front of an entire court of witnesses, discreetly slipped behind a gathering of richly dressed men in his company to test Joan and see if she was *really* sent by an angel. If it was, in fact, God's angelic messenger who inspired the meeting, this same messenger would have the power to lead Joan straight to him, past the opulently dressed lords of the court, and directly to the authentic king.

When Joan arrived, she glanced about the room until her eyes fell on him behind the others, and she instantly headed for his location, disregarding the men gathered near his throne. This was done to the amazement of all those present, as the king's lords were reportedly as opulently dressed as he, providing no visible clue to help a young shepherdess distinguish the king from an array of wealthy aristocrats and advisors.

One legendary retelling of the event in the historic *Chronique de Charles VII* states that King Charles took the test even further: When Joan knelt and humbly greeted him as king, he openly denied his identity, redirecting her to another man who had previously been prepared to impersonate him. This test, too, was passed quickly, thanks to the angel's leading: "Wherefore he [the king] answered Joan: 'I am not the King,' and pointing to one of the lords said: 'There is the King.' To which Joan responded: 'In God's name, gentle dauphin, it is you and none other.'"[18] Joan's words during trial reflect: "When I entered the king's room I recognized him among many others by the counsel of the voice, which revealed him to me."[19]

As if that weren't enough, Joan proceeded in a private meeting to tell the king secret arrangements nobody could have known about his upcoming coronation ceremony. There were other secrets the king and Joan shared that, to this day, nobody knows the nature of, but they were significant enough to make the skeptic Charles a believer in the Maid of Lorraine. At that, the king vetted Joan to the court and acknowledged she had to have been sent by an angel of God.

The ensuing bloody battles Joan led were victorious, and when it no longer politically suited the king to keep her around, he turned his back on her, refusing to pay her ransom when she was captured by the English. Left in the hands of the Church of England for trial, she was badgered about the nature of her relationship with God and His alleged angelic messengers. No matter how many times the bishops tried to overwhelm her with insinuations about the origins of the voices, she remained steadfast. More than once, she warned her prosecutors that they should proceed with caution.

Joan: You say that you are my judge; take good heed of what you do, because, in truth, I am sent by God, and you put yourself in great peril.... I firmly believe, as firmly as I believe in the Christian faith and that the Lord redeemed us from the pains of hell, that this voice comes from God, and by His command.

Judge: Does this voice, which you say appears to you, come as an angel, or directly from God, or is it the voice of one of the saints?

Joan: This voice comes from God; I believe I do not tell you everything about it; and I am more afraid of failing the voices by saying what is displeasing to them, than of answering you.... My voices told me to say certain things to the king, and not to you.... I will not tell you everything, I have not leave, nor does my oath [the oath of truth she swore in front of the tribunal] touch on that. This voice is good and worthy; and I am not bound to answer you....

Judge: Are you in God's grace currently?

Joan: If I am not, may God put me there; and if I am, may God so keep me.[20]

This last statement is by far the most heavily quoted from Joan's trial. It shows her ability to sidestep rhetorical traps with the cleverness and skill of a person who had spent fifty years in court. At only nineteen, she baffled the prosecution, who had to spin many words to rise to her unexplainable level of intelligence and verbal dexterity. In light of her success at war, over and over, the bishops and judge asked her if the voices had told her to hate her enemies, or if they had inclined her toward violence. Each time, instead of confirming that God or His angel would inspire such impulses, she offered a different viewpoint instead, stating that she was obedient to God in delivering His oppressed people, betraying only her patriotic devotion for the king and nothing more. (Note that throughout the trial she was also repeatedly asked about details concerning her king, and she refused to answer, even at the threat of a beheading. Many times, she explained that the angelic voices—which she heard at night during her personal prayer time—were giving her guidance on how to answer her interrogators.)

As mentioned earlier, ultimately, the shock to the jury was not that she believed she had been visited by angels or saints, or that voices in her head told her step by step what she was to do in her role of liberating France. Citizens of both France and England had been well acquainted with that part of her story by this time. The surprise, and essentially what damned her in the eyes of the Church, was her eventual caving in to the prosecution's relentless attempts at coercing her to describe her encounters with the angels, even though she avoided going into deep detail.

Judge: Which of your apparitions came to you first?

Joan: St. Michael [the archangel] came first.

Judge: Was it a long time ago that you first heard the voice of St. Michael?

Joan: I do not speak of St. Michael's voice, but of his great comfort.

Judge: Which was the voice which came to you when you were about thirteen?

Joan: It was St. Michael, whom I saw before my eyes; and he was not alone, but accompanied by many angels from heaven....

Judge: Did you see these angels corporeally and in reality? [A corporeal visitation, in the eyes of the Church, by default made the statement that angels had physical substance, and that they were not wholly *spirit*.]

Joan: I saw them with my bodily eyes, as well as I see you; and when they left me, I wept; and I fain would have them take me with them, too....[21]

Judge: In what form did St. Michael appear to you?

Joan: I did not see his crown, and I know nothing of his apparel. [Note that elsewhere in her trial, Joan *did* state that the saints had been crowned.]

Judge: Was he naked? [Yes, the presiding judge *did* just ask Joan of Arc if the archangel Michael had come to her naked... This seems like a bizarre and inappropriate question at this point in the reflection. Make a mental note for now, and stay tuned.]

Joan: Do you think God has not wherewithal to clothe him?

Judge: Does he have any hair?

Joan: Why should it be cut off? I haven't seen St. Michael since I left the Castle Crotoy, and I do not often see him. I do not know whether he has hair.

Judge: Does he have scales? [By "scales," he is referring to the measuring instrument, not what grows on the exterior of snakes or lizards. Again, note this question for later.]

Joan: I do not know. I was filled with great joy when I saw him; and I felt, when I saw him, that I was not in mortal sin....[22]

Judge: Does he have wings?

Joan: Yes.... I have seen St. Michael and the saints so clearly that I know they are saints of paradise.

Judge: Have you seen anything of them besides the face?

Joan: ...I would rather have you cut my throat than tell you all I know; I will willingly tell you all I know about the trial [referring to earthly/political matters between France and England].

Judge: [Relentlessly:] Do you believe that St. Michael and St. Gabriel have natural heads?

Joan: I saw them with my two eyes, and I believe it was they I saw as firmly as I believe in the existence of God.

Judge: Do you believe it was God who created them in the form and fashion that you saw?

Joan: Yes.

Judge: Do you believe that God from the beginning created them in that form or fashion?

Joan: You will learn no more from me at present than I have told you.[23]

Though Joan continuously tried to keep the trial focused on matters relevant to war and her actions as a soldier of France, the bishops were determined to snare her into sharing too much about her angelic companions. If they could just keep her talking, the uneducated and theologically oblivious girl would eventually slip and say something about her angels that didn't align with God's Word.

Judge: In what guise and shape, size and dress did St. Michael come to you?

Joan: He was in the guise of a most upright man. I will answer no more. As for the angels, I saw them with my own eyes, and you will not get any more from me than that. I believe what St. Michael, who appeared to me, did or said as firmly as I believe that Our Lord Jesus Christ suffered death and passion for us. I was moved to believe it by the good counsel, comfort, and teaching which he gave me.[24]

When the bait given Joan didn't render a slip, her descriptions of the angels—in and of themselves, entirely vague—were enough to earn her (alongside a cross-dressing charge) the stamp of heretic. The trial transcript barely mentioned any of her actions for France or against England, but obsessively returned to Joan's claims about the angels. The summation on page 209 of the English translation of the trial shares the court assessors' opinion:

To say this of archangels and of holy angels must be held presumptuous, rash, deceitful; especially seeing that it is not written that any man, however upright, nor even Our Lady, Mother of God, received such reverence or greetings. Often she [Joan] said that there came to her the archangel Gabriel, St. Michael, and sometimes a million angels.... These are less divine revelations than lies invented by Jeanne [Joan], suggested or shown to her by the demon in illusive apparitions, in order to mock at her imagination whilst she meddled with things which are beyond her and superior to the faculty of her condition.[25]

Why was the act of describing angels so instantly and naturally heretical?

In order to provide the exceedingly fascinating answer that question provides, we have to travel further back in time, to the First Byzantine Iconoclasm in AD 726–787.

The Iconoclasm Changed Everything

"Iconoclasm" literally means "struggle over images." This iconoclasm was the first of two major eras when religious images or icons (works of art, usually in the form of a painting, although occasionally involving a statue, a carving on a church ceiling, or ornately whittled figurines around a loved one's tomb, etc.) were destroyed for religious or political reasons. During the Byzantine Empire, angels were believed to be great guardians over humankind and were taken seriously because of how powerful they were. Since the formation of the first-century Church, they had already been pictured with humanlike qualities in drawings, sculptures, and paintings—both because they appeared in the shape and form of humans in certain narratives of the Bible, and because the human form is a familiar starting place for the painter/craftsman to develop a scene. Though the Bible makes many references to nonhuman spirits appearing in our likeness (an "anthropomorphic" appearance), there was no question in the teachings of the early Church that they were *spirits*. (Obviously, the exception to this was Christ, who was wholly human and wholly God at the same time.) As messengers of God, these spirits would have access to His unlimited power while accomplishing His work, thus were serious forces to reckon with.

Because women were viewed as the weaker sex in Greco-Roman cultures, any strong, mighty, *holy* angel would naturally have been rendered as a male in ancient art from that region, as we clearly see in many famous images from AD 300 forward that are still in existence today. (Note that females may have been used to depict *evil* angels in antique art, but those instances are generally unrelated to any works reflecting Christian doctrine or theology.)

Not only were angels not yet being depicted as women during this time, the idea that they might be babies or toddlers was absurd; further, at least at first, the concept of angels having wings was likewise bizarre, if not entirely unbiblical. Whereas the cherubim and the seraphim are described in Exodus and Isaiah as having wings, those angels are distinctly different from the messenger angels that have been known historically and biblically to make appearances here on earth, and the early Church was aware of that. Thus, the earliest artistic portrayals of angels after the Ascension of Christ (at least based on the art we still have access to, which would be those that survived the iconoclasm) show only fully grown, masculine figures.

Then, somewhere between AD 379 and 395, probably while Emperor Theodosius the Great was on the throne, the "Prince's Sarcophagus" was carved from stone, featuring two angels with wings, both attached to a wheel at the center of the side of the casket. This work was found in the Imperial Cemetery a few decades into the twentieth century, and to date, we still don't know the identity of the child buried within, or what the angels with the wheel were supposed to indicate, since winged angels hadn't yet become the norm. (The closest biblical link between wings and wheels would be the cherubim in Ezekiel 10, which we will look more closely at later, but they definitely didn't look like regular men with wings, so that's a stretch.)

In any case, though wings were starting to come onto the scene, *women and children were not.*

The Church understood that throughout the Bible, when angels appeared to mankind, they were so transcendently fierce and commanding—*frightening even!*—that the people they visited had to be immediately reassured by the angel's "Fear not" greeting. A gentle female or a baby weren't the artists' best choice for conveying the awesome countenance of these beings. Artists saved the use of feminine and innocent for their works featuring the Virgin Mother and her Blessed Babe.

Though religious icons had been a part of the Christian Church from its very beginning, over time, the veneration of these holy paintings began to resemble idol worship: The paintings were involved in rituals, given a place of honor at family gatherings, affectionately kissed, etc. Since the times described in the book of Genesis, idol worship was expressly forbidden, so, periodically within the first eight centuries AD, important Church leaders questioned whether images of Christ, Mary, the saints, and such would be allowed for believers. Although censoring all religious artwork was tragic, it was a far lesser offense than standing idly by while Christians engaged in activities such as the pagan-style worship of a *picture* of Christ rather than the true Messiah Himself.

Before long, certain secular leaders such as Emperor Leo III discovered that they could earn extreme favor with important religious personalities within the Church if they joined forces and legally sanctioned the destruction of religious art. Under these new political and religious strategies, the very act of owning icons or images of God or the Virgin Mother ironically became, at certain times and under certain leaders, heresy against God.

As a result, the posture quickly adopted by secular authorities (obviously influenced by religious authorities) was equivalent to the following summary: God is abstract. All Trinity Persons are abstract. The chief servants of God whose role it was to prepare or build the Church—Mary, the apostles, the saints, and the angels—are all abstract. God and the key players of His grand design cannot be wholly depicted within human means, no matter how great the artist. To define the appearance of any of the aforementioned with human-designed images when their appearance can't be capably and efficiently captured by any human endeavors, or to portray the relationship between any of the aforementioned and humanity in art when such an infinitely complicated relationship surpasses human comprehension is to place unfounded limits upon God's magnitude and/or plan, diluting the Trinity and the Divine Order of life and eternity down to only that which fits the narrow boundaries of human logic and imagination. Thus, such endeavors should be viewed as blasphemy, a sin worthy of the charge of heresy.

More simply put, human-created "art" of any religious nature served only to diminish God and bring Him down to the human level. Therefore, iconoclasts (the destroyers of the art) maintained, it was a slap in God's face to create art, and an even more profane offense to venerate the images.

Iconophiles ("icon lovers") lashed back at these drastic restrictions, proving themselves even willing to die to protect their art. Persecution—at times by religious groups, and at other times by secular authorities—increased and decreased throughout the years, and the consequences of possessing icons was inconsistent from one epoch to another, depending on what religious and political leaders were in charge. So, the pattern emerged: Some leaders would allow the possession of religious artwork, then others would impose a ban and confiscate the works. Yet others would step in and, with formal apologies, return the pieces, but still others would come along and destroy the works and punish (persecute) the owner.

In response to this tumultuous predicament, the Church met for the Seventh Ecumenical Council (otherwise called the Second Council of Nicaea) in order to decide, once and for all, whether religious icons and images would be allowed.

These meetings, spanning four centuries, were organized gatherings for central, early-Church authorities within Eastern Orthodoxy and Roman Catholicism to weed out rising heresies and reestablish existing

Christological doctrines. By extension, they set out to determine ecclesiastical practices in each church and outline what would be expected of the clergy's personal conduct (both inside and outside the house of the Lord). Consolidating many varying opinions and convictions into one common system of governance naturally sparked much back-and-forth discussion, which explains why it took almost four hundred years and seven complicated councils to produce any results—and the conclusions didn't always go unchallenged, nor were the final decisions universally respected and adhered to.

Research on the tension between the Western Church and Eastern Church frequently draws back to the matters addressed at these councils. Historians have spent well over a thousand years discussing the influence these councils ultimately had over the development of early Christianity, and hundreds of exceptional collections of literature exist on the subject, so I won't give a lengthy explanation of them here. Relevant to our thread on Joan of Arc and her archangel visitor is only one tiny piece in a larger puzzle called the Seventh Ecumenical Council (*or* Second Council of Nicaea), which relates to the Church's cemented "legalization" of angel, deity, or saint images and icons (and more specifically for this book, how the identity of angels as perceived within the Church would soon take a 180-degree turn for the worse, theologically speaking).

In the trails of devastating iconoclasmic warfare against religious art—where lovers of the painted image of Christ and His angelic messengers were persecuted and identified as deviant iconophiles—the Church gathered for one final council in hopes of healing these wounds once and for all. Intermittently from September 24 through October 23, AD 787, notable bishops took the stand and presented their rationale for or against the legalization of icons and imageries. Here is a general outline of the proceedings:

Session 1, September 24: Basil of Ancyra, Theodore of Myra, and Theodosius of Amorium each begged for an official Church pardon from a heresy/excommunication charge for having been caught treasuring religious art. Theodosius' bold statement best captures the three men's collective plea:

Theodosius, the humble Christian, to the holy and Ecumenical Synod: I confess and I agree to and I receive and I salute and I venerate in the first place the spotless image of our Lord Jesus Christ, our true God.… [In other words, he bravely asserts himself as honoring early Christian artwork without shame or remorse. Then, he goes on to clarify:] Not indeed as gods—God forbid! [the artwork, itself, is *not a god*, so this is not a matter of idol worship]…for in this I am but showing forth more clearly the affection and love of my soul which I have borne them from the first [in loving his art, he feels closer to the incorporeal Trinity, as well as the work of Mary, the mother of Christ, and the apostles]…

Moreover, I am well pleased that there should be images in the churches of the faithful, especially the image of our Lord Jesus Christ and of the holy Mother of God, of every kind of material, both gold and silver and of every colour, so that his incarnation may be set forth to all men [i.e., so that Jesus' life, works, death, resurrection, and ascension would be visualized by all]. Likewise there may be painted the lives of the Saints and Prophets and Martyrs, so that their struggles and agonies may be set forth in brief, for the stirring up and teaching of the people, especially of the unlearned [i.e., so that those who cannot read will otherwise be taught through pictures].…

Even as also St. Basil says: "Writers and painters set forth the great deeds of war; the one by word, the other by their pencils; and each stirs many to courage."[26]

The logic in this last comparison is clear: If war soldiers are "stirred" to act courageously because of the paintings of heroes who have gone before them in battle, then it is by religious works of art that certain men will be "stirred" to come to faith in the Lord. Theodosius ended his appeal with a passionate assertion that he should not only be received back into the Church, but that his reentrance should be met with celebration, and that it is those who oppose veneration of images who should be accursed:

> O all-holy lords! Let them who do not venerate the holy and venerable images be anathema! Anathema to those who blaspheme against the honourable and venerable images! To those who dare to attack and blaspheme the venerable images and call them idols, anathema! To the calumniators of Christianity, that is to say the Iconoclasts, anathema! To those who do not diligently teach all the Christ-loving people to venerate and salute the venerable and sacred and honourable images of all the Saints who pleased God in their several generations, anathema! To those who have a doubtful mind and do not confess with their whole hearts that they venerate the sacred images, anathema![27]

So far, so good. The Church heard the pleas of these three bishops, previously charged with heresy, and they were restored to the fold. Additionally, the leaders who accepted them back went on (as recorded in the minutes) to identify the "iconoclasts" (the "breakers of icons") as guilty of the worst of all heresies, "as it subverts the incarnation of our Saviour."[28]

Session 2, September 26: A letter written in Greek by the hands of the then-current pope—Hadrian I—was read in front of the council. In it, he asked for full cooperation in legalizing the veneration of images (though, if we're being perfectly honest, his letter was plum-full of the grandest promises regarding the many blessings and protections that God would pour out from the otherworld if they agreed…which felt a bit "leading," as if it were an inch away from selling indulgences).

Another letter from the same pope was read, and it stated similar convictions. Unanimously, the presiding bishops agreed with the contents of the letters and voted in favor of heeding Hadrian's advice.

Session 3, September 28: Clarification was given once again to reiterate that holy images and icons should be honored, but that worship and adoration would be offered "alone to the supersubstantial and life-giving Trinity," and anyone who continued to worship the inanimate art would be "cast out of the holy Catholic and Apostolic Church."[29]

Session 4, October 1: A series of writings from the early Church Fathers were read aloud. Within them, the Church Fathers spoke of their connection to art. One particular entry was noted above the others: St. Gregory—bishop of Nyssa for many years in the fourth century, key player in the development of the Nicene Creed written at the First Council of Nicaea, and an unparalleled expert on the subject of the Trinity—wrote that he paused to reflect every time he passed a certain painting depicting the scene when Abraham nearly sacrificed his son, Isaac. So moved was St. Gregory by the character of God and His provision through that moment—a moment now forever preserved *visibly* through a painter whom God, Himself, had gifted with the talent to do so—that he was unable to walk past the image without giving in to the temptation to cry.

Bishop Basil of Ancyra, at this point only restored to his position within the Church for a week and a few hours since their first council meeting, stood to share his thoughts about St. Gregory's tears: "Many times the father had read the story, but perchance he had not wept; but when once he saw it *painted*, he wept." Another bishop spoke up on the matter, and then another. An excerpt of this historical exchange is as follows:

> "If to such a doctor [Father Gregory] the picture was helpful and drew forth tears, how much more in the case of the ignorant and simple will it bring compunction and benefit."

The holy Synod said: "We have seen in several places the history of Abraham painted as the father says."

Theodore the most holy bishop of Catanea, said: "If the holy Gregory, vigilant in divine cogitation, was moved to tears at the sight of the story of Abraham, how much more shall a painting of the incarnation of our Lord Christ, who for us was made man, move the beholders to their profit and to tears?"

Tarasius the most holy Patriarch said: "Shall we not weep when we see an image of our crucified Lord?"

The holy Synod said: "We shall indeed—for in that shall be found perfectly the profundity of the abasement of the incarnate God for our sakes."

For a while, it seemed like the attending bishops of the council had already said all there was to say on the matter. It *seemed* clear, if for only a few minutes, that the worship of art was forbidden, regardless of who or what was depicted within that art; yet, in an odd but beautiful balance to the discussion, it was also acknowledged that God, Himself, bestows talent to specific artists to tell *His* story. That benefitted the illiterate (a great many men and women in those days) as well as the greatest theologians whose education would only grow deeper through stunning visual displays. Art, it appeared, was a win-win for the Church.

What might have wrapped up into a clean-cut ending to the whole council was further complicated and recycled back to reflections upon what had started the iconoclasm in the first place. Yes, these bishops comprehended the *healthy* relationship between God and images of God, but not everyone did, and if images and icons were allowed amidst the laity, then they could potentially be *worshipped* by the laity, and God's people could be once again defiled by the pagan trends of the Old Testament. This was a path the bishops knew well enough not to travel down again, so they found themselves back at the drawing board of the discussion.

After a lot of talk and of weighing pros and cons, one of the lengthiest clarifications of all the Seven Ecumenical Councils put together was set in stone at this juncture of the debate. It begins:

> Thus we confess, thus we teach, just as the holy and ecumenical six Synods have decreed and ratified: We believe in one God the Father Almighty, maker of all things visible and invisible; and in one Lord Jesus Christ, his only-begotten Son and Word, through whom all things were made, and in the Holy Ghost, the Lord and giver of life, consubstantial and coeternal with the same Father and with his Son who has had no beginning. The unbuilt-up, indivisible, incomprehensible, and non-circumscribed Trinity; he, wholly and alone, is to be worshipped and revered with adoration; one Godhead, one Lordship, one dominion, one realm and dynasty, which without division is apportioned to the Persons, and is fitted to the essence severally.[30]

This type of dissertation went on for pages. There was no chance that any man, woman, or child who had heard about the council would still be confused afterward. Eventually, we reach their opinion about what happens when someone knows better and *still* chooses to worship icons and images: "As for such as turn back unto their own wickedness, the Lord shall lead them forth with the evil doers; and peace shall be upon the Israel of God."[31]

Session 5, October 4; Session 6, October 6; Session 7, October 13; and Session 8, October 23: Many of the charges of the original iconoclasts were read aloud to the assembly and openly refuted in turn over the next several sessions. This was so the Church leadership could jointly address what offense initially triggered the entire Byzantine Iconoclasm, and what theological assertions were made to justify persecution of Christians who honored holy images. Without understanding which crucial figures were first angered, whether they belonged to the

Orthodox Church or to a secular conviction, whether their concerns were politically or theologically motivated (and so on), the bishops would never be able to return home with assurance that history would not repeat itself. It would only be through letting the complaints of the opposing side speak for themselves and get shut down there, in that room full of learned men, that religious art could be legalized with confidence moving forward.

As one example of the iconoclasts' propaganda: In a royal decree, Leo III and his son, Constantine V, stated that misguided men, influenced by Satan, himself, "gradually brought back idolatry under the appearance of Christianity" each time they pointed to a picture of Christ and said it was "Christ." (You would think that the reference to the Man *within* the picture, and not to the framed work itself, would have been obvious, but it was trivial details like this that had started this whole muddied mess, and it didn't help that the images were actually being worshipped here and there throughout Rome.) We won't list the entire royal statement here, as it is lengthy, and it just so happens to be one of the wordiest criticisms in existence…but it is important to view, at least in part, the brand of words that were weaved around this issue both in secular and religious governing groups, because certain personalities (such as Joan of Arc) would be persecuted later as a result of the outlandish convictions championed at this time. Many of the statements below have been rephrased for clarity in brackets:

> …we found that the unlawful art of painting living creatures ["living creatures" here refers to God, Mary, apostles, saints, or angels] blasphemed the fundamental doctrine of our salvation—namely, the Incarnation of Christ….
>
> Wherefore we thought it right, to show forth with all accuracy, in our present definition the error of such as make and venerate these [rephrase: "Therefore we thought it right to point out the error of those who paint or venerate art"], for it

is the unanimous doctrine of all the holy Fathers and of the six Ecumenical Synods [rephrase: "because the early Church Fathers and the bishops of the six prior councils all agree"], that no one may imagine any kind of separation or mingling in opposition to the unsearchable, unspeakable, and incomprehensible union of the two natures in the one hypostasis or person [rephrase: "that Christ—who was both entirely human and entirely God—is so metaphysically incomprehensible to us regular, finite humans that no one man, not even the greatest artist, may imagine Him accurately enough to capture in a painting both the God nature and the human nature as they are fuse into the one Person of Christ"]. What avails, then, the folly of the painter, who from sinful love of gain depicts that which should not be depicted— that is, with his polluted hands he tries to fashion that which should only be believed in the heart and confessed with the mouth? ["Gain," might have meant monetarily, as in one who sells a painting, but it also might also have been referring to a painter who uses his art to make himself look pious.] He makes an image and calls it "Christ." The name "Christ" signifies God *and* man. Consequently it is an image of God and man, and consequently he has in his foolish mind, in his representation of the created flesh, depicted the Godhead which cannot be represented, and thus mingled what should not be mingled. Thus he is guilty of a double blasphemy—the one in making an image of the Godhead, and the other by mingling the Godhead and manhood. Those fall into the same blasphemy who venerate the image, and the same woe rests upon both.[32]

Just as the bishops' reiteration of the core doctrines of Christianity went on for pages in Session 4, so, too, does this royal decree. The emperor must have hired himself quite the scribe to create this document, because it cleverly finds every logical loophole to presume that any artist who has the gall to represent a viewable version of God can only be in it for his or her own gain—and, in forcing God into an artistic box, the incomprehensible divinity of God's nature has been depreciated, cheapened if you will, which earns the painter or sculptor a charge of blasphemy.

(I'm sure you can see where this might be going as it relates to Joan of Arc. Extremely powerful and royal authorities cemented this kind of thinking into both Rome and the Church of Rome during this time, to the point that it wasn't just about painting or sculpting anymore. Even telling a story about an angel visitation elicited finger-pointing, skepticism, and concern. Although equally powerful and royal authorities eventually relegalized religious art, the damage would not be reversed for centuries, so long as there would be men in control of secular and/ or religious government who benefitted from whistleblowing on certain personalities they didn't like.)

Noteworthy about the kind of "law" or procedure being passed around by iconoclasts just prior to this council were the emperor's "19 Definitions," recorded at the Iconoclastic Conciliabulum (commonly called the "Mock Synod") at Constantinople in AD 754. Here are a few of those (note that the word "anathema," used in the context of a religious [or theocratic] council, is a pronouncement of official excommunication at the very least; in these settings it also occasionally represented an impassioned speaker proclaiming an eternal curse of damnation upon one's soul):

Definition 8: If anyone ventures to represent the divine image of the Word after the Incarnation with material colours, let him be anathema!...

Definition 10: If anyone ventures to represent the hypostatic union of the two natures in a picture, and calls it Christ, and thus falsely represents a union of the two natures, let him be anathema!...

Definition 12: If anyone separates the one Christ into two persons, and endeavours to represent Him who was born of the Virgin separately, and thus accepts only a relative union of the natures, let him be anathema....

Definition 14: If anyone endeavours to represent by material colours, God the Word as a mere man, who, although bearing the form of God, yet has assumed the form of a servant in his own person, and thus endeavours to separate him from his inseparable Godhead, so that he thereby introduces a quaternity into the Holy Trinity, let him be anathema....

Definition 16: If anyone shall endeavour to represent the forms of the Saints in lifeless pictures with material colours which are of no value (for this notion is vain and introduced by the devil) [my goodness...], and does not rather represent their virtues as living images in himself, let him be anathema.[33]

Definition 19 ends with an all-consuming "anathema" that damns the offender to earthly excommunication from the Church *as well as* eternal excommunication from all three Persons of the Trinity. This document (and others), written and stamped with royal approval in 754, led to many arrests and countless destruction upon church property across the Roman Empire.

Needless to say, the bishops of the Seventh Ecumenical Council were outraged over the "Mock Synod Definitions" from the emperor, and after the definitions were read aloud, they spent the rest of their remaining council time recording their own official confession of faith, reinstating the artists' right to freely express themselves and the rest of God's people the right to own and enjoy it. This final document was, in the last council session (which took place in Constantinople), read in the presence of Empress Irene (more on her in a moment).

To make our confession short, we keep unchanged all the eccle-siastical traditions handed down to us, whether in writing or verbally, one of which is the making of pictorial representations, agreeable to the history of the preaching of the Gospel....

We, therefore...define with all certitude and accuracy that just as the figure of the precious and life-giving Cross, so also the venerable and holy images, as well in painting and mosaic as of other fit materials, should be set forth in the holy churches of God, and on the sacred vessels and on the vestments and on hangings and in pictures both in houses and by the wayside, to wit, the figure of our Lord God and Saviour Jesus Christ, of our spotless Lady, the Mother of God, **of the honourable Angels**, of all Saints and of all pious people. For by so much more frequently as they are seen in artistic representation, by so much more readily are men lifted up to the memory of their prototypes, and to a longing after them; and to these should be given due salutation and honourable reverence.[34]

Certainly, the original confession was far longer than this, but this excerpt communicates the bottom line: All art depicting any of the three Trinity Persons, Mary, the saints, the apostles, "the honourable Angels," and anyone else considered "pious" is to be allowed in all churches, altars, homes, and anywhere else that might draw the believer or nonbeliever alike closer to God. There was no room left for additional confusion or interpretation; if royalty and the authorities of the Roman Catho-lic Church could be convinced to agree with this confession, believers would once again be free to express their personal appreciation and understanding of God through the illustration and craftsmanship tal-ents God instilled in them in the first place.

At this point, it all relied on Empress Irene.

I know this part is a little hard to follow, what with this dynasty's bend toward naming every boy Constance or Leo, but here's the familial breakdown:

- Leo III was the first to place a ban on the icons, launching the tumultuous Byzantine Iconoclasm Era.
- Leo III's son and successor, Constantine V, carried the ban and prosecution through his rule.
- Constantine V also bore a son, Leo IV, who also upheld the ban on icons through his rule.
- Leo IV married Irene and had a son, Constantine VI.
- Constantine VI did succeed his father Leo IV's rule for a time, but it didn't last, because he was overthrown by his stepmother, Leo IV's wife, Empress Irene.

Empress Irene, known primarily for ending this chaotic iconoclasm, heard the bishops' confession of faith as it was penned in Nicaea and agreed that the war over paintbrush and chisel needed to come to an end. Before Session 8 (the final meeting of the final Ecumenical Council) ended, Empress Irene signed the document, cementing *at last* the legalization of religious art. (Note that there was another iconoclasm circa 814–842 under Leo V, but the freedom that was solidified at this time under Irene would maintain a certain staying power despite subsequent flip-flops.) Both the Church and State were in agreement that it had gone on long enough, and that *individuals* needed to be accountable for themselves when it came to what or whom they worshiped.

All of a sudden, it was over, and the destruction of icons ceased. As the dust settled from the colorful war, painters and sculptors were once again free to direct their artistic imagination back toward Mary, Christ, the saints, the apostles, and the angels.

But soon, God's "honourable Angels" would be depicted a lot less honorably…

The Greeks from Iconoclasts to Renaissance

Although the belief in Christ as both wholly human and wholly God was well known and respected at that time, the only side of Christ any artist knew how to capture was the "human" angle (as hotly debated during the council). As such, drawing, sculpting, or painting Christ and Mary, as well as all the saints and apostles, provided the natural human form and likeness as a starting point for any artist to begin a new piece after the religious art prohibition had been lifted. Whereas almost any picture of these chief religious figures would have been given *some* visual distinction (such as a "glory" [circle of light or pointy rays of light] around their heads and so on) to differentiate them from nonreligious portraits of regular men or women (or children, as was often the case with "Christ Child" style paintings), the person or Person in the picture would have still resembled a human. That might always have been a point of contention for certain religious personalities who believed Christ's "deity side" should be part of the image, but for the most part, it wasn't offensive anymore that Christ looked like a man, or that Mary looked like a woman, or that any of the saints and apostles looked like regular people. All those arguments had effectively been silenced by Empress Irene and the council.

But what of the angels? What did *they* look like? Where did an artist even start with a concept as incorporeal and mystifying as a *spirit*? Considering that the Holy Scriptures gave but few detailed descriptions, some of which are impossible for mankind to fully comprehend (let alone bring visual likeness to), what were the now-liberated artists to do with pictures depicting angelic visitations or interventions…and what guidelines had been put in place by the Church to ensure that God's messengers would always appear in icons with decency and respectful treatment?

The documentary, *Angels: Messengers of the Gods,* involves insight from Jewish scholar and author Rabbi Avraham Zvi Schvarcz, who, along with the narrator, reflects on this time in history:

Schvarcz: What do they look like? I would guess that you would have to answer, if I would have seen one, then I wouldn't have been able to explain how they looked.

Narrator: Judaism mistrusted any illustration. Manifestations of God's word could not take on physical form.

Schvarcz: They are not tangible. They are something that you see only because you have a different perception.

Narrator: By the fifteenth century, the Catholic Church was reaching the same opinion. The Church elders had failed to foresee that allowing the depiction of angels would undermine one of its most precious principles: that all things holy are abstract. Allowing the painting of angels had given them form, not just on canvas, but in the minds of believers.[35]

Unfortunately, even if there had been iconography guidelines, there almost wouldn't be any way to prevent what would begin to take place in the following generations. The Church of Rome, so heavily surrounded with the sensual pagan gods and goddesses of the Greco-Roman mythological culture, would only be able to keep these two worlds separate for so long...

Although there were historical clashes involving the Romans and the Greeks from the beginning (back during the Greeks' "vase-painting" days), it is blatantly clear when studying both cultures that the Romans held a great appreciation for the way Greeks celebrated life, especially when it came to their artistic or recreational customs. It's well known that their belief systems were very similar—and in some cases, were identical concerning certain pagan gods, their role and function on the earth, and their relationship with humanity—though they differed in their views of the afterlife: The Romans generally held the idea that spectacular works and good behavior would transform them into gods upon death, which is a stark contrast to the rather bleak general beliefs the Greeks held about floating aimlessly around in the Underworld (or "the Realm of Hades"). Despite a few deviations, anyone who has studied both groups at length knows that when the Romans conquered the Greeks, they *did not* conquer their cultural traditions or expressions. To the contrary, they adopted the Greeks' appreciation for theatrics and drama unto themselves, and this most certainly included the panache of their brushstrokes and chisel strikes. Roman art—from paintings to music, stage, and beyond—espoused the flamboyant Greek flair in countless ways, making the depictions of the gods in paintings or sculptures nearly indistinguishable from Roman to Greek, and vice versa (minus diminutive differences that only the anthropologically tuned eye would spot). This, of course, meant that regardless of political unrest between them, they would at least be merged in the breathtaking masterpieces they designed, and without a doubt, the Greco-Roman culture, as a united front in the world of artistic expression, was the greatest influence over imaginative creations in the ancient world for well over a thousand years.

Another thing the Romans and Greeks had in common was their view of women. The Greeks viewed women as the satisfiers of men and little else. If a baby girl was born in an ancient Greek household, it was up to the man of the house to decide whether the baby would be left outside until she starved to death, sold into slavery or prostitution (a practice that paved the way for the "career prostitutes" of the pagan temples in New Testament times), or raised in his household (an option that guaranteed she would simply grow to be *his* slave—which, for a hundred-plus disturbing reasons, had the potential of being an equally terrible fate). Women weren't allowed to participate in political affairs, and their social lives were largely limited to their husbands and children. Unlike the Greeks, Roman women, if they were born into wealth, were allowed to have an education and hold the status of a citizen, but otherwise the two cultures agreed on the near uselessness of the female gender, with only one exception: a woman was *beautiful.*

In both the Greek and Roman systems of religion (which, as stated, frequently merged to the point that they appeared indistinguishable to the untrained eye), the pantheon of the gods and goddesses was predominantly built upon sexually deviant relationships including (but certainly not limited to) marital infidelity, rape, incest, homosexuality, bestiality, and even necrophilia. No Greek or Roman mythology is ever as sanitized as Disney's *Hercules*… Even the most rudimentary romp down Research Lane in the subject of their pantheons reveals intensely sickening sexual desires and the fulfilment thereof (as was the case for many ancient religions, as far back as early Babylonian sex-magick cults), and the reward of these satisfied appetites often manifested in additional power and control instead of reprimand. In other words, violence and sex were often a means of increasing status and domination amidst the gods of the ancient world religions, not only as means of getting revenge or quenching lust. Therefore, blood and nudity (oh so much nudity!) was prevalent in Greek/Roman "religious" (mythological) art for centuries before Christ was born. Naturally, this means that the dominating artistic finesse of this geographical territory before Christianity was an established religion of the Empire that was related to false gods, repulsive domination tactics, death, and proudly displayed genitalia.

When Christianity *did* become an established religion of the Empire, it pushed against this immoral trend quite successfully. By medieval times, most human forms appearing in mainstream art (not including the pornographic art that still circulated under the radar) were modestly covered with long robes, so, since it wasn't really an issue, the Seventh Ecumenical Council didn't have to address nudity; their main concern was whether Christ's humanity and deity were both coming through on a single canvas. A few generations *following* the Seventh Ecumenical Council saw the earliest stages of the Renaissance (which holds its roots right there in Rome), and it was probably about that time when many a bishop wished that the council had drawn some harder lines in the sand about what would and what would *not* be allowed in "Christian" art.

As the Renaissance dawned and countless numbers of citizens ran toward science, humanism, realism, academia, and nearly every other form of intellectualism, all in the pursuit of trumping the mere medieval "scholasticism" of yesteryear, Rome experienced a *major* revival of Greek philosophy.

Historians as of yet cannot agree on what year the Renaissance started. It has been acknowledged unanimously that there was a "Renaissance of the Twelfth Century," but between that social movement and the famous older-brother movement known simply as "the Renaissance" (sometimes "the Italian Renaissance")—which launched several celebrated polymath superstars like Leonardo da Vinci and Michelangelo into permanent fame—hundreds of smaller social developments carried all of Europe into a new era of thought. In the first of these two movements, Aristotle's writings and teachings were brought back into light, which inspired one scholarly wave after another of philosophy, and before long, people were questioning Orthodox doctrine of the Roman Catholic Church. Scholasticism (critical and academic analysis of theology) was born and spread quickly into secular universities, resulting in a significant exodus of students from Christian monastic schools and into irreligious educational settings.

Although there were Church leaders who railed against such a progressive cultural shift on the grounds that students of the Word were being polluted with worldly thinking, others embraced the shift and celebrated the sharp increase of focus on medicine, science, and law, seeing it as an opportunity for God's Word and will to be taken into secular outlets and careers.

As history does tell, religion thrived inside and outside the Church throughout both Renaissance movements, but a central side effect to the sudden and extreme demand for increase in education was an equal increase in the process of intellectual inquiry over and about every fathomable thing in the world: *Everything* had to be questioned—every knowledge base in existence was in need of revision. It was no longer sufficient to simply believe in something. One had to explain *why* and *how* they believed in something, and be able to provide a scholastic breakdown of their rationale. If they couldn't do so, they were socially expected to keep studying until they had all the answers. Additionally, because humans are capable of logical and rational thought, we are by default supremely individual, and are therefore encouraged to break away from the majority and explore our own spiritual and philosophical convictions—regardless of whether they line up with the teachings of the Church or the worldview shaped by our upbringing.

(Funny how history repeats itself. This era reminds these authors much of today's postmodernist America: Nobody knows what truth is because *your* truth is not the same as *my* truth. Even the word "truth" itself has to be questioned to the point that nobody knows what we think or believe while we ironically claim to know everything because of the increase of intellectualism that spawned the questioning of truth in the first place. *Wheeze, gasp...* Are you confused yet? Us too...)

So, regardless of when *the* Renaissance began, the seeds of liberal reform had already more than paved the way for it to commence as early as the twelfth century. Europe's focus on philosophy in turn championed the ancient Greeks, not only in the pursuit of enlightenment and inquiry, but once again in a widespread, cultural appreciation for *artistic expression*—including the deep appreciation for the form of the human body, and shamelessly so.

Back to square one, but with a few tweaks: All the gods and goddesses were back in paintings, just like before—equipped with gender, blood, and genitalia—but now painters and sculptors had both legal *and* societal support for bringing some of those same impressions into *any* spiritual/religious sphere, including Christianity.

Greek art and mythology had for so long conditioned people to visualize a spirit being or deity's power through sex, seduction, or sensuality that when the revival of Greek art hit Europe, it wasn't unnatural at all for artists to subtly suggest in their images that even a chaste spirit—or, in this context, an angel of God—would be viewed as stronger, mightier, or more influential on earth if the finished piece held provocative insinuation. Again, not *all* artists' work was born out of a religious conviction. Some of the artists were devout Christians, some of them adopted parts of several religions, some were working out their beliefs through their art, and so on. The deep questioning that had become routine at this time, along with the great appreciation for the beauty of the human body, encouraged artists to be open to a new blend of spiritual expression that reflected each artist's personal journey of faith.

That's not to say that all the angels of God around this time were portrayed in a sexually explicit way. (And it's not to say that many artists depicting Christian icons were confused about their beliefs. That would be an overstatement. However, it would be just as inaccurate to say that every painting or sculpture conveying a Bible character or spirit created at this time was modestly and respectfully designed by a theologian of the Church.) There is a *world* of difference between sexual explicitness and subtle suggestion. Although many of the angels (and demons, by the way) were presented wholly in the buff, that was simply a part of the ancient Greek culture—now revived in the early stages of the Renaissance—and didn't immediately suggest eroticism or anything sexual at all. Whereas there would *always* be conservative personalities in the Church who balk even at an exposed collarbone in a painting, the trend of Greco-Roman/Renaissance art had for so long been featuring unashamed nakedness that it would take a certain something extra to insinuate indecency.

Consider the works around this time showing the Garden of Eden; it's not hard to locate classical images of Adam and Eve's fully exposed bodies, including breasts and genitals, but to the Europeans during the Renaissance, this wasn't considered erotic *unless* the image conveyed suggested sensuality. The human body, in and of itself, was a natural thing that no one needed to blush about, and centuries of nudity in art made the idea of unclothed spirit beings no big deal, so to speak. (This was especially true for any art showing young boys, which is why the "Christ Child" paintings often illustrate a naked baby Jesus.) However, if the character in an image was female—and if she held even the slightest note of sexual innuendo in her eyes, facial expression, hands, arms or legs, or pose—even a modestly clothed (or "robed") character in art could insinuate something erotic, because the picture itself had the potential to convey *intent*. Perhaps put more simply: A strong, male angel of God standing like a warrior ready for battle could be stark naked and nobody would bat an eyelid. He would only be seen as a powerful entity from a realm where clothing was not a factor, and the focus would not be upon his nudity, but upon his function as a soldier. (This is true as a general rule. However, there were, of course, Christian theologians alive at that time who would have held a strong opinion about a nude male angel because of the Genesis 6 and Enochian references to fallen angels sleeping with the daughters of Israel. The very depiction of an angel with reproductive function would pose an awkward question about whether the artist had intended to suggest the holy angel in the image was "equipped" to commit the same grievance as the evil angels had at the beginning of the world. But if the angel was not intentionally depicted in any way as wicked, conservative Christians and theologians would have little choice but to dismiss it as a cultural norm.)

On the other hand, a female angel painted with gentle, delicate, swooping lines, whose nudity is cleverly obscured by long locks of hair or floating cloth—featuring a confident and serene face, outstretching her pale, white arm delicately across the canvas as she intervenes for a human below—*that* was something worth writing home about, because art is subjectively interpreted, and anyone could confuse an unclothed female angel with a Greek goddess with the intent to seduce (or worse).

Obviously, we shouldn't assume that all artists had a dark or pagan motive for changing the way they presented God's angels after the Seventh Ecumenical Council and leading into the early Renaissance. (In fact, as some historians reflect, as the Byzantine era slowly crawled into medieval times, many male angels resembled the descriptions recorded about the powerful eunuchs of the Imperial Court, which gives the impression that their inspiration was neither Christian nor pagan, but of a political origin.) Logic alone can quickly identify the draw toward imagining a female angel with wings, *regardless* of what a culture thought of women, simply because every culture from the beginning of the world has mothers who represent something men (or fathers) cannot. As a *spirit*, the *female* angel of God on canvas or in stone would have naturally been a thing of loveliness and mystery, enticing a passerby to consider the soothing, caring side of God's provisionary plan: Yahweh's choice to utilize spirits that bring ease and peace like a nurturing mother—sweet, gentle, maternal, and ethereal—communicating a comforting presence that a strong, dominant male couldn't equally capture. But to many within the Church, she would have popped off the canvas like a brazen Jezebel, regardless of how innocently she hovered around those she protected. Yes, a woman was beautiful, but she was also the object of carnal desire, even to the gods of the surrounding pagan religions.

Nevertheless, these delicate lines that traced even the exposed ankle of a female angel was at least initially a scandal to many Church leaders of the Middle Ages, because God's angels were to be fierce soldiers in His army, not sensual, alluring women sent to entice anyone for any reason. Regardless of the spiritual nature of the image, at the end of the day, to many within the Roman Church, a nurturing/soothing/maternal angel was hardly different than Aphrodite/Venus, the sometimes-hermaphroditic Greek/Roman goddess of love, reproduction, and sexual pleasure. The Seventh Ecumenical Council, having paved the way for the incorporeal and spiritually abstract nature of God and His subjects to be captured in art, inadvertently paved the way for God's angelic messengers to be, at least in the minds of religious leaders, suggestively indiscreet. The character of the woman in the picture might have shifted from Aphrodite/Venus to God's pretty angel—and the artists might choose to avoid scrutiny by painting/sculpting something floating over the woman's nudity—but as Christian art was heavily influenced by the pagan art that had dominated the Greco-Roman world for centuries, the brushstrokes now defining the pure angel were heavily influenced by those that had previously defined half-naked and malicious goddesses of lore involved in sexually deviant sports.

Additionally, for any early Renaissance artist, Christian or otherwise, an angelic messenger from Yahweh to His people would naturally possess the wings necessary for travel between heaven and earth. (Also, when glancing at a work of art, it wasn't always possible to recognize a figure as an angel unless there was some visual distinction between spirit and human. However, this certainly would not be the only way a creative artist could identify a spirit. With all the "glory" bursts around the heads of all God's key players in icons from the beginning, there could have been other ways. So, whereas the wings were a quick fix for an identification problem, it can't be the only explanation for why they were introduced.) Thus, over the years, wings were born into the artwork and placed on every angel, a cultural norm introduced by mankind's attempt to rationalize a divine and supernatural concept.

Yet, there was also a cultural factor that seems the most plausible. *Throughout ancient Greek and Roman mythology as well as the Renaissance, goddesses of the pagan pantheons were no strangers to wings.*

(*Every time a bell rings…* I wonder who keeps ringing these things.)

How strikingly similar classic Christian angels look in Roman/Renaissance artwork to the depiction of the winged goddess Nike/Victoria! Nowhere in the Bible is an angel described as a being a woman with wings, wearing a robe, yet now this portrayal was popping up as a norm. The link between modern Christian, pretty, female angels and the pagan Nike/Victoria is one that art historians and critics are quite open about, often treating the subject as if it's so obvious that nobody still questions it. As for the male angels with wings in this era: Those, too, are said to have been adapted from the pagan *genii* (plural of *genius*) of Roman mythology—protector spirits, each assigned to a person (much like contemporary concepts of guardian angels), especially for royalty—and Mercury (also Roman), the winged messenger between gods; Mercury is the father of Cupid (which we will soon discuss).

But another argument that comes up in this arena often relates to the lack of gender accuracy within these earlier periods. Gods haven't always been immediately distinguishable as male or female from the beginning. Many images or statues of Apollo (one example among many) could easily be mistaken to represent a woman, based on his facial features and hair: For example; he doesn't have a beard, his hair is long and curly, and his facial countenance is entirely gender-neutral. When Apollo *does* have on clothing—almost never in classical art—it's a long and flowing robe— which, again, could easily be mistaken for a woman's attire. Yet, the same is true for women or goddesses in these depictions, as they are easily confused with males at times, with their wide jawlines and short-cropped hair. Gender, therefore, was usually identified only by physical features such as exposed chest muscles, breasts, male genitalia (female genitalia was almost never depicted), or by actions, such as a woman washing a man's feet; a man slaying a beast; or, in the case of a god or goddess, an act, token, or symbol associated with that god or goddess, such as Apollo's harp). However, even these distinguishing features could be ambiguous, since some of the gods were hermaphroditic—both male and female.

So yes, it could be argued that the reason "female angels" were showing up in art after the lifting of the prohibition is that the original artists actually painted and sculpted "male angels" with feathered wings and long flowing robes and hair (or the equivalent), and they just weren't recognized as the "men" they were supposed to be… But how does that argument make it *better*? It's obvious that this potential reasoning for all the "female angels" around this time is actually far, *far* worse! Could it be that they were supposed to be male but were mistaken as female because the pagan art for centuries had—at times *intentionally*—confused the sexes to the point that they were indistinguishable?

When we arrive at a day in history when a pretty, blonde, feminine, maternal, gentle angel of God is actually a *man*—the less-offensive gender to appear as an angel according to patriarchal culture, but more controversial to the Church in his potentially hermaphroditic and effeminate appearance—we have major issues with Christian art.

The patriarchal *male* angel was transformed into what could only be described as a *sensual woman*...

It's no wonder that the Church at one point had such an issue with an artist's attempt to capture a spirit-being anthropomorphically. (And, as I'm sure you've already seen coming, it's no wonder that the Church would take such offense to Joan of Arc's admission that she saw God's archangels "corporeally and in reality." Such constant, *ceaseless* controversy around the pagan/angel connection would give cause for the Church to react swiftly, if not entirely impulsively, about Joan's visitations.)

Perhaps one of the greatest grievances that many within the Church have had with angel art appearing between the end of the iconoclasts and the Renaissance centers around the "cherub" or the "cupid." The biblical "cherub" (plural "cherubim") is a complex kind of angel that we will delve into later on, but for now, suffice to say that it is anything *but* a small toddler shooting "innocent love arrows" at unsuspecting couples every February 14. These naked, harmless, little "angels" spring from an important god in the Greek pantheon who, although not violent or malicious, had a sexually deviant nature. So many things are wrong with this picture, especially the idea that the words "cherub" (biblical angel of Yahweh) and "cupid" (which could also be described as the "Greek baby-god of deviant sex") inspire the same mental imagery in the minds of most people today.

First, the name of the Greek god *Eros* (from which we eventually derive the English word "erotic") translates to "sexual desire"—and, far from being an innocent love-arrow-flinger, he was the winged god of erotic love, carnal lust, passion, fertility, and illicit affairs who mischievously meddled with the other gods and goddesses of the pantheon. When the Romans adopted Eros into their pantheon as well, he was given the name Cupid, which again, translates as "desire." In pagan art, the cupids are most popularly connected to the mystery cult of Aphrodite's brother, Dionysus/Bacchus, the god of wine, sex, ecstasy, and unrestrained consumption. In ancient Greek epics and poetry, Eros/Cupid flies wherever he wants and bestows uncontrollable sexual desire for another by shooting subjects in the chest with an arrow. Occasionally, this act is accompanied with a kiss. Once Cupid's target has been hit, the victim is defenseless against the overwhelming lust until the flesh has been repeatedly satisfied. Furthermore, Eros/Cupid is viewed in ancient art and literature as a great advocate for homosexual intercourse. (These two elements of his nature together represent the potential of a heterosexual person being forced, against his or her will, to feel burning passion for a member of the same sex.) Depending on the version of the myth, Eros is either an original god from the "Chaos" void, and therefore has no birth account, or he is depicted as the son of Aphrodite. (This would explain how he would become the god of eroticism; the apple doesn't fall far from the tree in ancient Greece, apparently. In Roman mythology, Cupid was the son of Mercury and Venus, so it plays out the same way there also.)

Second, although Eros was originally shown in artwork to be a slender young man, and at times a naked youth around the teen or preteen age, artists and tales continuously have represented him as younger and younger, and by the Hellenistic period, he appeared mostly as a chubby infant. (The perversion behind this concept is as depraved as it can get—a nude *child* or *baby* god stirring up lustfulness and wicked sexual acts by shooting people in the chest with arrows... Wow. It's one thing to have a culture built upon a pantheon of deviant sex between consenting adults. It's another thing to bring the image or likeness of a little boy into it, let his "boy parts" show in a context that is sexual, keep his innocent appearance, yet knowingly depict that all the warped sex originated from him. I can't imagine a faster way to sponge the purity away from the image of a child.) Poetry and works of satire have sometimes state that Eros' arrows were released while he was blindfolded, and it is from that idea that we eventually arrive at the blindfolded Cupid of the Renaissance.

Third, as Eros/Cupid tended to be in many places at one time, he was eventually viewed as omnipresent. (This is why, later, during the Baroque Era of the Renaissance, the cupid/cherub in art represents the omnipresence of God.) As such, the lore surrounding him involved a certain multiplicity, and, instead of always appearing as Eros/Cupid (singular), he appeared as erotes (plural): tiny babies or toddlers flitting about in several areas of the same scene at once, which is why we almost never see a modern picture with only *one* cupid or cherub, *and* it's why they all tend to look identical (some are even depicted as mirror images). However, while in plural and omnipresent form, erotes sometimes took on their own love traits, and therefore oversaw different functions. Perhaps for this useful reason, erotes became part of Aphrodite's retinue. Then, under Aphrodite's supervisory rule, many other gods of the pantheon occasionally began appearing as erotes here and there, complicating the identification of which god or goddess shows up in what image, and when. In other words, not every classical Greek or Roman cherub or cupid is a depiction of Eros, Cupid, or erotes. At times, other independently fundamental gods emerge in imagery as chubby-baby, arrow-shooting erotes, primarily Hermaphroditus, Pothos, Anteros, Himeros, and Hymenaeus (the god of weddings and marriage, from whose name eventually developed the word "hymen" describing part of the female anatomy).

As to how these cherubs became so popular in classical works during the early Renaissance, expert Elisabetta Valenti of the *Galleria Nazionale d'Arte Antica* (National Gallery of Ancient Art) at the *Palazzo Barberini* in Rome says:

During the Renaissance, angels were often portrayed as children. The artists of the time were striving to capture the ideal of beauty. Children were seen as the embodiment of well-rounded, physical harmony, with minimal muscle definition, which allowed the painter to achieve delicate effects with chiaroscuro [the relationship between light and shading]. Besides, the image of the child was the epitome of tenderness. So, children provided ideal inspiration in keeping with the iconography of angels.[36]

Louise Grover from the National Gallery in London approaches the subject from the angle of mortality: "We have to remember that when these paintings were made, many, many babies died, and even though the idea that 'angels are dead babies' souls' is heretical according to the Church, this, perhaps, was something of a comfort."[37]

Remember the next time you buy that adorable Valentine's Day card—the one with the sweet, pure angel babies making men and women fall in love—that it draws its origins from an exceptionally immoral and sexually explicit branch of paganism.

As you can easily see, learned theologians at the first signs of the Renaissance who had familiarity with Greek/Roman roots in art were bombarded with an ongoing conundrum. Certainly we haven't covered all the ways that pagan iconography was redressed as Christian (for your information, some of the earliest depictions of Jesus were tweaked versions of the Greek Apollo and Hermes, the "ram-bearer"), but by now in our reflections, it's clear that the Church faced one of two decisions: 1) Instigate another iconoclasm (or convince a secular leader to do so) in an attempt to stop Christian art from syncretizing pagan iconography—which, for reasons stated at the Seventh Ecumenical Council, wouldn't set well and might touch off a mass kickback from Church leadership all over the world; or 2) Deal with the worst offenders case by case.

That wouldn't be as easy as it sounded, either, because art is naturally subjective and personal. Nobody knows for *sure* what each artist was thinking or intending when painting or sculpting a new piece. Artists either didn't know the biblical role and function or angels, or they knew and pretended *not* to. Whether it was intentional or not, after being around paintings of *genii* protecting emperors for enough years, it's not a stretch that the archangel Michael would also have wings as he protects Bible characters in Christian art, even if the Bible doesn't describe him that way. But whatever the causes behind the blending of pagan and Christian iconographies, many masterpieces left the door wide open for conflicting interpretation.

For instance, consider a Roman painting showing a winged angel descending to earth with a laurel crown in her hand and chaos beneath her. Christians with untrained eyes might see an "angel" carrying the all-too-familiar Grecian crown of sportsmanship (from where we get our modern Olympic medal emblems) while en route to assist a soldier of God on the ground. On the other hand, pagans might see in the same image the goddess Nike/Victoria her way to help Zeus crush the Titans during the battle for Mt. Olympus.

Or, here's another example: A chunky, naked baby with wings is depicted as sitting on a cloud in the heavens, looking down on a man and woman engaged in a sweet embrace. Christians might see a baby angel in God's care—the soul of a deceased human child, perhaps (a comforting "theology" of many parents during such times as when infant-birth casualties were extremely high)—gently influencing the couple below toward virtuous, innocent love. Alternatively, a pagan might spot a mischievous erote, one of the homoerotic, child-aged sex representatives of Aphrodite's retinue wickedly tempting the couple toward extramarital fornication. Or, perhaps, a pagan might even comprehend an appearance of Aphrodite's and Hermes' sexually androgynous son, Hermaphroditus, who was commonly known to appear in art as an erote.

Were these paintings Christian or pagan in origin? One or the other, or both? Did images like these glorify or offend God? Unless the work was done by a famous artist whose religious beliefs were widely known (and even that is suspect, knowing what we know now about the most famous painters/sculptors of that time), nobody could be sure that a piece of art had been created in reverence to God, or if it had been a contracted work by an unbelieving artist who wanted to make a buck on yet another household Madonna. (Many sources online involved in this discussion state that the artists of this time were obviously religious and had respect for what/who they painted, simply because their life's work was dedicated to religious art. That argument is as reliable as saying that anyone today who sells paintings of Buddha for a living in a tourist city in India is a devout Buddhist. Understand that artists at this time in history were in in extremely high demand, and the most heavily requested form of art *by a longshot* was Christian iconography. In the meantime, individualism—and the emphasis that placed on breaking away from social, political, and religious norms [shedding "group mentality," perhaps]—drove many painters to wear the "Christian iconographer" hat one moment and the "nude/pagan gods iconographer" the next.) Christian homes were decorated with more and more pagan iconography by the decade, and these images/icons began showing up within church walls, at times even upon liturgical tools. These pictures were everywhere, and before long, this style of "Christian art" was the societal norm.

When something becomes a societal norm, it is much, *much* harder to stop.

What a mess this whole thing had become!

Tragically, fighting against iconoclasts and legalizing religious art in the interest of permitting *respectful* depictions of holy, Christian images backfired. Even when the artists' intentions were wholesome, the finished products simply couldn't be. For every innocent brushstroke, a thousand theologians would cry "pagan idolatry" with the same iconoclastic voices that solidified the religious art prohibition in the first place. As history tells, though there was another iconoclasm beginning circa AD 814 (it, too, would not be the last), ultimately the liberty granted by the council bishops and Empress Irene would hold, so the Church was left to accept what such unrestricted artistic expression had earned for all of Christendom, whether they liked it or not.

What of Joan?

Within the next several centuries leading up to the birth of Joan of Arc, any time a notable, influential Christian with a significant audience or following dared to describe a member of the Trinity, Mother Mary, the saints, the apostles, or the angels in a concrete, corporeal likeness, the leaders of the Roman Catholic Church got nervous. Unlike what readers might be expecting—that the tense issue of religious art eventually calmed over the period of centuries and everyone decided to relax—in some ways, the problem only got worse.

One famous (and artistically stunning) painting that dates to around the time of Joan's trial is *The Annunciation* by Jan van Eyck, a masterful Belgian painter of the Northern Renaissance who was lived during Joan's life, and whose home was a mere 154 miles from the city of Rouen where the young martyr was executed. In the painting, as he delivers the news to Mary about the Son she is carrying in her womb, the archangel Gabriel is depicted with multicolored, peacock-style wings that smoothly transition from one vibrant hue to the next, like a gradated rainbow. More controversial than the bizarre wings, however, is the fact that Gabriel is draped in a dalmatic (the familiar, wide-sleeved tunic worn by Church clergymen), then covered with a cope (a kind of liturgical cape that clasps at the neck). These are not the garments of a priest, but of a *deacon*! Based only on his clothing in this image, Gabriel, in all his God-given might and authority, would *not be allowed to perform the Eucharist, and is therefore outranked by human priests*. Just like before, however, it would be up to the observer to decide whether Eyck had intended to make an ecclesiastical statement about how much authority Gabriel would have within the walls of a church, or if the artist had simply seen religious garments and decided to paint a pretty picture with what clothing clung to his memory. Either way, the painting would not go unquestioned.

By Joan's birth, a claim that an angel had appeared "corporeally and in reality" was indecent. No longer limited to the painted or sculpted angel, testimony of even *seeing* an angel—especially coupled with the description of it—was cause for major controversy. Now, with fresh eyes tuned into the backdrop of Joan's tragic trial, let's look again at some of the questions the interrogators were asking, followed by clarification (in brackets) about what they were likely suggesting in light of the historical icon-related circumstances:

Judge: Did you see these angels corporeally and in reality? [In other words: "Are you actually suggesting these angels were more than just spirit—that they would leave thousands of artists for hundreds of years without any clue as to how they look, and then suddenly appear to a teenage girl?"]

Joan: I saw them with my bodily eyes, as well as I see you [this confident claim shocked the jury, most definitely]; and when they left me, I wept; and I fain would have them take me with them, too....

Judge: Was he naked? [This question should make more sense now. Basically, he was asking: "Was he naked like the winged, pagan *genii* or Nike/Victoria?"]

Joan: Do you think God has not wherewithal to clothe him?

Judge: Does he have any hair? [No doubt he was planning to follow up by asking for a description of the hair to see what pagan gods matched her portrayal.]

Joan: Why should it be cut off? I haven't seen St. Michael since I left the Castle Crotoy, and I do not often see him. I do not know whether he has hair.

Judge: Does he have scales? [As mentioned earlier, "scales" refer to the measuring instrument. Michael was, according to Catholic Church tradition, responsible to weigh each soul on Judgment Day. Thus, he was depicted in art during Joan's day as holding his scales, with which he would weigh the good and bad deeds of mortal souls as they go on to meet their maker. Often, the scales would be shown as holding a righteous, pious person on one plate and either an evil presence or a sinner on the other. By asking Joan about the scales, the English Church leaders could have trapped her either way: If she had said no, she would be refuting or dismissing iconography that the Church had deemed suitable for his nature and character; if she said yes, she would be assigning Michael to the likeness of painted iconography…which the Church knew very well had been redressed from pagan origin.]

Joan: I do not know. I was filled with great joy when I saw him; and I felt, when I saw him, that I was not in mortal sin.…

Judge: Does he have wings? [Translation: "Does he look like the *genii* of the Roman pantheon?"]

Joan: Yes.… I have seen St. Michael and the saints so clearly that I know they are saints of paradise.

Judge: Have you seen anything of them besides the face? [More accurately: "Have you seen any other details that link your idea of Michael to pagan concepts? Is there anything else you remember that we can trap you with?"]

Joan: …I would rather have you cut my throat than tell you all I know; I will willingly tell you all I know about the trial.

Judge: Do you believe that St. Michael and St. Gabriel have natural heads? [Before we assume that the head of the body (as opposed to arms or legs, etc.) is the focus of this question, it must be understood that the emphasis was on whether the parts she *could* describe were either "in the natural," and therefore *flesh*, or "not in the natural," and therefore *spirit*. The nature of this question shows that the Church—though in agreement at the Seventh Ecumenical Council over the issue of corporeal/incorporeal depictions in *art*—was still milking a constant debate over whether the abstract nature of God's "spirit messengers" could be captured in the image of human description.]

Joan: I saw them with my two eyes, and I believe it was they I saw as firmly as I believe in the existence of God.

Judge: Do you believe it was God who created them in the form and fashion that you saw? [Another trap. If she said no, she would be claiming that some portion of the angels' creation was without God's hand; if she said yes, she would be stating that God created angels in "a form and fashion" that was corporeally perceptible to people, which denies the orthodox concept that they are spirits.]

Joan: Yes.

Judge: Do you believe that God from the beginning created them in that form or fashion? [Similar question, but this is an attempt to goad Joan into admitting the angels were like that "from the beginning," which would suggest they hadn't another form prior.]

Joan: You will learn no more from me at present than I have told you.

Judge: In what guise and shape, size and dress did St. Michael come to you? [They just *won't* let it go...]

Joan: He was in the guise of a most upright man. I will answer no more.

We can easily see that Joan's entire trial centered on the controversy of how people viewed angels. Again, recall that it wasn't that she answered incorrectly about how angels appeared; it was that she *answered at all.* As mentioned earlier, the sin wasn't in the claim of the visitation; the blasphemy was in the *description.* One documentary about Joan's trial notes stated:

> After *centuries* of debate, the theological principal accepted by the Church was that an angel was not a physical being, but a spiritual one. So the more real, physical details Joan described, the more like a demon her visions sounded, but Joan stood no chance of understanding this scholarly argument, and as she tried to demonstrate the truth of her visions by adding more and more detail, she damned herself in the eyes of her judges.[38]

(Note that when questioned about Michael having wings, Joan answered that he did. This may raise questions in the reader's mind, as we've already established that the Bible doesn't describe angels as having wings. The authors of this book will make no statement as to *why* Joan may have answered that way or as to what *specifically* she had seen to give her the impression that her visitor had wings. While the first obvious issue to many people is the fact that Joan of Arc had *some* type of visions that rendered a victory for France, our reason for discussing her in this book is to explain *the religious and political climate of this era, and how these events shaped lingering concepts and depictions of spiritual and angelic beings over the long term.*)

There were, throughout the years, certain leaders of the Roman Catholic Church who had discovered that this ongoing and relentless tension related to what God's key players really looked like could be manipulated for political gain…which is ultimately what happened to Joan. But for our purposes, it's not all about how they found a tool to manipulate her case on paper so they could justify having her killed (obviously, hers was a political death), it's that the tool—which forms itself as the question "What do angels look like?"—was powerful enough to kill her.

The world may never know for certain what Joan *really* saw, but we do know that those trial bishops barely mentioned the political strain between England and France and her role in the war. Her unabashed willingness to describe God's archangels as they had appeared to her was—after hundreds of years of angels-depicted-in-art controversy—the ruse they needed to condemn her. Any Joe Smith off the road might have earned the stink-eye for claiming he met angels and describing the incident, but when *Joan* opened her mouth about them, *two* entire countries tuned in to hear, for once and for all, what angels *really* looked like.

If Joan had been sent by God, she would bring answers to questions that humankind had been asking since the first generation under Adam and Eve. If she had *not* been sent by God, then her description of the saints and angels would be more misleading—and therefore more vile, indecent, and corrupt—than the *worst* of the "Christian idol worshipers" who made the Byzantine Iconoclasm a necessity.

However, if the people believed she had been sent by God, which most of the surrounding world did (even the English, who had feared her on the battlegrounds)—and, if the people believed her when she said her faithful angels would rescue her from the English, which many did due to her accuracy before—*then what happened to the peoples' trust in angels when she was horrifically burned at the stake?*

Ahhh... Now we've arrived at the *key element* of why Joan's life *must* be shared in this book! Everything about Joan, the iconoclasms, and art history has been building to this crucial moment.

The Church "found they needed to apologize for the angels who left the righteous to perish, so the idea evolved of the angel who could do nothing to help. The angel could only watch and weep.... Belief in the angels, the 'guardians,' was severely shaken, as was the belief in a benevolent God, *and still the angels wept.* Soon, questions would be asked about the existence of the heavens, themselves."[39]

England, France, and the world watched as the once-powerful and commanding Joan was defeated in court and carried to her fiery execution, and as the flames increased, people's faith in the messengers of God decreased. From every side, an unspoken questioned dawned:

Where were Joan's angels *now?*

Her last word, which she cried out six times, was simply the name of Jesus.[40]

Once again, this wasn't the execution of any ordinary citizen. The reach of this woman's story was profound.

After the unnerving and ominous event drew to a close, the embers beneath her stake hadn't completely cooled yet before even the secretary to the king of England (a man obviously expected to be staunchly opposed to Joan as a servant to the political adversary) said, "We are lost; we have burned a saint."[41] This is merely one of many similar recorded statements by people in comparable positions, who were either present or arrived shortly after her execution. Little did any know at the time how prophetic their sentiments were.

About twenty years after Joan's death—at the request of her surviving mother, Isabelle Romée, alongside Inquisitor-General Jean Bréhal—

Pope Callixtus III sanctioned a posthumous retrial of Joan's case. The retrial began in 1452 and concluded on July 7, 1456, when she was pronounced innocent of all the charges set against her in 1431. Pierre Cauchon, the judge and bishop presiding over Joan's first trial, was thereby declared a heretic for the judgments he made over her decades earlier, and he was posthumously excommunicated from the Church (he died in 1442). In May of 1920, 489 years after her death, Joan of Arc was canonized as a saint of the Roman Catholic Church.

(Note: Not every word said about Joan after she died was pleasant, as she *obviously* had enemies. Even immediately after death, some people started to question whether she had just gotten lucky for several years, and all her voices were a ruse. Though it would be irrelevant to go into detail about that feedback, one shocking and atrocious rumor about her will herein be corrected: the idea that Joan was sexually involved with Gilles de Rais, the notorious child serial rapist and murderer allegedly responsible for the torture and death of hundreds of children. Although de Rais was Joan's companion-in-arms during some of their crusades, no evidence suggests that the pair ever so much as shared a lingering glance. Quite to the contrary: Cauchon had Joan examined during the trial to ensure that she had not lied about being a "maid," and the virtuous result of that exam was brought into court evidence. Based on how Joan's descriptions about her treatment by the English guards in prison are interpreted, there is a strong possibility that she was sexually violated just before death, so those who claim she wasn't a virgin when she burned could possibly be right by accident, but it still has *nothing* to do with any secret affair with France's most hated man.)

The questions the world continues to ask about Joan of Arc may never cease this side of eternity: Were the voices in her head the side effect of mental illness? Was she clinically insane? Were the voices proof of divine intervention? Or might they have been simply lies? If the voices *weren't* legitimately from God, then how could Joan possibly have accomplished all she did for France within her own finite power? Or, as for the other obvious angle: How could she have accomplished all she did with the help of sinister or wicked forces if every step of the way they glorified Jesus Christ? How could she be a false prophet if her prophecies were both given to her and delivered by her in the name of Christ? First John 4:1–2 says: "Beloved, believe not every spirit, but try the spirits whether they are of God: because many false prophets are gone out into the world. Hereby know ye the Spirit of God: Every spirit that confesseth that Jesus Christ is come in the flesh is of God." Many Christians interpret all of the information in 1 John 4 as suggesting that she couldn't have been controlled by evil…a stance that some mainstream Protestants are uncomfortable with because of Joan's open communication with the saints. Yet, because the Protestant Reformation didn't occur until a century later, Joan's form of worship followed the Christian mainstream (read: "*Catholic* mainstream") at that time, which would have involved identifying with and communicating with a patron saint. That simply *was* Christianity at the time when Joan lived, and she was as devout as they come in following the ways of the Church. Might God have been willing to use a young girl who sought Him in the ways she knew how?

If the numbers of those who believe her to have been legitimately sent by God to liberate France—as well as her own words—are any indicator of reality, there's definitely a chance that Joan was the Lord's servant and nothing else, as she many times claimed to be nothing more than the servant of the Christian God. But that presents another problem: If Joan's voices *were* from God, then why wasn't she saved from execution? Certainly, God and His angels were powerful enough to deliver her…

Then again, God and His angels were also powerful enough to save Christ from the cross, but the Messiah's death was necessary for a much greater cause. Could that be the same for Joan? Was the testimony of God's provision over France drastically amplified in her execution than in her living? Might God have allowed her to leave this earth when and how she did to spare her from a crueler fate later on?

For goodness' sake: Was she ultimately sent by God to armor up and liberate France—or wasn't she?

Dr. Rachel Gibbons, professor at the University of Bristol (west of London) and expert of medieval history who is considered a key authority on Joan of Arc, acknowledges the diverse perspectives associated with Joan today, outlining briefly her vast résumé in the statement: "She is a saint. She's a knight. She's a heretic. She's a witch. She's a feminist champion. She's a prophet."[42] But for as many opinions as there are about her—ever circulating between the folk world of legend, the research world of academia, and the many theological hiccups that clash with her story from one denomination to another—many peculiar details about her time on earth point to something enormously supernatural...and angels are at the center of it all.

From the testimonies of only one girl, the entire world was willing to view angels as strong, mighty messengers of God.

From the death of that same girl, that same world saw their view of these angelic beings shift dramatically to remote, weepy spectators who hover helplessly above.

Where Does This Leave Us?

It always has been and always will be dangerous to base assumptions about the spirit world on what the culture or people lead us to believe. The act of describing angels might be without controversy now, and we may be legally allowed to paint or sculpt whatever we want, but the image portrayed in public about God's holy spirits is far from accurate.

Every time a bell rings... It doesn't seem so silly anymore. It's a curious thing, indeed, that we would dismiss one concept because it came from an old, black-and-white movie we know is campy and adopt another concept through gradual imprinting and lifelong exposure to misconceptions. The grievance is the same, is it not?

Nobody on the production side of this book would identify as an iconoclast. However, *everyone* behind the making of this book believes that it's time for some of our erroneous, culturally shaped concepts about angels to be destroyed. In Joan's day, those misconceptions were the alluring, chubby babies shooting arrows of love; in our day, they are the mystical angels of New Age meditation and Hollywood.

If we don't respect what history teaches us, we're doomed to repeat it. Angels have *always* been a mysterious subject around which many false claims cluster. It's imperative that we never allow ourselves to grow so accustomed to the "angel" we want to see—the paganized angel that parts of society dictate—that we lose sight of what the Word of God actually says.

With so many people across the world today praying to or worshiping angels directly—and with so many "clairvoyants" saying they can see and speak to them on our behalf with requests for material blessings or protection—we are constantly perched on the edge of accepting or perpetuating false ideas about what and who these messengers are. However, angel worship isn't a new trend. It's been an issue since the Council of Laodicea circa 363 (not officially a part of the Seven Ecumenical Councils), in which Canon 35 states:

> Christians must not forsake the Church of God, and go away and invoke angels and gather assemblies, which things are forbidden. If, therefore, any one shall be found engaged in this covert idolatry, let him be anathema; for he has forsaken our Lord Jesus Christ, the Son of God, and has gone over to idolatry.

Even farther back, in the first century, Paul addressed angel worship in the city of Colossae:

> Let no man beguile you of your reward in a voluntary humility and worshipping of angels, intruding into those things which he

hath not seen, vainly puffed up by his fleshly mind. (Colossians 2:18)

We should approach to the subject of angels with caution, of course. But we should also approach it with a focus only on what's *biblical*. Our first and last authority on the topic should be the Bible—not a young girl in France, not the presiding bishops of a Church council, not the frescoes on the ceiling of Renaissance homes, and not today's psychics or mediums.

But for as many "amens" that paragraph might have just drawn from readers, we must remember that the information in the following pages might challenge us away from traditions *within* the Christian Church as well…and even if that's uncomfortable, if it forces our ideas and beliefs to more appropriately align with the Word of God, it's ultimately the right thing to do.

In Colossians 2:8, Paul wrote: "See to it that no one takes you captive by philosophy and empty deceit, according to human tradition" (ESV). In Matthew 15:3–6, Jesus, Himself, said: "Why do you break the commandment of God for the sake of your tradition?…for the sake of your tradition you have made void the word of God" (ESV). The Word is clear that we should be willing to *immediately* let go of traditional concepts birthed through society and the imaginations of humans whenever the Word disagrees with them. And yes, this rule applies even when it's the Church that's perpetuating the inaccurate concept.

But wait… Didn't Paul say in 1 Corinthians 11:2 that we are to "hold firmly to the traditions"?

Not so fast. If we keep that verse *in context*, we will see that the "traditions" Paul was referring to were his teachings of the Messiah and the kind of Church we're supposed to be today. Because Paul's words to Corinth were included in the canon of Scripture, the "traditions" he referenced have actually *become* a part of the Word of God. In fact, many translations (including the NIV) translate this word as "teachings." So, it circles right back around: Yes, we are to "hold firmly" to what the Word of God says and not to the traditions of mankind or society.

Therefore, even when popular beliefs about angels exist *within the Church*, we must be willing to let those beliefs go if what we think and what the Bible says are not in precise alignment.

I wonder how many nasty problems the council bishops, Joan, England, France, royal families, and all the great artists of history could have avoided by obtaining a copy of this book...

3

The Origin and Nature of Angels

*N*o true reflection upon the nature of angels and their role in modern times would be complete without at least a brief look at the nature of the Creator God who made them. Too many questions about the existence and purposes of angels relate to the existence and purposes of God to simply skim past them. So, even though this work will not include an exhaustive record of all He was, is, and will forever be, we'll address a few of the basics here. God is so unfathomably all-powerful, and His relationship to the world and everything in it is so profound, that it would take a million pages to scratch the surface of who He is, so we should consider the following ruminations about Him as just a simple reminder.

Fundamentals of God

Creator

Proof of God's existence is all around us. He cannot be seen with the physical eye (John 1:18; 1 Timothy 6:16; Luke 24:39; 1 Corinthians

2:10–15), but much like the wind—an invisible force with clearly visible effects—those with eyes to see the properties of God's handiwork around us at all times (in both physical and spiritual ways) have all the proof they need that He exists and that He created the earth. Though science continues forever to determine the origins of all life through completely random events in space a number of billions of years ago, the mathematical probability that the world we see today is still biologically successful in both maintenance and reproduction by means of random happenstance is, at the very least, a logical conundrum. If we were to accept the Big Bang Theory (which, as the name states, is *only* a theory, though today's culture often treats it as fact), we would still be left wanting the answer to the question of who or what created the universe that the Big Bang occurred in, as well as all the particles involved in the event.

Even human DNA and DNA Replication Machineries presents the unanswerable question: "Since they all rely on each other to function, which came first between DNA, RNA, and proteins, and how could one exist without the other in the beginning of all life?" Questions like this and many others make the base of what scientists and scholars refer to as "the Cosmological Argument"—theories relating to the "first cause" of the "cosmos" (universe). The systematic arrangement of the universe and all life as we know it (including the earth's interdependency between weather patterns, seasons, plants and animals, and human biology) is complicated enough that, to believers, assuming it was all a random accident makes as much sense as throwing rocket parts the air and having them "accidentally" or "coincidentally" fall together to make the first fully functional and operational NASA space shuttle. On the other hand, the Word openly acknowledges a Designer who created the world with order and purpose (Psalms 19:1–2, 8:3–4; Genesis 1:12, 21, 25).

Evolution has always been problematic in answering all the questions that brilliant human minds have postulated throughout history. And with every scientific discovery related to life's origins comes another season of science that refutes yesterday's "facts" about the world and everything in it. As such, faith in a divine Creator appears to believers to be the far more rational conclusion. As this book is not an apologetics piece to argue creationism, we'll proceed to focus on the nature, character, and existence of God and His angels via the assumption that the Creation-versus-evolution question has been satisfied for our readers.

Essence, Character, and Sovereignty

The Bible approaches God's existence from the very beginning as an obvious assumption, because of His handiwork through every page. In other words, there was never a moment in time when God was created by something or someone else. He is the beginning, the present, and the forever (Revelation 1:8, 22:13) of all existence—a concept that we humans cannot easily wrap our brains around. The book of Genesis reveals that He made the world and everything in it, and His nature can be seen from every angle *within* His creation—a concept modern Christians have no problem accepting—but it again becomes challenging to accept that while He is *in* it, He is also independent *of* it.

He is:

- Omnipresent, everywhere at once (Jeremiah 23:23; Psalm 139:7–12; see also Matthew 18:20);
- Omniscient, knowing all things at once and from every aspect of time—past, present, and future (Psalm 139:1–6; Proverbs 15:3; 1 John 3:20); and
- Omnipotent, holding infinite power over all things (Job 42:2; Jeremiah 32:17; see also Matthew 19:26 and Ephesians 2:20).

He doesn't need planet earth or its inhabitants to prove Himself powerful to angels, demons, or any other spirits of the universe. Additionally, He is:

- Immutable—unchanging and unchangeable (Malachi 3:6; James 1:17; Numbers 23:19; see also Hebrews 13:8).

Nothing has, can, or ever will change God, nobody has the right to challenge His authority, and He has eminent charge over all things as He sees fit (Job 23:13; Psalm 115:3; Daniel 4:35). When Moses asked God how to respond when the Israelites asked who had sent him prior to their Exodus from Egypt, God, Himself, did not feel He needed to provide a detailed explanation. He is who He is (his literal response in that situation), and that was good enough (Exodus 3:14).

Yet, though the universe and every person or thing in it are subject to His ultimate prerogative, He proved Himself to be eminently all-loving and personally approachable when He extended Himself to us as Advocate, Friend, Teacher, and Counselor (John 14:26)—providing His only Son so that no matter how ugly humans get in this temporal condition known as life, *anyone* who believes will share eternity with Him in a glorious and pain-free afterlife (John 3:16; Revelation 21–22). How amazing that He would allow for such provision.

What a mighty God we serve, right?

John 4:24 states that God is Spirit—note that it does not say "*a* spirit*," as in one among many. He is unconfinable and omnipresent, and since He is the beginning and the end, He is everywhere all at once and in observation of all things and all times, not limited to our linear comprehensions of time. He is the *ultimate* Spirit, unlimited by any and all of our own expectations of what He should be. As the Spirit who creates humans—each with his or her own spirit—He is the *supreme* Spirit, forever alive and everlasting (Jeremiah 10:10). In fact, Scripture goes on to say, not only is He the source of life, He is *the* life (John 14:6). We finite humans are privileged to share in His image (Genesis 1:27), and because He is Spirit, we, too, are spirit, sharing incorporeal attributes alongside Him, such as conscience, emotions, will, intellect, and an intrinsic draw toward goodness and morality, manifesting itself in how we value humans and nature around us.

We frequently reflect upon how God is all-knowing, but unfortunately, today's Western Christianity tends to dilute the fullness of that idea as describing a God from whom we cannot hide. To us, this quality often simply means that you can't get by with stealing that car or telling that lie, and so on. Whereas it is true that He sees and hears all we do and think, this attribute likewise includes a limitless intellect, meaning that God is also the most intelligent entity over the universe. Nobody can know the depths of His mind or even imagine giving Him advice (Romans 11:33–36). He is the Supreme Engineer, Artist, Designer, and Stylist of the world He created.

Emotions

Likewise, we struggle to wrap our brains around the personality and emotions of God. Today, it's perhaps easier to imagine a God of wrath and judgment, especially after the historically famous *Sinners in the Hands of an Angry God* works and sermons by Jonathan Edwards of the First Great Awakening that profoundly affected modern cultural ideas of how God views us in our sinfulness.

(Actually, this is a bit ironic, because the biographical accounts of Edwards' life attribute the aggressive, pulpit-pounding oratory style to Edwards' *grandfather*, not to Edwards personally. When Edwards became the famous preacher of the First Great Awakening, he borrowed the theology [and the titles] of his grandfather's sermons, so it is Edwards who is remembered as the fiery deliverer of God's wrath, but he, himself, was a calm and tranquil man behind the pulpit. His teaching brought people in droves to accept the loving depiction of Jesus. Unfortunately, to this day, many acquaint *Sinners in the Hands of an Angry God* with this gentle spiritual giant, viewing him as forceful and insistent upon their repentance, but he was quite tender in his delivery. His focus was upon repentance through reverence for an amazing God, not repentance out of fear of His judgment.[43] Nevertheless, after the Great Awakening in the 1700s, Western Christianity was influenced for hundreds of years, viewing God as the thrower of lightning bolts if we miss the mark in our daily lives. To many of those in the early formation of the US, God was perhaps *only* a judge, instead of "judge" being merely one of His many characteristics. It took a lot of cultural shifts and powerful voices throughout the years to heal our Church from that concept, but to many outside the Church today, our God is still "a vengeful God" perhaps partly as a result of Edwards' enormously popular and widely published sermons [read often by those who never heard him speak in person]. It just goes to show what kind of damage can occur across entire countries when preachers and teachers of the Word choose to teach what is trending instead of sharing the inspired and living Word. Even more tragically, Edwards' own teaching was a hundred times more inspiring than his grandfather's, leading people to the Lord because He *loves*, not because He *hates*, and I imagine that soft-spoken country preacher of Northampton, Massachusetts Bay Colony would have never used his grandfather's sermons if he would have known they might have canceled out the tender, redemptive power of his own over time.)

However, we know from Scripture that God also feels compassion (Psalm 135:14; Judges 2:18; Deuteronomy 32:36), grief (Genesis 6:6; Psalm 78:40), joy (Zephaniah 3:17; Isaiah 62:5; Jeremiah 32:41), jealousy (Exodus 20:5; Exodus 34:14; Joshua 24:19), and *most of all*, love. The Word is packed with testimony of God's love, including beautiful verses like John 3:16 and Jeremiah 31:3, but the most mind-boggling example is 1 John 4:8, which states that God *is* love.

He not only feels and experiences love...He "is" love.

The Word could have said that God "is" anger, jealousy, or a number of other emotions, but in this sweet Scripture, God "is" love. God, in

His perfection, cannot contradict Himself, so whereas His standards of holiness and righteousness result in His expression of anger or jealousy when His people turn away from Him toward evil or paganism, of all emotional attributes, the only one that He perpetually "is," is love.

But note that we shouldn't associate Him with emotions like we do other humans; God doesn't have "mood swings," and His emotional expressions aren't impulsive. On the contrary, God's expressions of anger, wrath, judgment, etc., are consistent with His character. He *will always* be angry when His people worship false gods (simply as one example), and His consistent expressions are not "reactions," but are a solid, set position upholding righteousness. He wouldn't be a "completely and wholly righteous God" if He tolerated and allowed wickedness (Habakkuk 1:13). Therefore, though He has the final prerogative and does as He wills (Job 23:13; Psalm 115:3; Daniel 4:35), He is not capricious. It is to the standard of the greatest intelligence, rationale, and compassion in all the cosmos from the One who "is" love that He acts consistently with His character in all that He does, including emotions or actions that we humans perceive to be in contrast to His soothing, loving hand.

(Though it doesn't completely capture the same concept, one might more clearly understand God's emotional side by imagining a good mother disciplining a child for bad behavior. Though the mother seems angry, ultimately, her emotions reflect her attempt to care for the health and welfare of her child. When she scolds her tiny son for trying to play with an electrical outlet plug for the thirty-ninth time, her reproach is a direct result of her intent to show provisionary love. In this moment, you might say she "*is*" love" for displaying her "anger" during scolding, because love and provision are the genesis of her discipline. Therefore, in this analogy, the good mother who shows "love" and "anger" at the same time is not at all inconsistent or capricious. Again, it's not a perfect analogy of God, but because *nothing* is a perfect analogy of God, this word picture might be helpful.)

Resemblance to Humanity

In addition to emotions—though God is invisible, as discussed—other poetic instances within the Word describe God with physically human-like qualities (anthropomorphisms): His "hands" (Hebrews 1:10), His "face" (Genesis 32:30), His ability to "hear," "see" (Isaiah 37:17; Genesis 1:4), "speak" (Genesis 1:3), "walk" (Genesis 3:8), "smell" (Genesis 8:21), and even "sew" (Genesis 3:21)! (This is by no means an exhaustive list; another interesting anthropomorphism is in Isaiah 66:1, where the earth is described as His footstool.)

Yet, for all these expressions (i.e., the "image" of God that we share in common—the "invisible" becoming "knowable" through picture words we can comprehend), the Word makes a clear distinction between God and humans, going as far as to describe a Being so magnificent and vast that we will never *completely* understand Him on this side of eternity: "'For my thoughts are not your thoughts, neither are your ways my ways,' saith the Lord. 'For as the heavens are higher than the earth, so are my ways higher than your ways, and my thoughts than your thoughts'" (Isaiah 55:8–9). Romans 11:33–34 goes on to say: "O the depth of the riches both of the wisdom and knowledge of God! how unsearchable are his judgments, and his ways past finding out! For who hath known the mind of the Lord? or who hath been his counsellor?" Still yet, in 1 Corinthians 2:11 we find: "Even so the things of God knoweth no man, but the Spirit of God."

One Person (Jesus) within the Godhead/Trinity submitted Himself to the incarnation, becoming wholly human in the literal sense, but He still remained wholly God, as the following verses illustrate:

- "And Thomas answered and said unto him, My Lord and my *God*" (John 20:28).
- "Looking for that blessed hope, and the glorious appearing of the great *God* and our Saviour Jesus Christ" (Titus 2:13).

- "But unto the Son he saith, 'Thy throne, O *God*, is for ever and ever: a sceptre of righteousness is the sceptre of thy kingdom'" (Hebrews 1:8).
- "Concerning his Son Jesus Christ our Lord, which was made of the *seed of David according to the flesh*" (Romans 1:3).
- "Hereby know ye the Spirit of God: Every spirit that confesseth that Jesus Christ is come in the *flesh* is of God" (1 John 4:2).
- "For many deceivers are entered into the world, who confess not that *Jesus Christ is come in the flesh*. This is a deceiver and an antichrist" (2 John 1:7).

And rather than leaving us to believe blindly, although there is virtue in believing without seeing (John 20:29), Jesus displayed the multiplicity of both natures by: a) carrying out acts that *only* God can accomplish while in human form, such as when He forgave sins (Mark 2:1–12; Luke 7:48–50); and b) showing Himself to be vulnerable to common limitations of the human body, such as when He was thirsty (John 19:28). Hebrews 2:17 also provides a glimpse into the deeply complicated and mysterious purpose behind Christ's incarnation: "Wherefore in all things it behoved him to be made like unto his brethren, that he might be a merciful and faithful high priest in things pertaining to God, to make reconciliation for the sins of the people."

Despite this, we learn from John 1:1 and 14 that Jesus was never a "created being" (despite what Arian heresies arose in the fourth century requiring the First Ecumenical Council at Nicaea): "In the beginning was the Word, and the Word was with God, and the Word was God.... And the Word was made flesh, and dwelt among us, (and we beheld his glory, the glory as of the only begotten of the Father,) full of grace and truth." Humanity was not the beginning of Jesus' life, because He is eternal.

So, whereas God is abundantly above humanity and therefore incomprehensible to us—to the point that He cannot be completely and accurately summarized in any earthly tongue—He has also condescended Himself to be exactly what we are from birth to death (but without sin). In this, there will always be an obvious resemblance to and connection with humanity, while simultaneously being abundantly more than mere human.

Our God really is an awesome God.

Although this isn't an exhaustive outline of who *God* is and how He functions (as if there is such a thing), the information in the last several pages will launch us into the theology of who *angels* are (the messengers that *God* created) and how they function as outlined in the Word. Moving forward, God—including all three members of the Trinity—will still be the "main character" of this book, because all of His creation is a reflection of Him, so we aren't changing the subject away from Him. Rather, we're dedicating the rest of this book to one aspect of His design, now that we've taken a few minutes to establish a starting place from which to grow our understanding of His heavenly handiwork.

Treatment of Terms

Before continuing, we must dispel the common misconception that the word "angel" represents *all* the spirit beings within the heavenly host of God. There are many different spirit beings with unique roles in the supernatural realm under God, and each is given an exclusive name.

Maybe the following will help illustrate:

A hunter goes into the woods in pursuit of game. To assist him, he takes along three breeds of dog, each known for being excellent hunting collaborators, and each useful in ways unrelated to the others. The experience plays out like this:

1. The first dog, the "pointer breed," locates nearby game hiding in a thick bush. He stands perfectly still, with one paw off the ground

and his tail as straight as possible. With his snout and intense gaze, he assumes the "pointing" position to alert his master that he has pinpointed exactly where the game is hiding.

2. The second dog, the "flusher breed," without ever recklessly chasing the birds *away* from the hunter, corners the game from just the right angles and charges to flush the flock straight into the open air, where the hunter can get a great shot.

3. The third dog, the "retriever breed," waits until the hunter has successfully completed a kill, then races to the dead animal. With the expert, "soft-mouth" handling characteristic of his breed, the retriever carries the game back to his owner without biting into the flesh.

All three of these breeds are equally *canine* in nature—and all three are equally assisting their master in accomplishing the act of a hunt. However, none of the animals looks just like either of the other two, and none carries out the same function as the others. People who aren't interested in hunting would simply call all three of these breeds "dogs," and the general population would agree that the term is accurate. However, it would *not* be correct to look at all three—the pointer, the flusher, and the retriever—and say they are all "retrievers."

Yet, this is the mistake we often make when using the term "angels." We might hear someone in church on Sunday morning say, "Oh, yeah, the 'seraphim' in God's throne room are those fiery angels with six wings." Whereas that kind of terminology is common, it's fundamentally flawed. Using our hunter illustration, it would be similar to saying, "The 'pointers' are those dogs that carry the game to their master," a sentence that *names* the "pointer" but *describes the function of* a "retriever."

To make it perfectly clear: Just as the names "pointer" and "retriever" shouldn't be interchanged, neither should "angel" and "seraph." Just as the pointer and the retriever are *dogs*, the angel and the seraph are members of the same heavenly host of spirit beings under God's authority.

Calling a seraph (or a cherub, etc.) an "angel" is as inaccurate as calling a retriever a "pointer."

Interestingly, the word "angel" (Hebrew *mal'ak,* Greek *aggelos;* commonly transliterated *angelos*) means "messenger." Frequently throughout Scripture, this term refers to a spirit being within the heavenly host; i.e., a messenger of God directly:

- "And God heard the voice of the lad; and the angel of God called to Hagar out of heaven, and said unto her, 'What aileth thee, Hagar? fear not; for God hath heard the voice of the lad where he is'" (Genesis 21:17; Old Testament example).
- "Then the devil leaveth him, and, behold, angels came and ministered unto him" (Matthew 4:11; New Testament example).

Because the root words *mal'ak* and *angelos* can mean "messenger" in a generic application, the reference also appears in regards to a *human.*

- "That confirmeth the word of his servant, and performeth the counsel of his [human] messengers; that saith to Jerusalem, Thou shalt be inhabited; and to the cities of Judah, Ye shall be built, and I will raise up the decayed places thereof" (Isaiah 44:26; Old Testament example).
- "And when the [human] messengers of John were departed, he began to speak unto the people concerning John, What went ye out into the wilderness for to see? A reed shaken with the wind?" (Luke 7:24; New Testament example).

Right away, it is clear that "angel" isn't as exclusive a term as we may have thought. Because the word can also describe a "messenger" generically, we have to view it as a description of a *function.* An angel is called an "angel" because it is a "messenger," not because it is the only "breed" of spirit beings that serve God's will.

As such, this book—unlike *so many* others in this genre—will not use the word "angels" as an all-encompassing term referring to all the members of the heavenly host. Instead, we will refer to the term "Celestial Order" as referring to *all* of the spiritual beings who serve God's purposes, and we'll refer to the term "angel" *singularly* as meaning a member of the order of beings by the same name.

So, to clarify: Anytime readers see the capitalized term "Celestial Order" in the upcoming pages, it represents not only the "messengers" (angels), but the seraphim, cherubim, and all the other spirit beings that have the same goal of serving the Lord in the spiritual realm, such as the: "sons of God" (Genesis 6:2–4; Job 1:6–12, 2:1; 38:7), "holy ones" (Job 5:1; Daniel 8:13; Zechariah 14:5), "ministers" (sometimes translated "servants"; Psalm 103:21), and simply "hosts" (Psalm 103:21).

Created Beings

Where do angels come from? They aren't a part of the Genesis Creation account, are they? Whereas the answer to these questions is *no*, we shouldn't assume that they, like God, never had a beginning. We can safely understand, however, that, like human souls, their existence will carry on. The Celestial Order is a product of God's creation, though it takes stepping away from Genesis to locate that fact within Scripture.

Psalm 148 covers many created things in one long list. Observe this chapter in its entirety:

> Praise ye the Lord. Praise ye the Lord from the heavens: praise him in the heights. Praise ye him, all his angels: praise ye him, all his hosts. Praise ye him, sun and moon: praise him, all ye stars of light. Praise him, ye heavens of heavens, and ye waters that be above the heavens. Let them praise the name of the Lord: for

he commanded, and they were created. He hath also stablished them for ever and ever: he hath made a decree which shall not pass. Praise the Lord from the earth, ye dragons, and all deeps: Fire, and hail; snow, and vapours; stormy wind fulfilling his word: Mountains, and all hills; fruitful trees, and all cedars: Beasts, and all cattle; creeping things, and flying fowl: Kings of the earth, and all people; princes, and all judges of the earth: Both young men, and maidens; old men, and children: Let them praise the name of the Lord: for his name alone is excellent; his glory is above the earth and heaven. He also exalteth the horn of his people, the praise of all his saints; even of the children of Israel, a people near unto him. Praise ye the Lord.

Now, if we cut to only what's relevant to angels, we arrive at: "Praise ye him, all his angels…[and] hosts…for he commanded, and *they were created*. He hath also *stablished them for ever and ever*" (emphasis added.)

More loosely, Paul writes in Colossians 1:16: "For by him were all things created, that are in heaven, and that are in earth, visible and invisible, whether they be thrones, or dominions, or principalities, or powers: all things were created by him, and for him." This verse makes it clear that God created not only "all things," but that also, each of these is delegated a location (heaven *or* earth) and a natural role (thrones, dominions, principalities, and powers), which of course encompasses the Celestial Order as well.

As far as *when* the Celestial Order was created, read Job 38:4–7:

Where wast thou when I laid the foundations of the earth? declare, if thou hast understanding. Who hath laid the measures thereof, if thou knowest? or who hath stretched the line upon it? Whereupon are the foundations thereof fastened? or who laid the corner stone thereof; When the morning stars sang together, and all the sons of God shouted for joy?

If this passage can be correctly interpreted to say that these "sons of God" were present when God "laid the foundations of the earth," then it could mean that the angels were created before our planet.

Errant Concepts and Common Questions about Angels

Some may find the order of this chapter a bit odd—starting with wrong teachings before approaching the correct teachings—but be assured, there's a sound reason for this approach. Some readers have questions about their preconceived ideas, and others want confirmation that what they believe about angels is true. I'd like to hit the ground running on this topic so that those readers don't have to skim the pages ahead to find what they're looking for.

I see evidence that there are far more errant than correct teachings about angels. We're in an age when, sadly, many Christians who regularly attend church don't know what the Bible says about the subject, because many of us are too busy to stop and read it personally. We tend to rely on our pastors to give us a weekly dose of verses and explain them. Not only does this mean we aren't personally sharpening ourselves with God's truth daily and are therefore open to being misled by New Age ideas of angels (which are rampant, even within some churches); it also means that we leave our entire theological worldview up to others, hoping they render an appropriate interpretation.

In light of that, let's look at a few popular, but incorrect teachings about angels.

The Source of Errant Teachings

Where do errant teachings come from? Answers to that question range from incorrect interpretation to intentional misleading. The truth is, the reasons misconceptions exist are varied. However, one common denominator is human logic and its capacity for error.

When we don't understand something, it's our first impulse to appeal to our own logic and experience to "fill in the blanks." Often, we do this by identifying what we'd like more information about and then looking for ways to connect it with what we already know. In other words, we play a "connect-the-dots" game, leaning on our own reasoning to guide us. As we map this course out between what we *know* and what we *want to know*, we lean on our rationality, leaving opportunity for flaws.

In mathematics, this type of problem-solving approach is called the *working backward heuristic*, which "translates to working backward from the answer to the given information in the problem."[44] An example of how this works appears in the simple calculation below:

$10 - ? = 3$

This simple subtraction problem is quickly and easily solved by taking the *answer* and factoring in the *provided information*. In doing so, we can determine the missing element. What most of us do, without even thinking, is rearrange the information within our minds to the following:

$10 - 3 = ?$

Because we know that $10 - 3 = 7$, we're able to fill in the number "7"—confident that we've come up with the accurate missing number and never giving the original equation much of a second thought. We have quickly filled in the blanks and solved the problem—and we can move along with our busy day. Whether it' a simple math problem such as this or other, non-abstract issues we face, this can be a great problem-solving strategy that helps us save time and headaches.

There are simple, nonmathematical ways that we use this same method in daily life without even realizing it. For example:

(I am hungry) + (?) = (I am no longer hungry)

We quickly conclude that the missing element indicated by the "?" is food. Thus, the necessary action is to eat. As the question becomes more complicated, the "?" becomes more ambiguous:

(I am cold) + (?) = (I am warm)

In this scenario, the answer is not as readily available. We must take a step back, considering and exploring more variables in order to assess the missing information: *Why is it* that I am cold? Perhaps I am standing in the rain without a coat, or maybe I am building a snowman with my kids, or it is even possible that I am at home where I *should be* warm, but I have not built a fire and/or my furnace is broken. In each of these situations, I can easily look around and assess *why* I am cold, because all of that information is *readily available to me at a glance.* But what about when the missing information takes a little more digging to unearth, or when the world offers myriad confusing counterinformation? As situations become more complicated, the "?" likewise becomes increasingly vague. The spiritual implications can be detrimental. A quick, devastating, yet common example of how this can confound theological matters is below:

(I am a sinner) + (?) = (I will go to heaven when I die)

Those of us who have Scripture-based faith know that the "?" is accepting Christ as Savior and asking Him to forgive our sins. But many false teachings in the world today (and sadly, sometimes even within the Church) replace the "?"with things such as "good works," "being a good person," or… (the list goes on).

Additionally, because we live such busy lifestyles (and due to the earlier-mentioned fact that so many of us rely on preachers and pastors to decipher and interpret Scripture for us), many don't find or make the time to investigate scriptural matters for themselves. The trap of using this heuristic to answer questions of all types—*without even realizing that we are doing it*—skews our discernment regarding what we do *and* do not know about Scripture. Without investigating, we easily find ourselves grabbing a loosely related concept—biblically supported or not—and fill in the blanks without so much as a backward glance to confirm the truth of the conclusion that we've just jumped to.

Furthermore, when we continually, unknowingly process information this way, the method can begin to affect how we view other spiritual matters, because, as we search for (and believe we find) "answers," we use those concepts as foundations upon which to build other beliefs. But, as proven in the Garden of Eden (and oh so often since), our own logic is defective and unreliable. Our "answers" *should be* based on the information provided in Scripture. The available information—evidence that is visible, physical, or tangible—is what we're able to directly assess as physical human beings. However, the path between the two may not connect in the way our logic would try to link it. The result can be errors and misconceptions that are allowed to enter the equation as a byproduct of our being spiritual creatures while trapped in physical bodies with limited knowledge. By applying human logic and experience in an effort to find the biblical—or even merely the abstract, missing—information, we must align it with the given evidence, which in this case would be the clues provided by the Bible. It requires us to redirect our thinking and start with what God's Word tells us, then apply our own reasoning while taking care not to contradict or add to Scripture.

Beyond this, at times we must simply accept that the Lord has told us that there are some things we will not understand in full while in this life: "For now we see through a glass, darkly; but then face to face: now I know in part; but then shall I know even as also I am known" (1 Corinthians 13:12.)

As emphasized, regarding theological issues, the information isn't always as clear as our mathematical example showing the addition and subtraction of two simple numbers. It should be noted, however, that *these authors believe that while some spiritual matters can require extra effort on the part of the seeker, or even seem to be more vague than others, the salvation plan provided by Christ on the cross and His redemptive work is available to all who ask, and indeed is as simple as the math problem above (10 - ? = 3).* For those who want answers to more complicated issues, God's Word makes it apparent that we are expected to actively seek answers:

Study to shew thyself approved unto God, a workman that needeth not to be ashamed, rightly dividing the word of truth. (2 Timothy 2:15)

For the word of God is quick, and powerful, and sharper than any two-edged sword, piercing even unto the dividing asunder of soul and spirit, and of the joints and marrow, and is a discerner of the thoughts and intents of the heart. (Hebrews 4:12)

Contrasting the aforementioned passages, it is reasonable to believe that while we aren't given all the answers in this lifetime, we are expected to study the Word of God and attempt to understand everything we can within our power and capability. It is for these reasons that we strive to address such questions in the first place. However, it is imperative—especially in biblical matters that are complicated or debated—for each person to seek answers not only from scholars, pastors, and others, but *by reading the Word of God personally*. Ultimately, each of us will account for our own actions and knowledge:

That at the name of Jesus every knee should bow, things in heaven, and things in earth, and things under the earth; and that every tongue should confess that Jesus Christ is Lord, to the glory of God the Father. Wherefore, my beloved, as ye have always obeyed, not as in my presence only, but now much more in my absence, work out your own salvation with fear and trembling. For it is God which worketh in you both to will and to do of his good pleasure. (Philippians 2:10–13)

With this stated, we'll address some common questions about angels in the following pages.

Believers Don't Become Angels upon Death

Matthew 22:24–30 addresses a moment when Jesus clarifies angelic status with the Sadducees who tried to entrap Him with their doctrine. Observe the exchange:

> Moses said, "If a man die, having no children, his brother shall marry his wife, and raise up seed unto his brother. Now there were with us seven brethren: and the first, when he had married a wife, deceased, and, having no issue, left his wife unto his brother: Likewise the second also, and the third, unto the seventh. And last of all the woman died also. Therefore in the resurrection whose wife shall she be of the seven? for they all had her."
>
> Jesus answered and said unto them, "Ye do err, not knowing the scriptures, nor the power of God. For in the resurrection they neither marry, nor are given in marriage, but are as the angels of God in heaven."

This conversation is repeated nearly word for word in Mark 12:19–25. The final sentence stating that humans will be "as the angels" does sound a bit confusing at first, especially in the KJV, where "as" is used instead of the word "like" in more modern translations.

The word for "as" here is the Greek *hos*, which means "as, like, even as…in that manner."[45] Already, it sounds like a comparison, not a literal transformation.

However, if we allow the circle of context to spread a little wider to Luke 20:34–36, we see a perfect explanation ("the rest of the story," one might say). Let's look at the verses as they appear in the KJV:

> And Jesus answering said unto them, "The children of this world marry, and are given in marriage: But they which shall be accounted worthy to obtain that world, and the resurrection

from the dead, neither marry, nor are given in marriage: Neither can they die any more: for they are equal unto the angels; and are the children of God, being the children of the resurrection."

Let's break it down a little bit. Pay attention not only to what Jesus is saying here, but to the *order He's saying it in*:

And Jesus answering said unto them, "The children of this world marry, and are given in marriage [that's us humans, marrying here on earth]: But they which shall be accounted worthy to obtain that world [true believers worthy of inheriting the Kingdom of God], and the resurrection from the dead [eternal life], neither marry, nor are given in marriage [we don't "get married" again in heaven]: Neither can they die any more [we live forever]: for they are equal unto the angels ["equal unto the angels" is from one Greek word, *esangelos,* a compound word made up of *esos,* "through the idea of seeming" or "similar,"[46] and *angelos,* "angels"]; and are the children of God, being the children of the resurrection."

Luke explains that we will not "become" angels; according to *esangelos,* we will be "similar" to them.

How?

We will be similar in that we will inherit eternal life in a place where we will not marry.

Note that there are other similarities—while again not identifying *sameness*—between the "celestial bodies" and the "terrestrial bodies," as well as between the "natural body" and the "spiritual body" in 1 Corinthians 15:35–54, and this has also confused some into thinking that our physical bodies will be transformed literally into the same bodies as the celestial beings (i.e., angels). However, this doesn't identify *which* bodies we will be transformed into. Philippians 3:20–21 speaks first about

Jesus, then goes on to say that He will make our bodies look like *His*. If we apply an absolute interpretation for 1 Corinthians 15:35–54, then we would need to apply the same absolute for Philippians 3:20–21, which leads us to the question: Which of these bodies are we inheriting—Christ's or the angels'?

It can't be both, so the transformation is simply what it sounds like: Upon death, we get new bodies, *similar to* those of the angels and of Christ (glorious, etc.), but not "exactly like" anyone or anything that we know.

"Angels" Don't Have Wings

Contrary to popular belief, angels are never described in the Bible as having wings. While flight is referenced as one of their abilities, it was actually the seraphim and the cherubim—*not the angels*—that were associated with "wings" in Scripture. The contrasting references to actual "angels" makes it reasonable to believe that they look much like humans: "Be not forgetful to entertain strangers: for thereby some have entertained angels unawares" (Hebrews 13:2).

This passage suggests that these creatures look so much like humans that, at times, they're *mistaken* for them.

The Gender of Angels

This topic is often the subject of debate for a few reasons. Beyond the influencing factors discussed previously in this book regarding the historical implications of angelic portrayal in religion, culture, and art, there remains the question of whether the Bible itself assigns gender to these beings. Again, our working-backward heuristic throws us for a loop:

Those who try to assign male or female status to angels find themselves leaning on outward attributes, such as strength or ability to nurture as evidence. Others find the thought off-putting, stating that to ascribe gender to angels is too closely related to sexualizing them.

On one hand, many associate the nurturing nature of angels with qualities that are maternal, and therefore slant arguments toward the female. Others observe that Scripture refers to these entities as men, which naturally supports the concept that they are male. In addition, the ability of fallen angels to procreate with women in Genesis chapter 6 lends confusion to the entire debate by suggesting that at least some angels, or fallen angels, are masculine. As if all of this weren't enough, we have the information gleaned in Matthew 22:30, which says, "For in the resurrection they neither marry, nor are given in marriage, but are as the angels of God in heaven." While this verse refers to whether angels *marry*, many believe it doesn't directly address whether angels indeed possess *gender*. In the following pages, we'll attempt to answer such questions.

The Nurturing Nature of Angels

Because angels often appear to be caring for and helping others, it's easy to conclude that they are maternal—female. However, the Bible never refers to an angelic being as a woman. On the contrary, all biblical references to angels use male pronouns. As we've already addressed, the very essence of God is love, and He continually provides those He loves with comfort. God Himself is always referred to using masculine pronouns, yet He is the ultimate source of nurturing peace:

> Cast thy burden upon the Lord, and he shall sustain thee: he shall never suffer the righteous to be moved. (Psalm 55:22)

Blessed are they that mourn: for they shall be comforted. (Matthew 5:4)

Blessed be God, even the Father of our Lord Jesus Christ, the Father of mercies, and the God of all comfort. (2 Corinthians 1:3)

These verses (and many more!) make it evident that the nurturing, comforting spirit often carried by angels is simply a byproduct of their proximity to God. As they do His bidding, they carry His mission and thus these attributes. We can't presume that maternal, nurturing qualities are an argument for angels being female. Jumping to the conclusion that they have gender simply because they carry certain attributes is only another way that we misinterpret Scripture by filling in the gaps based on our knowledge of what it is to be human. But if we presume that angels are female, we leave out an important factor: the nature of God and how that influence affects His servants, as well as how varying forms of creation reflect this in different ways. In making this mistake, we confine our view of God's ability to our finite understanding. Allow us to elaborate.

Scripture states that both male and female were created in God's image: "So God created man in his own image, in the image of God created he him; male and female created he them" (Genesis 1:27). With our limited mindset, we tend to recognize and project attributes that we recognize as part of our mortal experience onto spiritual beings, and thus categorize such traits according to our own knowledge. (We are still working with backward logic.) For example, simply because a female in the physical realm has a maternal, nurturing instinct, and an angel has similar traits, this does not mean that the spiritual entity is female. What it *does* mean is that the woman, created in the image of God, inherited a likeness of God's ability to love, nurture, and comfort. On the other hand, men display part of His likeness through their independence and strength. Similarly, noting the warriorlike power of an angel doesn't indicate that the creature is male, but that God has entrusted that being with the power of the Almighty, through which the warrior will carry out the will of God with great strength.

Scripture doesn't say *anywhere* that angels are made in God's image, but it's clear that members of the Celestial Order dwell in close proximity to God, love Him devotedly, and carry out His mission as their purpose (we will cover each of these points later in this book). As humans, *we are reflections of God's nature that has been shared with us.* When we note that a human holds certain attributes specific to masculinity or femininity, we're observing how *that gender* carries and mirrors God's image. In short, spiritual beings can't be said to reveal identifying attributes the way that the human mind reasons, but the reverse is true: We observe spiritual qualities connected to the innate, God-given nature of both genders as it pertains to his or her likeness of the Almighty. By the same argument, it is reasonable to see many of the same characteristics in angels, *not because they have genders*, but because of their *proximity to God*, their likemindedness with His cause, their dedication to his mission, and their love and devotion for Him.

Genesis 6: Does It Prove Angels Are Male?

Those who understand the fallen angels' procreation with human women presume that this physical capability stems from the concept that these entities were male.

> There were giants in the earth in those days; and also after that, when the sons of God came in unto the daughters of men, and they bare children to them, the same became mighty men which were of old, men of renown. (Genesis 6:4)

The idea of fallen angels procreating with human women opens the dialogue that it was indeed possible for them to appear in physical, male form. This is further backed by the argument that they look enough like people that when they appear in physical form, they could be mistaken for humans (thus necessitating attributes that would blend in with other fleshly beings), such as in the case of Hebrews 13:2. Added to this is the already established fact that all scriptural references to angels use masculine pronouns. Moreover, there is no question of the angels' ability to perform other human functions, such as eating food, when they appear in physical form (Genesis 19).

However, many scholars believe that while angels appear in Scripture to be male, in the spirit realm they are without gender. Such individuals explain the difference between a *spirit being appearing in physical form* and a biological being who has a soul, such as a human. Michael S. Heiser clarifies:

> The assumption [the concept that angels could be female] presupposes the idea that angels have gender. They do not—indeed they *cannot* be gendered, since they are spirit beings and gender is a biological attribute. When angels assume visible form or flesh to interact with human beings, Scripture always has them male. The flesh they assume is gendered because it is flesh, not because that corporality is an intrinsic part of angelic nature. [47]

Some argue that Zechariah 5:9 describes angels as being female and having wings. At first glance, this appears to be the case:

> Then I lifted up mine eyes, and looked, and, behold, there came out two women, and the wind was in their wings; for they had wings like the wings of a stork: and they lifted up the ephah between the earth and the heaven. (Zechariah 5:9)

In context, however, Zechariah is actually having a conversation with an angel, during which he sees a vision of two other entities. He then resumes his conversation with the angel. Let's review this with its surrounding narrative:

> Then the angel that talked with me went forth, and said unto me, Lift up now thine eyes, and see what is this that goeth forth. And I said, What is it? And he said, This is an ephah that goeth forth. He said moreover, This is their resemblance through all the earth. And behold, there was lifted up a talent of lead: and this is a woman that sitteth in the midst of the ephah. And he said, This is wickedness. And he cast it into the midst of the ephah; and he cast the weight of lead upon the mouth thereof. Then I lifted up mine eyes, and looked, and, behold, there came out two women, and the wind was in their wings; for they had wings like the wings of a stork: and they lifted up the ephah between the earth and the heaven. Then I said to the angel that talked with me, Whither do these bear the ephah? And he said unto me, To build it and house in the land of Shinar: and it shall be established, and set there upon her own base. (Zechariah 5:5–11).

Perhaps Heiser's explanation of this passage provides more detail:

> Despite the fact that even some scholars speak about these women with wings as angels, there is no textual basis for identifying the women as angels. The "women" (Hebrew, *našîm*) are never described as angels. In the very next verse the prophet speaks to an angel (*mal'āk*), a figure distinct from the women (Zech. 5:10). When the angel speaks (Zech. 5:11), the writer used the masculine form of the verb (*yō'mer*), not the feminine form (*tō'mer*). The text is clear.[48]

The Pronoun Question

As stated earlier, every reference in Scripture refers to angels with the masculine pronoun. But if they have no gender, why is this the case? Many scholars assert that we in the physical realm are wired for duality where masculinity/femininity is concerned. We do not have (nor do we want to create) any third, "non-gender" pronoun that would refer to a spiritual, living *individual*. To clarify, if we were to remove both the male and female identity from such a creature, we would be left with only one option when referring to that entity: a pronoun such as "it." To use "it" to refer to powerful heavenly beings such as the Lord God Almighty or His Celestial Order would be to strip the being's authority and notoriety—not to mention that it would be an act of disrespect to address any member of the Trinity (all of which are also always referred to in masculine terms) with a pronoun that negates their capacity for free will, intellect, emotion, personality, intelligence, and relationship. Pronouns that fall into the "non-gender" category are suited for inanimate objects that are incapable of thinking, feeling, or acting on their own accord. To depersonalize God and His Celestial Order in this way would not show Him due praise and authority.

Furthermore, when God delivered His inspired Word to the men who wrote the Bible, Scripture was conveyed in language that applied to their time and culture. Thus, being that mankind has nearly always operated under a patriarchal culture—*especially* during the era when the Bible was written—it would have been an act of outright disrespect to refer to God or any member of His Celestial Order as anything but male.

Not "Given in Marriage" = No Gender?

Some maintain that Scripture doesn't *deny* that angels have gender. Ironically, this theory, just as it's contradicting countertheory, stems from

Matthew 22:30: "For in the resurrection they neither marry, nor are given in marriage, but are as the angels of God in heaven." The foundation for this point of view is that this passage doesn't *specifically* say that angels are without gender, nor is such a statement anywhere else in Scripture. The fact that all angelic references are male only fuels this theory (although we've already discussed the use of the male pronoun). Matthew 22:30, however, merely states that those who will become "as the angels of God in heaven," will not *marry* in heaven. Some scholars, hence, argue that the issues of gender and marriage are separate and should be treated as such.

The catalyst for this perspective is the concept that within the union of marriage, children are formed. We see in Scripture that angels were created, not born (we also see in Genesis 6 what a disaster occurred when this boundary was violated). Those who support this also explain that it is a sin to participate in sexual intercourse outside of marriage. Thus, the logic is that by not *marrying*, the possibility of reproduction is ruled out completely in a society where there is no sin (heaven). Likewise, the concept of procreation was introduced to human beings who at the time were living *in physical form on earth*, which likewise delegates these circumstances as the time and place for such activity.

> And God blessed them, and God said unto them, Be fruitful, and multiply, and replenish the earth, and subdue it: and have dominion over the fish of the sea, and over the fowl of the air, and over every living thing that move it upon the earth. (Genesis 1:28)

Up to this point, God had created everything that existed without the involvement of man. Through this instruction, he extended an invitation—even a command—to man to be a participant in that creation. Many scholars maintain that this level of contribution on the part of man is an element only intended for humans, and exclusively for our time here on earth. Approaching the situation from this angle, one would believe that spiritual beings—including human beings who go to heaven—could indeed be male or female, but literally would not marry or bear children because the era for human, *physical* procreation will have ended.

Does Scripture Promise Everyone a Guardian Angel?

Matthew 18:10 says, "Take heed that ye despise not one of these little ones; for I say unto you, That in heaven their angels do always behold the face of my Father which is in heaven."

This Scripture has become the basis for the belief that each of us is assigned a guardian angel. However, many disagree. While it is established that He has given His angels charge over us: "For he shall give his angels charge over thee, to keep thee in all thy ways" (Psalm 91:11), the concept of angels being dispatched on a *one-to-one ratio for a person's whole life* is the subject of debate. Notice that in Matthew 18:10, the word "their" refers to those being guarded, which lends to the idea that these "little ones" are the subject of specific, individual assignment.

On a different note, some theologians state that while the "little ones" are possibly assigned to specific, individual protectors, this passage promises such status for those who are *young and defenseless*. Others maintain that angelic defense is guaranteed to anyone and everyone who will inherit salvation: "Are they not all ministering spirits, sent forth to minister for them who shall be heirs of salvation?" (Hebrews 1:14). This last point opens a new, further discussion of whether—because God has knowledge outside the realm of time and can see the future—this protection is applied a) to *anyone* who will receive salvation during his or her lifetime, or b) if that protection is given, once the salvation decision is made, to those who *are now* inheritors of salvation.

While some might be skeptical of the concept that angelic guardianship is extended to those who *someday, over the course of their lives on earth,* will receive salvation, consider the number of testimonies that exist of sinners who were converted to Christianity after what they later claim to be a divine, miraculous, or even life-saving intervention. Such accounts tend to be given by those whose lives were radically changed during or due to these occurrences, and often the individual links the astounding event to God's plan for his or her own conversion and subsequent ministry. Such stories support the notion that angels intervene for those who haven't yet accepted Christ, but who eventually will.

Regardless of interpretation of some of the details rendered in Matthew 18:10, this passage does clarify at least two facts: a) the "little ones" have a specific enough angelic assignment that the (possessive) pronoun "their" is used, and b) those angels "always behold" the face of God the Father, which places them in the throne room of God. Whether the passage in Matthew indicates that specific guardianship is only for small children or all believers everywhere, it is made obvious by Psalm 91:11 and Hebrews 1:14 that all who trust in the Lord are put under the charge of angels. Considering the two preceding verses along with Matthew 18:10, it is reasonable to believe that children, Christians, and possibly even anyone who, over the course of his or her life, will receive salvation are continually guarded by angels, who stand in the throne room in direct communication with God regarding our well-being and circumstance.

Should We Ask Our Angels for Advice?

Scripture makes it clear that we're never to worship angels:

And when I had heard and seen, I fell down to worship before the feet of the angel which shewed me these things. Then saith he unto me, See thou do it not: for I am thy fellowservant, and of thy brethren the prophets, and of them which keep the sayings of this book: worship God. (Revelation 22:8–9)

However, a common claim we hear these days (especially within the New Age movement) involves asking one's angel for advice. It seems that many people regard angels as mere living assets who live at their beck and call, constantly available for their smallest needs—not unlike paid staff members or employees.

Is it wrong, then, to ask angels for advice, as long as we don't worship them? Scripture repeatedly directs our attention back to God Himself, never to angels, when we petition for anything. In fact, God wants to be the first and only Being we turn to for help. We recently discussed Psalm 91:11, but let's broaden the spectrum a bit by including the surrounding verses:

Because thou hast made the Lord, which is my refuge, even the most High, thy habitation; There shall no evil befall thee, neither shall any plague come nigh thy dwelling. For he shall give his angels charge over thee, to keep thee in all thy ways. They shall bear thee up in their hands, lest thou dash thy foot against a stone. Thou shalt tread upon the lion and adder: the young lion and the dragon shalt thou trample under feet. Because he hath set his love upon me, therefore will I deliver him: I will set him on high, because he hath known my name. (Psalm 91:9–14)

As noted in the personal accounts of magnificent intervention featured in the beginning of this book, God delivers us when we call out His name. Recall that each time someone was in trouble, it was *the* Lord that the person in distress cried out to before help arrived through a heavenly creature. This passage clearly explains that our refuge and protection is God Himself. When we surrender to Him and ask Him for help, He often responds by sending angels to help us. Members of the

Celestial Order don't take instructions from us, and when these beings deliver any sort of message—whether it is one of hope, advice, or warning—it has been directly dispatched by God. This is different than independently seeking conversation with such a spirit being. Scripture repeatedly instructs us to seek our help from the Almighty Himself, and it continually reinforces the fact that *He* is the one who will guard and keep us:

> I will lift up mine eyes unto the hills, from whence cometh my help. My help cometh from the Lord, which made heaven and earth. He will not suffer thy foot to be moved: he that keepeth thee will not slumber. Behold, he that keepeth Israel shall neither slumber nor sleep. The Lord is thy keeper: the Lord is thy shade upon thy right hand. The sun shall not smite the by day, nor the moon by night. The Lord shall preserve thee from all evil: he shall preserve thy soul. (Psalm 121:1–7)

This passage, along with so many others, directs our request to God, and makes no mention of petitioning an angel. Likewise, pleas for comfort, wisdom, knowledge, or advice of any nature must be directed toward Him; He may or may not choose to answer with an angelic intervention. As Mike Kerr noted in the beginning of this book, *how and when* God chooses to dispatch angels is never up to us.

Now that we've explained the nature of the Almighty God, clarified how that reflection appears through mankind and the Celestial Order, and hopefully eradicated some age-old myths about these beings, we'll spend the upcoming pages attempting to bring some truth to light about what angels are, their ministry, their abilities and limitations, and their mission.

4

Fundamentals of Angels

The idea of what angels truly are is often so misconstrued that, by the time we've stripped away the misconceptions, we're left with little knowledge about them at all. Yet, they play an enormous part in God's plan, His ongoing ministry to believers, and future fulfillment of prophecy. It is easy, once we address falsehoods regarding angels, to wonder how our understanding of angels became so skewed in the first place (although the historical information highlighted earlier in this book does shed some light on that). Regardless, now that we've torn away the structures built by errant notions, we'll attempt to rebuild our perception of these heavenly beings by using truths found in Scripture.

Holy Angels: Loyal Army of the Almighty God

The Lord hath prepared his throne in the heavens; and his kingdom ruleth over all. Bless the Lord, ye his angels, that excel in strength, that do his commandments, hearkening unto the voice of his word. Bless ye the Lord, all ye his hosts; ye ministers of his, that do his pleasure. (Psalm 103:19–21)

This passage illustrates that angels are strong, mighty creatures who follow God's commandment, listen to His Word, and minister according to His will. These sentiments are echoed throughout Scripture, along with many others that show angelic rejoicing at the pleasure of their maker:

> When the morning stars sang together, and all the sons of God shouted for joy? (Job 4:7)

> Likewise, I say unto you, there is joy in the presence of the angels of God over one sinner that repenteth. (Luke 15:10)

There are also many passages indicating that these entities worship the Lord intensely and constantly:

> And again, when he bringeth in the firstbegotten into the world, he saith, And let all the angels of God worship him. (Hebrews 1:6)

Likewise, we read that members of the Celestial Order worship the Lord passionately, but below we also see that angels are innumerable:

> And I beheld, and I heard the voice of many angels round about the throne and the beasts and the elders: and the number of them was ten thousand times ten thousand, and thousands of thousands; Saying with a loud voice, Worthy is the Lamb that was slain to receive power, and riches, and wisdom, and strength, and honour, and glory, and blessing. (Revelation 5:11–12)

> I beheld till the thrones were cast down, and the Ancient of days did sit, whose garment was white as snow, and the hair of his head like the pure wool: his throne was like the fiery flame, and

his wheels as burning fire. A fiery stream issued and came forth from before him: thousand thousands ministered unto him, and ten thousand times ten thousand stood before him: the judgment was set, and the books were opened. (Daniel 7:9–10)

These passages indicate that there are more holy angels than can be counted. The closest number we're given in Scripture is "ten thousand times ten thousand," equaling one hundred million!

Considering this description of the population, we can quickly substantiate claims that angels are a militia force—an army of light! Although, as previously discussed, our modern media often depicts angels to be small, soft, baby-like creatures with wings, these images are quickly erased when the sheer size of this populace is coupled with the following descriptions:

And I saw another mighty angel come down from heaven, clothed with a cloud: and a rainbow was upon his head, and his face was as it were the sun, and his feet as pillars of fire: And he had in his hand a little book open: and he set his right foot upon the sea, and his left foot on the earth, And he cried with a loud voice, as when a lion roareth: and when he had cried, seven thunders uttered their voices. (Revelation 10:1–3)

While this passage wasn't written regarding a physical, flesh-and-blood experience, but rather was the prophetic vision of an angel's role in future events (more on this later), it still bears saying that this must have been an intimidating sight for the writer. Imagine what this must have looked like (and *will* look like)—particularly regarding the brilliance of the being's face and the element of fire at his feet. (We've already discussed the use of the word "as" in Scripture and its use in comparative form, and established its meaning to be "like" or "similar to." With this in mind, we can understand that the angel bears literal, physical resemblance to such elements as the sun, fire, and so forth). The description in the next passage is even more intimidatingly vivid, and likewise gives us many other details about these beings.

Daniel 10: Great Insight Regarding Angels

Then I lifted up mine eyes, and looked, and behold a certain man clothed in linen, whose loins were girded with fine gold of Uphaz: His body also was like the beryl, and his face as the appearance of lightning, and his eyes as lamps of fire, and his arms and his feet like in color to polished brass, and the voice of his words like the voice of a multitude. And I Daniel alone saw the vision: for the men that were with me saw not the vision, but a great quaking fell upon them, so that they fled to hide themselves. (Daniel 10:5–7)

In each biblical description of an angel, there is a characteristic that is seemingly difficult to relate. As a result, the writers tend to use earthly elements such as brass or lightning to convey an accurate image. In addition, those who are writing about angels always seem to have a hard time communicating about the angel's voice; they often compare it to natural phenomena such as a lion's roar or lightning. While the Bible makes it clear that angels appearing in physical form look enough like humans to be mistaken for them, it quickly becomes apparent that when they manifest in spiritual form, they *do not* fly under the radar. In fact, they're quite a force to be reckoned with, carrying with them a presence, strength, and power that writers can only liken to the very strongest elements we humans can imagine.

Furthermore, Daniel makes us aware that he is the only person who can see the being, meaning that angels can appear to select individuals within a crowd. However, this revelation is followed by the prophet relaying that the angel brought with him an earthquake that everyone experienced. Not only did the ground shake, but the seismic activity was apparently so terrible and frightening that, while those around Daniel couldn't *see* the vision, they were *affected* by the angel's delivery enough that they ran and hid.

Imagine what a force ten thousand times ten thousand of these beings would be! Worlds away from the mainstream depiction of soft, effeminate creatures, the *real* countenance of angels equates to thunder-evoking beings of light, with radiance so bright it can only be compared to brass, lightning, or fire. When they open their mouths, such a strong power is emitted that the only way humans can understand the force is to liken the voice to noises such as thunder. Even more awe-inspiring, these beings have the power to control the natural elements of this planet!

Let's be transparent here for a moment: Many of us would be scared to death if we saw *even one* of these beings, much less could we handle the sight a hundred million! Considering how intimidated we would feel, it seems outright arrogant (or embarrassing) that we would ever assume such creatures exist to fulfil our selfish, human petitions.

As we've well established regarding the Daniel passage, this creature made a fear-invoking entry. Reading on, however, we discover that although his arrival is one of tremendous power, the entity is actually a ministering being who reflects God's love, reassuring and encouraging Daniel:

> And he said unto me, O Daniel, a man greatly beloved, understand the words that I speak unto thee, and stand upright: for unto thee am I now sent. And when he had spoken this word unto me, I stood trembling. Then he said unto me, Fear not, Daniel: for from the first day that thou didst set thine heart to understand, and to chasten thyself before thy God, thy words were heard, and I am come for thy words. But the prince of the kingdom of Persia withstood me one and twenty days: but,

lo, Michael, one of the chief princes, came to help me; and I remained there with the kings of Persia. Now I am come to make thee understand what shall befall thy people in the latter days: for yet the vision is for many days. And when he had spoken such words to me, I set my face toward the ground, and I became dumb. (Daniel 10:11–15)

We've established that angels can present a frightful vision of power and that their greeting is often "fear not." However, in this case, beyond the presence of the entity himself, his arrival was accompanied by such forceful elements (via the earthquake), that Daniel would naturally be alarmed. The creature, however, immediately begins to minister, concerned for the prophet.

The next development also bears strong significance. The being explains to Daniel that the answer to his prayer has actually been coming for some time—twenty-one days, to be exact. In fact, he reassures Daniel that God dispatched the answer to his prayer *the moment he began to pray.* He then informs Daniel that he was delayed by the "prince of Persia," who, in this instance, refers to an evil spirit who interfered with the angel's course of action. Interestingly, the archangel Michael was transmitted to help in this episode of spiritual warfare, and twenty-one days after Daniel began to pray, the heavenly creature finally reached him.

During the next segment of this encounter, the celestial being makes Daniel aware that he has brought him a message. He informs Daniel of what will befall his people in the future. Daniel respons by falling on his face, unable to speak.

This indicates that angels can exist within the realm of time. If they didn't, then the spiritual battle that involved Michael and the prince of Persia wouldn't have claimed twenty-one days, and the being would've appeared to Daniel immediately. Instead, the holy entity appeared a significant length of time later, and he even explained the delay to Daniel. (This presents a unique perspective on prayers that sometimes seem to continue unanswered. We serve a mighty God, and He can do anything instantly should He choose; however, in matters of supernatural combat, we should keep the faith that a battle is being fought on our behalf, even when it feels in our finite, physical realm that nothing is happening.)

While angels can exist within the realm of time, significant scriptural evidence confirms that God exists completely outside it. Consider the following:

> But, beloved, be not ignorant of this one thing, that one day is with the Lord as a thousand years, and a thousand years as one day. (2 Peter 3:8)

> And he said to me, It is done. I am Alpha and Omega, the beginning and the end. (Revelation 21:6)

> And God said unto Moses, I AM THAT I AM. (Exodus 3:14)

Because God exists outside the realm of time and the angels are present in the throne room, it is likely that they're not always limited by the realm of time. However, it is apparent in this case that when interceding on behalf of those who *are limited by the realm of time*, these beings are at least sometimes required to operate within earthly dimensional constraints. We also can see from passages like the ones below that there are similar limitations on angelic creatures. These show that spiritual travel happens over a period; in other words, while angels are capable of traveling extremely quickly, it is not guaranteed that they instantly "teleport":

> Yea, whiles I was speaking in prayer, even the man Gabriel, who I had seen in the vision at the beginning, being caused to fly swiftly, touched me about the time of the evening oblation. (Daniel 9:21)

In this passage, the word "swiftly" indicates extremely fast, but not necessarily *instant*.

On another note, it's reasonable to believe that because Lucifer, before the fall, was a being of light who dwelt in God's throne room, many of his abilities are (or once were) similar to that of the holy angels. In Job 1:7 and Job 2:2—verses that repeat the other nearly verbatim— we see a spiritual creature who is trapped within time, whiling away unproductive hours (and likely suffering boredom), seemingly looking for a way to entertain himself: "And the Lord said under Satan, Whence comest thou? Then Satan answered the Lord, and said, From going to and fro in the earth, and from walking up and down in it" (Job 1:7). Despite the fact that this doesn't refer to a holy angel, it does reinforce the concept that, under certain circumstances, the element of time constraint applies to spirit beings other than God Himself.

Returning our attention to chapter 10 in Daniel, the last part of this passage is perhaps the most telling as it pertains to the true nature of an angel:

And, behold, one like the similitude of the sons of men touched my lips: then I opened my mouth, and spake, and said unto him that stood before me, O my Lord, by the vision my sorrows are turned upon me, and I have retained no strength. For how can the servant of this my lord talk with this my lord? for as for me, straightway there remains no strength in me, neither is there breath left in me. Then there came again and touched me one like the appearance of a man, and he strengthened me, And said, O man greatly beloved, fear not: peace be unto thee, be strong, yea, be strong. And when he had spoken unto me, I was strengthened, and said, Let my Lord speak; for thou hast strengthened me. Then said he, Knowest thou wherefore I come in to thee? and now will I return to fight with the Prince of

Persia: and when I am gone forth, lo, the prince of Grecia shall come. But I will shew thee that which is noted in the Scripture of truth: and there is none that holdeth with me in these things, but Michael your prince. (Daniel 10:16–21)

Despite the being's powerful, earth-shaking appearance, his ability to appear only to select individuals, radiant illumination permeating from the being, and a voice that is described as "a multitude," the angel, who dwells in close proximity to God, speaks in a loving, comforting, and nurturing way. He then proceeds to follow God's orders by delivering the message. When the vision he gives distresses Daniel, the holy servant assures Daniel that he is loved, tells him not to be afraid (again), and ministers strength and peace to him. Next, the angel literally, *physically* replenishes Daniel's strength. Once this task is complete, he bids Daniel farewell and departs with no further conversation.

Another element to consider in the interaction between Daniel and the angel: Every part of the event occurred *because Daniel prayed to God.* This is confirmed when the angel explains that the man's prayers resulted in this heavenly dispatch at the moment the prophet began to "chasten" himself "before [his] God": "thy words were heard, and I am come for thy words." Daniel had prayed to *God,* and an angel had been *dispatched by God on his behalf.* This confirms the mission-oriented function of these entities. There was no back-and-forth conversation between Daniel and the being, which supports the position stated earlier in this book regarding whether humans, on their own accord, should communicate with angels. Scripture likewise illustrates that when a holy being has completed a mission ordered by God, he leaves in peace without further activity.

Daniel 10 details many attributes of an angel, and other places in Scripture confirm similar ones. The holy warrior's commanding entry, contrasted with his ministering response to Daniel's vulnerability, certainly shows that angels reflect God's strong yet loving nature. This has been stated previously in this book, but bears repeating: Angels were not created—as humans were—in the image of God, but they *do* dwell in His throne room, worship Him, serve Him, and live to carry out His mission, thus they bear many of His characteristics.

Angels: A Company of Immortal Beings

Angels aren't eternal beings. This confuses many people, because Scripture says they live forever. However, they were *created*, which is an important distinction. An eternal entity has no beginning and no end; God is eternal, hence His ability to accurately claim that He is "Alpha and Omega." Angels, on the other hand, have a *beginning*, but no *end*; this is indicated throughout Scripture. Because of this, it's important to distinguish angels as immortal, not eternal.

> Praise ye the Lord from the heavens: praise him in the heights. Praise ye him, all his angels: praise ye him, all his hosts... Let them praise the name of the Lord: for he commanded, and they were created. He hath also stablished them forever and ever: he hath made a decree which shall not pass. (Psalm 148:1–6)

We must also recognize that Scripture repeatedly confirms that angels are *spirit* beings. While they can appear in the flesh, they are ministering *spirits*. Beyond this, given that they don't reproduce, they're not a *race*, indicating a population that replenishes itself. Rather, they're a *company* of created individuals who work together toward a similar goal.

Having established some fundamentals regarding the nature of these beings, we will next attempt to answer a question about the holy angels' loyalty to God the Father.

Can Holy Angels Rebel against God?

Angels were created by God to be with Him in the heavens, to serve, praise, and minister to Him. They were established in His dwelling place from the beginning, and the consequence of choosing to depart from that location is considered rebellion and punishable by being permanently cast out, with no chance of redemption:

> And the angels which kept not their first estate, but left their own habitation, he hath reserved in everlasting chains under darkness onto the judgment of the great day. (Jude 6)

> God spared not the angels that sinned, but cast them down to hell, and delivered them into chains of darkness, to be reserved unto judgment. (2 Peter 2:4)

It is apparent in Scripture that those who fell during the rebellion of Lucifer are unredeemable. However, a common question people ask regards whether a holy angel, at any time *after* the war in heaven, can defect to the dark side, joining evil forces. While Scripture doesn't spell out the answer in so many words, it does provide some very strong clues.

Important to consider is the issue of free will, which Scripture indicates that angels do have:

> Unto whom it was revealed, that not unto themselves, but unto us they did minister the things, which are now reported unto you by them that I have preached the gospel unto you with the Holy Ghost sent down from heaven; which things the angels desire to look into. (1 Peter 1:12)

To the intent that now unto the principalities and powers in heavenly places might be known by the church the manifold wisdom of God. (Ephesians 3:10)

These verses show that angels experience desire and are aware of matters taking place within the Body of Christ. Considering this along with the many instances in the Bible where the angels are said to rejoice at the fulfillment of God's will, it is apparent that they're aware of and interested in the success of the Church and the spread of the gospel. Because angels have the capacity for desire (and, for that matter, desire that is corruptible, as seen in the case of the fallen angels), there is support for the theory that God allows them the right to choose whose army they will serve in. After all, it's been well established by now that some angels are fallen—as the results of a decision that proves their free will.

The question then becomes whether a holy angel would *choose* to change sides. For some insight, we'll look—*as one should always do when answering such questions*—to Scripture. The biblical account of Lucifer's rebellion tells of God's response: He immediately cast the evil one and his followers out of heaven, because He *cannot and will not* tolerate the presence of evil. Because this book is primarily about holy angels, we won't thoroughly cover this conflict and the casting out of Lucifer and his followers, but for the sake of establishing a case for the loyalty of heavenly entities, this will be discussed briefly.

Thou [Lucifer] wast perfect in thy ways from the day that thou wast created, till iniquity was found in thee. By the multitude of thy merchandise they have filled the midst of thee with violence, and thou hast sinned: therefore I will cast thee as profane out of the mountain of God: and I will destroy thee, O covering cherub, from the midst of the stones of fire. (Ezekiel 28:15–16)

For thou art not a God that hath pleasure in wickedness: neither shall evil dwell with thee. The foolish shall not stand in thy sight: thou hatest all workers of iniquity. (Psalm 5:4–5)

As previously stated, when Lucifer and his cohorts rebelled, God responded by casting them out of heaven. The book of Revelation sheds further light on this. Although some scholars interpret the following passage to indicate a *future* event, it still shows God's attitude toward the permanency of rebellious beings who are cast out of heaven:

And war broke out in heaven: Michael and his angels fought with the dragon; and the dragon and his angels fought, but they did not prevail, nor was a place found for them in heaven any longer. So the great dragon was cast out, that serpent of old, called the Devil and Satan, who deceives the whole world; he was cast to the earth, and his angels were cast out with him. (Revelation 12:7–9)

Some may theorize that if this passage is referring to a future event, then it is possible that there is still division within the throne room today. However, everything Scripture mentions about Lucifer's fall indicates that angels chose sides at that moment, and since that event, the throne room has been a place of worship and praise—even in numbers equaling more than "ten thousand times ten thousand" angels worshipping simultaneously! This is not a picture of a crowd whose loyalty is divided or under temptation of changing sides. Scripture gives no indication that there is still a campaign for the loyalties of holy angels. Furthermore, when God cast the rebellious beings out of heaven, permanent lines between loyalties were drawn, as the Bible repeatedly *reinforces* the heavenly entitites' disposition of devotion and loyalty to God. Beyond this, nothing within the prophetic portions of the Bible indicates that there will be a coming rebellion among the angels. While angels are agents of free will, their love, loyalty, and alliance was established—permanently—long, long ago.

Angels' Appearances: Body, Spirit, and in Dreams

Because so much discussion of the nature of angels touches on the various forms by which they make appearances, we'll only briefly discuss here each of the types of manifestation, as we'll take a closer look at them throughout other areas in the book.

As a Physical Body

Angels appear in human form throughout Scripture. In fact, as we've already established, they look enough like humans that they can be mistaken for them, and they also can participate in human activities such as eating:

> And he [Abraham] took the butter, and milk, and the calf which he had dressed, and set it before them; and he stood by them under the tree, and they did eat. (Genesis 18:7–8)

As a Spirit

When angels appear in spirit form, humans usually respond with fear, because the beings are such mighty, powerful creatures; they're outside the spectrum of our human understanding or ability to describe in human tongue.

> Then a spirit passed before my face; the hair of my flesh stood up: It stood still, but I could not discern the form thereof: an

image was before mine eyes, there was silence, and I heard a voice, saying, Shall mortal man be more just than God? shall a man be more pure than his maker? (Job 4:15–17)

In Dreams

When angels appear in dreams, it's to deliver a message, often warning of things to come. Sometimes in Scripture, this was done through visions, and in other instances, it involved direct, spoken messages. Below are examples of when a holy being appeared to Joseph in a dream:

But while he thought on these things, behold, the angel of the Lord appeared to him in a dream, saying, Joseph, thou son of David, fear not to take unto the Mary thy wife: for that which is conceived in her is of the Holy Ghost. (Matthew 1:20)

And when they were departed, behold, the angel of the Lord appeareth to Joseph in a dream, saying, Arise, and take the young child and his mother, and flee to Egypt, and be thou there until I bring thee word: for Herod will seek the young child to destroy him. (Matthew 2:13)

Important to note about an angelic visitation in a dream: Angels are God's messengers. They deliver the message God ordains, then depart. This is contrary to some of the New Age concepts of dialoguing with angels throughout the night or having angel "spirit guides" that offer a mutually conversational type of "life coaching." As stated previously, communicating with a messenger sent by God is minimal, limited to the delivery of His message. Scripture tells us to:

…believe not every spirit, but try the spirits whether they are of God: because many false prophets are gone out into the world.

Hereby know ye the Spirit of God: Every spirit that confesses that Jesus Christ is come in the flesh is of God: And every spirit that confesses not that Jesus Christ is come in the flesh is not of God. (1 John 4:1–3)

Many teachings encourage individuals not only to consult "their angels" for advice, but also to engage in many types of dream visitations with what they *believe* to be benevolent entities to achieve various types of enlightenment, self-realization, and other versions of personal growth or success. This is flawed theology; nowhere in Scripture are we encouraged to pursue visitation from celestial beings in this way.

Can Angels Read Our Minds?

On the other hand, some individuals have raised the question of whether angels can read our minds because of their ability to appear in our dreams, or within our minds. First, a visitation from a God-dispatched messenger, even within a dream, will always operate within the parameters of what the Lord commands. Because we know that "all things work together for the good to them that love God, to them who are called according to his purpose" (Romans 8:28), we can be assured that any visitation *made by a holy angel* that *God sends on our behalf* in a dream will be completely safe and in line with God's will.

It is apparent from Scripture that angels are obedient servants of God, and they will communicate with anyone in whatever format God decrees. Whether that method is through physical, spiritual, or dream appearance is for God to decide. Satan cannot touch us beyond God's protecting hedge, as illustrated in the story of Job:

Hast not thou made an hedge about him, and about his house, and about all that he hath on every side? thou hast blessed the work of his hands, and his substance is increased in the land. But put forth thine hand now, and touch all that he hath and he will curse thee to thy face. (Job 1:10–11)

If even Satan is unable to touch us outside of God's permission, then surely a servant of the Lord is held to the same limitation. Therefore, those concerned that a dream visitation may not be a safe experience are either being approached by a spirit other than a holy angel (a topic for a different book altogether) or they offer the question in theory.

However, understanding that a heavenly messenger can appear to us in a dream doesn't automatically confirm that the entity can read our minds. In fact, everything in Scripture indicates that it is *God alone* who knows our hearts and minds:

I the Lord search the heart, I try the reins, even to give every man according to his ways, and according to the fruit of his doings. (Jeremiah 17:10)

Then hear thou in heaven thy dwelling place, and forgive, and do, and give to every man according to his ways, whose heart thou knowest; (for thou, even thou only, knowest the hearts of all the children of men;). (1 Kings 8:39)

Some argue that to know the *heart* is different than to read the *mind*. But again, Scripture supports the concept that our communication, whether through thought, prayer, or any other type of petition, takes place directly between the human being and God Himself, who in turn dispatches angelic intervention. Adding these truths together, it becomes apparent that even during a dream visitation when a message is being delivered to us, angels still don't read our minds.

Angels Can Fly

Although angels themselves don't have wings, they're able to fly. Recall that in Daniel 9:21, Gabriel was "caused to fly swiftly." In addition, many other passages in prophetic Scripture indicate that angels have this ability, including the following:

> And I saw another angel flying in the midst of heaven, having the everlasting gospel to preach unto them that dwell on the earth, and to every nation, and kindred, and tongue, and people. (Revelation 14:6)

Angels' role in prophecy, and in this particularly fascinating passage, will be covered at more length later in the book. For now, suffice to say simply that Scripture makes it clear that angels have the capability of flight.

Angels Can Manipulate Materials in the Physical Realm

Regardless of whether they appear in spiritual or physical form, these beings are capable of manipulating materials in the physical world. Many stories of intervention shared earlier in this book described such encounters, as does Scripture itself. For example:

> Peter therefore was kept in prison: but prayer was made without ceasing of the church unto God for him. And when Herod would have brought him forth, the same night Peter was sleeping between two soldiers, bound with two chains: and the keepers before the door kept the prison. And behold, the angel of the Lord came upon him, and a light shined in the prison: and he smote Peter on the side, and raised him up, saying, Arise up

quickly. And his chains fell off from his hands. And the angel said unto him, Gird thyself, and bind on thy sandals. And so he did. And he saith unto him, Cast thy garment about thee, and follow me. And he went out, and followed him; and wist not that it was true which was done by the angel; but thought he saw a vision. When they were past the first and second ward, they came unto the iron gate that leadeth unto the city; which opened to them of his own accord: and they went out, and passed on through one street; and forthwith the angel departed from him. And when Peter was come to himself, he said, Now I know of a surety, that the Lord has sent his angel, and have delivered me out of the hand of Herod, and from all the expectation of the people of the Jews. (Acts 12:5–11)

This passage is another where we see several different attributes of an angel within one narrative. Let's break it down: First of all, Peter was in an impossible situation—but the *church was praying for him,* without ceasing, even! On the night that Peter likely would have been executed, he was heavily guarded—bound by two chains between two soldiers, with more guards outside of his cell. When God sent an angel to help Peter, the first thing the angel did was smite him, or physically touch Peter urgently, in an attempt to wake him up. A brilliant light that apparently only Peter could see had filled the room. The captive, at that moment, believed it to be a dream, and both chains that had previously bound him fell off. Take note of the fact that these chains were likely extremely heavy and would have made a loud, "clanking" sound. Either the noise was audible only to Peter or the angel had blocked the hearing of the nearby guards. (On another note, contrary to the miraculous release of Peter's chains, he wasn't automatically, miraculously clothed. He was given orders from his rescuer to put on his garments, which he did. Even when God sends an angel to intervene on our behalf, our cooperation is expected.) Peter then was able to escape by walking directly past sleeping wards and out through a city gate, from which the locks miraculously fell.

This intervention shows many levels of an angel's supernatural power. They're able to influence our ability to see, hear, sleep, and even awaken. They likewise can cast light in a dark area, cause chains to be loosed from a person or locks to fall off of city gate, and much more. Yet, despite all of these capabilities, holy angels continue to act within the limitations set upon them by God. Additionally, when their job has been completed, they don't linger, seeking glory for themselves. They simply return to where they came from.

How Angels Interact with Animals

In Numbers, we read a story about a man named Balaam, who was in the process of going against an order from God. God stationed an angel on Balaam's path to stop him. However, it wasn't Balaam, but the donkey he rode, who initially interacted with the entity:

> And Balaam rose up in the morning, and saddled his ass, and went with the princes of Moab. And God's anger was kindled because he went: and the angel of the Lord stood in the way for an adversary against him. Now he was riding upon his ass, and his two servants were with him. And the ass saw the angel of the Lord standing in the way, and his sword drawn in his hand: and the ass turned aside out of the way, and went into the field: and Balaam smote the ass, to turn her into the way. But the angel of the Lord stood in a path of the vineyards, a wall being on this side, and a wall on that side. And when the ass saw the angel of the Lord, she thrust herself unto the wall, and crushed Balaam's foot against the wall: and he smote her again. And the angel of the Lord went further, and stood in a narrow place, where was

no way to turn either to the right hand or to the left. And when the ass saw the angel of the Lord, she fell down under Balaam: and Balaam's anger was kindled, and he smote the ass with a staff. And the Lord opened the mouth of the ass, and she said unto Balaam, What have I done unto thee, that thou hast smitten me these three times? And Balaam said unto the ass, Because thou hast mocked me: I would there were a sword in mine hand, for now would I kill thee. And the ass said unto Balaam, Am not I thine ass, upon which thou hast ridden ever since I was thine unto this day? was I ever wont to do so unto thee? and he said, Nay. Then the Lord opened the eyes of Balaam, and he saw the angel of the Lord standing in the way, and his sword drawn in his hand: and he bowed down his head, and fell flat on his face. And the angel of the Lord said unto him, Wherefore hast thou smitten thine ass these three times? behold, I went out to withstand thee, because thy way is perverse before me: And the ass saw me, and turned from me these three times: unless she had turned from me, surely now also I had slain thee, and saved her alive. And Balaam said unto the angel of the Lord, I have sinned; for I knew not that thou stoodest in the way against me: now therefore, if it displease thee, I will get me back again. And the angel of the Lord said unto Balaam, Go with the men: but only the word that I shall speak unto thee, that thou shalt speak. (Numbers 22:21–35)

Interestingly, aside from the donkey's interaction with the angel is the fact that the animal saw the spirit being well before the human did. The beast repeatedly avoided the path the entity stood blocking—and afterward, God's servant told Balaam that this action on the part of his mount actually saved the man's life! (This sheds an interesting light on instances when the behavior of some animals is inexplicably unruly and out of character.) While Scripture doesn't tell us that *all animals see into the spirit realm at all times*, it's probable that they're more in tune with it than we, as distracted human beings, are. This is alluded to in other places of Scripture as well: "And he answered and said unto them, I tell you that, if these should hold their peace, the stones would immediately cry out" (Luke 19:40). The Bible is clear that all of nature will glorify God, and we know that the angelic realm surrounds us at all times. Just because we don't see in the physical how these realms (earthly nature and spiritual beings) interact doesn't mean that they have no relationship with each other. It is probable that there are protective exchanges around us daily that, because we do not see with the naked eye, we take for granted.

We also see in Scripture that angels can *control* animals when necessary. When Daniel was thrown into a den of lions for refusing to abstain from his practice of prayer to the Living God, the Lord sent an angel to close the mouth of the lions:

> Then the king arose very early in the morning, and went in haste unto the den of lions. And when he came to the den, he cried with a lamentable voice unto Daniel: and the king spake and said to Daniel, O Daniel, servant of the living God, is thy God, whom thou servest continually, able to deliver thee from the lions? Then said Daniel unto the king, O king, live for ever. My God hath sent his angel, and hath shut the lions' mouths, that they have not hurt me: forasmuch as before him innocency was found in me; and also before thee, O king, have I done no hurt. (Daniel 6:19–22)

We should note, however, that angels don't actually *rule* over the animal realm. Genesis 1:26 says:

> And God said, Let us make man in our image, after our likeness: and let them have dominion over the fish of the sea, and over

the fowl of the air, and over the cattle, and over all the earth, and over every creeping thing that creeps upon the earth.

This Scripture establishes that the animal kingdom falls under mankind's sovereignty, and as such, it is sound to believe that angels only intervene within this realm when they're ordered by God to do so, whether for warfare, protection, or other causes. However, many animals have a "sixth sense," often seeing the true nature of people or "instinctively" knowing when or how to intervene for protection or healing on the part of a human being. Considering this, it's reasonable to believe that animals possibly see spirit beings—both good and evil— on a regular basis.

Angels Wage Warfare at God's Command

Angels serve the Lord with pure devotion and carry out His mission. They're also nurturing beings who minister the love of God to all of His creation. This, however, doesn't mean that they're soft, weak, or timid. They are conduits of God's will, reflecting His attributes through their actions. Thus, they're gentle when God would have them to be, and they wage warfare and execute judgment at His command.

The Significance of Genesis 19

The story in Genesis 19 gives quite a bit of insight to angels' role in carrying out judgment, but is also often a controversial and even misunderstood sequence of events. By taking a closer look at the entire series of occurrences, we can learn a lot more about angels, how they execute judgment, and when God may decide to order such action.

The story begins in Genesis 19:1:

There came two angels to Sodom at even; and Lot sat in the gate of Sodom: and Lot seeing them rose up to meet them; and he bowed himself with his face toward the ground; and he said, Behold now, my lords, turn in, I pray you, into your servant's house, and tarry all night, and wash your feet, and ye shall rise early, and go on your ways.

The angels had been dispatched, seemingly only moments before, to investigate the deeds of the town, move the righteous away before wrath was executed, and then carry out judgment (Genesis 18:20–33). Scripture indicates that God had told Abraham He intended to destroying Sodom and Gomorrah, and Abraham had petitioned the Lord to spare the righteous. Abraham had been with the angels for a portion of their journey, but at a certain point, they had parted ways, and Abraham returned home. There is no indication that Lot could have known that these angels were coming; however, Lot's immediate response was to greet them reverently and extend hospitality. When the visitors declined, explaining that they would stay in the street, it is reasonable to believe that Lot knew what types of adversity they would face from the townspeople. Lot's persistent offer of hospitality was finally accepted, and the angels went into his home. As we've already discussed, these beings are capable of physical acts such as eating, and during this visit, Scripture tells us that Lot provided them with a feast.

However, in verse 4, we read:

But before they lay down, the men of the city, even the men of Sodom, compassed the house around, both old and young, all the people from every quarter: And they called unto Lot, and said unto him, Where are the men which came in to thee this night? bring them out unto us, that we may know them.

This is a much different greeting than the one extended by Lot upon the angels' arrival. Let's analyze this, as certain segments of this passage often get overlooked. Lot saw the angels and immediately recognized them as distinct characters. He then approached them, bowed reverently, extended hospitality, then prepared and served them a feast. We also read in the previous verse that they would have "lay down" for the night as well, indicating that regardless of whether they actually would have *slept* while in Lot's house, they would have gone through the *motions* of doing so. However, imagine the deviant culture of this city; the verse literally says that "both old and young, all the people from every quarter," gathered and surrounded Lot's house, demanding that these men be sent out for the purpose of the crowd's carnal desires. What an irreverent response to heavenly travelers! If these holy servants were indeed there to gather information about the nature of the people living in this city (as Scripture states they were), they certainly got a good look from behind the door of Lot's home.

In verse 6, we read that Lot, *himself,* went out to talk to the mob, shutting the door behind him as he exited the home. He began to plead with the crowd to leave in peace, even offering his daughters to the horde, and giving them permission to do as they pleased with the two young women.

This is an extremely controversial part of Scripture. Unfortunately, there is significant vagueness about Lot's reasons for taking this action. While myriad ways that culture, history, and personal experience would have influenced Lot's action could be the subject of another book entirely (thus cannot be fully entertained here), let's consider a couple points before continuing.

Abraham and Lot had an extensive history together, and while there had been enough friction between them to cause them to part ways, their cultural roots likely were similar. Genesis 22 states that when Abraham was asked to sacrifice his son, Isaac, he readily obeyed:

And they came to the place which God had told him of; and Abraham built an altar there, and laid the wood in order, and bound Isaac his son, and laid him on the altar upon the wood. And Abraham stretched forth his hand, and took the knife to slay his son. (Genesis 22:9–10)

Many have asked why Abraham would be obedient to such a gruesome command. While the answer can be summed up in one word—faith—a more detailed explanation is found in Hebrews:

By faith Abraham, when he was tried, offered up Isaac: and he that had received the promises offered up his only begotten son, Of whom it was said, That in Isaac shall thy seed be called: Accounting that God was able to raise him up, even from the dead; from whence also he received him in a figure. (Hebrews 11:17–19)

This passage explains that Abraham's complied because his faith *ran so deep* that he knew God would spare Isaac, even if it meant the Lord would raise his son from the dead.

On a similar note, 2 Peter 2:6–8 indicates that God Himself acknowledged that Lot was a righteous man:

And turning the cities of Sodom and Gomorrah into ashes condemned them with an overthrow, making them and ensample unto those that after should live ungodly; And delivered just Lot, vexed with the filthy conversation of the wicked: (For that righteous man dwelling among them, in seeing and hearing, vexed his righteous soul from day to day with their unlawful deeds;).

It is possible that Lot was acting with a similar type of faith when he offered his daughters. Since Scripture acknowledges Abraham's willingness to sacrifice Isaac with faith so strong that he trusted God even to raise Isaac from the dead, then it is a reasonable theory that Lot was acting with comparable conviction, believing wholeheartedly that either no harm would come to his daughters or that they would be fully restored after any harm that might befall them.

Contrariwise, some theorize that Lot readily offered his daughters because their female status rendered them as property with little value. Others assert that cultural etiquette during this period dictated that when one was brought into a person's home as a guest, they were protected at all costs to the homeowner. Still other groups are angry at the Lord Himself about this; they claim that a loving God would never allow such an offering for the safety of His angels. In response, some point out that *God did not instruct Lot to make this offer* at the cost of his daughters' well-being. However, those who debate this matter miss the nugget of truth in this passage, which offers deep insight into our relationship with angels. Regardless of where one stands in this debate, it is critical to notice that the angels who were there quickly intervened, thus indicating *precisely* where God stood on the issue of the well-being of Lot's daughters, which will be discussed presently.

In verse 9, the throng pressed in on Lot, nearly breaking down the door. The mass turned their anger toward the man, threatening his physical safety. Recall our previous prompt to imagine what type of culture would exist in a city that unleashes such a sexually ravenous crowd on the arrival of two incoming travelers. Now the group was on the verge of violence.

At this point, God had seen enough.

The angels:

...put forth their hand, and pulled Lot into the house to them, and shut the door. And they smote the men that were at the door of the house with blindness, both small and great: so that they wearied themselves to find the door. (Genesis 19:10–11)

173

Regardless of Lot's reason for offering his daughters to the mob or risking his own safety by being the first to step outside and attempt to control the crowd, the angels intervened and protected the entire family from the horde, *daughters included.* Nothing in Scripture indicates that *mankind* protects *angels*, and these powerful, heavenly creatures had no intention of standing by and allowing human beings to suffer physical harm for their benefit. On the contrary, they immediately began to question Lot about his family: Are there sons-in-law? Are there more daughters? They instructed him to gather his family, because they were there to carry out judgment upon the evil city once they had ushered Lot's household to safety. While, sadly, the sons-in-law chose to ignore the warning, when the time came to escape, Lot took his wife and the two daughters who were with him and were escorted from the city by the holy messengers.

> And while he lingered, the men laid hold upon his hand, and upon the hand of his wife, and upon the hand of his two daughters; the Lord being merciful unto him: and they brought him forth, and set him without the city. And it came to pass, when they had brought them forth abroad, that he said, Escape for thy life; look not behind the, neither stay thou in all the plain; escape to the mountain, lest thou be consumed. (Genesis 19:16–17)

In response to this order, Lot asked the angel if he could retreat instead to a nearby city named Zoar, to which the angel consented, then replied, "Haste thee, escape thither; for I cannot do anything till thou become thither" (Genesis 19:22).

The angels were sent because God wanted to investigate whether the city was as evil as the outcry to God had indicated. The consequence was to be judgment by destruction, but these loving, commanding creatures were instructed not to carry out the Lord's order until the righteous individuals were out of harm's way. The situation that night outside the door of Lot's house separated the good people of the crowd from the bad: Scripture explains that the *entire* city had surrounded Lot's house. As previously stated, while it bothers many to know that Lot offered his daughters to such a demonized mass, it should likewise bring comfort to know that the angels *never had any intention* of allowing that to occur, and they intervened miraculously by blinding the crowd, rendering the multitude helpless, and evacuating the righteous in order to finalize Sodom's fate.

Note that in all of this, the heavenly servants told Lot that they were unable to carry out the order until he and those who would leave with him were taken to safety. Ultimately, Lot escaped with only two of his daughters, as his wife disobeyed the angel's order not to look back and was turned into a pillar of salt. Even when executing orders of destructive judgment, angels operate within the parameters given by God. Ultimately, verse 24 says that it was the Lord who rained fire and brimstone out of heaven onto Sodom and Gomorrah. Verse 25 tells us that the judgment was so thorough that it destroyed the cities, the surrounding land, all of the inhabitants besides those who fled with Lot, and even the vegetation in the area! It is commonly stated that the cities of Sodom and Gomorrah were destroyed, but often overlooked is the extent of the wreckage. Verse 28 indicates that the "smoke of the country went up as the smoke of a furnace." Many scholars assert that the "fire and brimstone" that rained from heaven, combined with the excessive smoldering, the killing of all vegetation, and even the description of Lot's wife turning to salt hint at nuclear implications.

Another interesting fact about this story is that archaeologists in recent years believe they have located the ruins of the ancient city. Judging from the rubble, theories regarding the source of the annihilation range from an earthquake to an asteroid. Steven Collins, professor of biblical studies and apologetics at Trinity Southwest University, stated that it would appear that a sudden event caused the fortified city to perish, based on his archaeological findings within the ruins, and that the area was likely a wasteland for the subsequent seven hundred years.[49]

Since the time the city was located more than a decade ago, many artifacts have been located and inspected. One tablet in particular is believed by some scholars, albeit controversially, to feature an eyewitness account of the massive city's destruction:

In 2008, mysterious circular clay tablets were identified as a witness' account of an asteroid that destroyed the cities. Two rocket scientists—Alan Bond and Mark Hempsell, who spent eight years trying to solve the mystery—believe that the tablet's symbols give a detailed account of how a mile-long asteroid hit the region, causing thousands of deaths and devastating an area of more than 386,000 square miles. The impact, equivalent to more than 1,000 tons of TNT exploding, would have created one of the world's biggest-ever landslides. The clay tablet, called the Planisphere, was discovered by the Victorian archaeologist Henry Layard in the remains of the library of the royal palace at Nineveh.[50]

Experts who have studied these elements estimate that the destruction took place on June 29, 3123 BC, and they believe it occurred suddenly, just as it is told in the Bible.

Despite the fact that angels are loving, nurturing creatures, they are simultaneously fierce, powerful, and can even perform violent acts at God's command. An angel who has been sent to execute wrath is swift, prevailing, and not to be trifled with. While the Bible is clear in the case of Sodom and Gomorrah that God Himself ultimately devastated the cities with fire and brimstone, other narratives in Scripture record that angels, in addition to delivering warnings, actually carried out judgment on God's behalf as well. While such cases are particularly prominent in prophetic events (which will be discussed at more length later), the Bible also records instances such as these that have already taken place.

Other Instances of Angels Executing Judgment

There are many examples throughout Scripture where angels have executed judgment, although some events have occurred on a much smaller scale than what appears to have been a nuclear attack large enough to destroy two cities and their surrounding territory. When Herod puffed himself up and indulged in the sin of pride, God sent His holy messenger to strike him dead, allowing him to immediately be eaten by worms. In Acts 12:20–23, we read the story of Herod's interaction with Tyre and Sidon. Because he was displeased with them and they relied on his approval for their continued food supply and economic success, they came to seek Herod's favor. In so doing, they paid such lip service as to say to him, "It is the voice of a god, not a man" (Acts 12:22). Herod's response was to bask in this worship instead of giving the glory for his position to God. Verse 23 says, "And immediately the angel of the Lord smote him, because he gave not God the glory: and he was eaten of worms, and gave up the ghost."

Exodus chapters 11 and 12 tell the story of how Moses and the Israelites witnessed the final in a series of plagues over Egypt, under which the firstborn human and animal of every house not covered by the blood of the lamb was killed. This was another instance wherein *God Himself* carried out judgment upon people of the earth. While some translations of the Bible use the phrase "destroying angel" or "angel of death," the King James Version does not, leaving some individuals confused about who actually carried death to the Egyptians' oldest sons that night. Let's take a moment to explore the true identity behind this powerful entity.

For the LORD will pass through to smite the Egyptians; and when he seeth the blood upon the lintel, and on the two side posts, the LORD will pass over the door, and will not suffer the destroyer to come into your houses to smite *you*. (Exodus 12:23)

In this passage, the word "destroyer" is derived from the Hebrew *shachath*,[51] which is a primitive root verb meaning "to decay, corrupt, ruin, or waste." Bearing this in mind, it is conceivable that the "destroyer" is sickness or disease, but before we conclude that this word refers only to physical illness and nothing more, consider this: The original term is the same as the one used in Genesis 6:11–12, which states that the earth and all flesh had been corrupted before God. In both cases, the word is associated with a condition that is irreversible and attached to the wrath or judgement of God. Let's read a little further:

> And it came to pass, at midnight the LORD smote all the firstborn in the land of Egypt, from the firstborn of Pharaoh that sat on his throne unto the firstborn of the captive that was in the dungeon; and all the firstborn of cattle. (Exodus 12:29)

In the original Hebrew writing, the word "LORD" translates from the Hebrew *Yĕhovah*, defined as a proper noun with reference to deity, specifically Jehovah, the One True God, or Eternal Lord. This passage clarifies and ends speculation about exactly *who* passed judgment upon the Egyptians that night.

Furthermore, recall the promise of safety made to the Israelites in the instructions they were given regarding how to put the blood on their doorposts for protection from this coming disaster:

> But against any of the children of Israel shall not a dog move his tongue, against man or beast: that ye may know how that the LORD doth put a difference between the Egyptians and Israel. (Exodus 11:7)

God literally promised that not so much as a dog's tongue would threaten His people. There was no room to doubt just who was in control during these circumstances. What a comforting thought that must have been for the Israelites during such a tumultuous time.

Some scholars assert an interesting perspective regarding these events: the concept that death was not selective *toward* Egyptians households, but that it was unleashed across the entire land, and that the blood created a covering *exempting* the Israelites. This may seem like a mere restatement of what has been many times before, but a unique distinction is up for interpretation here. Bear with me as I explain. One argument states that God selected *certain households* to inflict wrath *upon*, while another position states that wrath was *poured out upon the entire* land, but *isolated* households whose doorposts were covered in the blood were *spared* because they were protected by a deterrent shield put in place by God.

This interesting—albeit subtle—twist surfaces in a study of the original language of this passage. We'll take a moment to scrutinize the phrase, "When I see the blood I will pass over you, and the plague shall not be upon you to destroy you," which is translated from the Hebrew as *ra'ah dam pacach negeph mashchiyth nakah'erets Mitsrayim*. Consider the breakdown of the original Hebrew phrase:

- "when I see": *ra'ah*[52] — verb meaning "take heed," "look upon," or "perceive."
- "the blood": *dam*[53] — masculine noun meaning "blood," often associated with innocence.
- "I will pass": *pacach*[54] — verb meaning "pass over," "spring over," or "skip."
- "over you, and the plague": *negeph*[55] — masculine noun meaning "an infliction of disease" or "plague."
- "shall not be upon you to destroy you": *Mashchiyth*[56] — masculine noun meaning "corruption" or "destruction."
- "when I smite": *nakah*[57] — verb meaning "to strike," "beat," "kill," "slaughter," "punish," or "wound." Some lengthy

definitions of this word imply that it is forward moving while such blows are being dealt.

- "the land": 'erets[58] — taken from a Hebrew root word meaning "land," "earth," "nation," or "entire territory."
- "of Egypt": *Mitsrayim*[59] — an attitude or proper locative noun referring to Egypt.

While many scholars maintain that, in the story of Exodus 11 and 12, the Lord selectively went through slaying the firstborn human *and* animal in each household where doorposts did not display the blood, others view this phrase as saying something slightly different. In modern terms, many assert that the aforementioned phrase would look something like this: "When I move forward, slaughtering and punishing the entire land of Egypt with plague and disease, I will take heed of the blood proclaiming your innocence and cause it to skip over you." This theological position represents only a subtle difference in perception of this passage, and certainly brings about the same result. As a study of Exodus chapters 11 and 12 yields, those who obeyed God's orders and spread the blood on the doorpost of their dwellings were spared, and those who did not were not. But the peculiarity in this study remains that some individuals believe God passed over the land selectively delivering plague, while others believe He poured out wrath on *all of the land*, selectively protecting. This is where the potential involvement of an angel comes in. The second theory represents God performing two roles at once, which, of course, God is capable of doing. However, considering the connection between angelic beings and God's command for destruction as it pertains to wrath in other areas of the Bible, some believe that an angel accompanied the Lord and acted as the shield around each household the Lord intended not to smite.

This concept of mass wrath and discerning safeguard is not entirely out of the question, considering that this is precisely how God handled matters in Genesis chapters 6–8, where He is described as pouring out His wrath on the entire world, selecting only certain individuals to be spared. This viewpoint is further reinforced in passages such as Luke 21:35–36:

> For as a snare shall it come on all them that dwell on the face of the whole earth. Watch ye therefore, and pray always, that ye may be accounted worthy to escape all of these things that shall come to pass, and to stand before the Son of man.

The use of the word "destroyer" in other passages of the Bible where God's wrath is concerned also serves, to many scholars, as a link to a living entity—particularly to an angel whom God has ordained to carry out judgment.

Psalm 78 reinforces this by adding, in verses 43–48, an extensive list of the damages God, in His wrath, caused the Egyptians. Then, at the list's completion, we read:

> He cast upon them the fierceness of his anger, wrath, and indignation, and trouble, by sending evil angels *among them.* (Psalm 78:49)

In fact, many individuals link the same or a similar angel whose involvement might have been present in Exodus chapters 11 and 12 to the events of 1 Chronicles 21, claiming these passages and others to confirm that a "destroying angel" exists. Some scholars look to 1 Corinthians 10 as further validation that God uses His subordinates to perform destruction:

> Neither let us tempt Christ, as some of them also attempted, and were destroyed of serpents. Neither murmur ye, as some of them also murmured, and were destroyed of the destroyer. (1 Corinthians 10:9–10)

Based on the fact that the destruction referred to in this passage is distinctively dealt from one of two places—either at the hand of "serpents" or "the destroyer"—some believe this to further confirm the existence of a holy angel performing the act. The importance is that, by this Scripture specifying *two* sources of damage, some scholars see the contrast of reward for evil deeds being those received at the hand of "serpents," while "the destroyer" represents the hand of God as judgment.

1 Chronicles 21

At times, God has even allowed people to choose for themselves how judgment will be executed. When David sinfully numbered Israel in 1 Chronicles 21, placing faith in his resources over God's promises (verse 1 says that Satan stood up against Israel, provoking David to this action), God immediately spoke to Gad, sending him to deliver a message to David:

> Go and tell David, saying, Thus saith the Lord, I offer thee three things: choose thee one of them, that I may do it unto thee.... Either three years' famine; or three months to be destroyed before thy foes, while that the sword of thine enemies overtaketh thee; or else three days the sword of the Lord, even the pestilence, in the land, and the angel of the Lord destroying throughout all the coasts of Israel. (1 Chronicles 21:9–12)

In this passage, the term "angel" is taken from the Hebrew *mal'ak*,[60] a masculine noun meaning "messenger" or "representative," and "of the LORD" comes from the Hebrew *Yĕhovah*[61] (the same term as in Exodus chapter 12, identical to its previously discussed translation). From this we know that although there are instances in Scripture that report that

God Himself smote individuals, there are other times when an angel does so as His direct representative.

The Bible then says that the Lord sent pestilence to Israel, killing seventy thousand men:

> And God sent an angel unto Jerusalem to destroy it: and as he was destroying, the Lord be held, and he repented him of the evil, and said to the angel that destroyed, It is enough, stay now thine hand. (1 Chronicles 21:15)

This punishment was devastating to David, who recognized that *his* sin had brought judgment to his people. He repented with a burnt offering—one he insisted upon paying a heavy monetary price for despite being offered the necessary goods for free—to which "the Lord commanded the angel; and he put up his sword again into the sheath thereof" (1 Chronicles 21:27).

God has dispatched spiritual beings to fight human battles, sometimes executing judgment by wiping out entire armies. When Sennacherib, king of Assyria, kindled God's anger by his blasphemy, arrogance, and threats to the Lord's people, God's response was:

> Whom hast thou reproached and blasphemed? and against whom hast thou exalted thy voice, and lifted up thine eyes on high? even against the Holy One of Israel. (Isaiah 37:23)

God continues in subsequent passages to explain how He will make his people prosper and deliver them from the hand of their enemies:

> For I will defend the city to save it for mine own sake, and for my servant David's sake. Then the angel of the Lord went forth, and smote in the camp of the Assyrians a hundred and fourscore

and five thousand: and when they arose early in the morning, behold, they were all dead corpses. (Isaiah 37:35–36)

Angels Engage in Spiritual Warfare

The preceding example of angels enacting judgment at God's command also shows that they are active in spiritual warfare. Throughout Scripture, when God decided to defend His people, He sent holy servants to reinforce their armies during a battle of good versus evil. Just as the stories at the beginning of this book reflect angelic intervention in modern-day supernatural combat, this age-old role played by these warriors is found throughout the Bible. Similar to the situation that Israel was in against Sennacherib, king of Assyria, Elisha found himself at odds with the king of Syria in 2 Kings 6. Elisha was renowned for his intuition, and it was said to the king of Syria that Elisha could even tell "the king of Israel the words that thou speak just in my bedchamber" (2 Kings 6:12). The king was closing in, preparing to make war on the Israelites, when Elisha's servant walked outside early in the morning and realized the city was surrounded by horses and chariots. Quickly, the servant ran to Elisha, panicked.

Elisha answered:

Fear not: for they that be with us are more than they that be with them. And Elisha prayed, and said Lord, I pray thee, open his eyes, that he may see. And the Lord opened the eyes of the young man; and he saw: and, behold, the mountain was full of horses and chariots of fire round about Elisha. (2 Kings 6:16–17)

It is easy for us, when we're surrounded by obstacles, to feel outnumbered and alone. If only our spiritual eyes could be opened during these times to see the supernatural forces surrounding us, ready to do battle on our behalf!

> Plead my cause, O Lord, with them that strive with me: fight against them that fight against me. Take hold of shield and buckler, and stand up for mine help. Draw out also the spear, and stop the way against them that persecute me: say unto my soul, I am thy salvation. Let them be confounded and put to shame that seek after my soul: let them be turned back and brought to confusion that divides my hurt. Let them be as chaff before the wind: let the angel of the Lord chase them. Let their way be dark and slippery: and let the angel of the Lord persecute them. (Psalm 35:1–6)

> The angel of the Lord encampeth round about them that fear him, and delivereth them. (Psalm 34:7)

Scripture assures us that when we are persecuted for our faith, there will be a day that the Lord's mighty angels avenge this:

> Seeing it is a righteous thing with God to recompense tribulation to them that trouble you; And to you who are troubled rest with us, when the Lord Jesus shall be revealed from heaven with his mighty angels, In flaming fire taking vengeance on them that know not God, and that obey not the gospel of our Lord Jesus Christ. (2 Thessalonians 1:6–8)

Ultimately, the battle we see before us each day is only a physical-realm reflection of what's happening in the spiritual world around us, unobserved. Although our petitions for help are to be made directly to God, who then sends angelic intervention (seen or unseen), we are surrounded day and night by a battle that rages on, just beyond our peripheral vision.

> For we wrestle not against flesh and blood, but against principalities, against powers, against the rulers of the darkness of this world, against spiritual wickedness in high places. (Ephesians 6:12)

5

Angels' Involvement in Jesus' Mission

*I*t may seem contradictory to begin the subject of angelic involvement in Jesus' mission here on earth with a look at the Old Testament, knowing that Jesus Himself did not arrive in the flesh until the times of the early New Testament. However, a common question often surfaces when studying angels' appearances in the Old Testament. For our purposes, it serves us well to prelude our study of Jesus' interaction with these beings in the New Testament with a little history from the Old.

Angel with a Capital A

Sometimes in Scripture, the word "angel" appears with a capital *A*. There's obviously a reason. Often a person asking about this seemingly sporadic capitalization also questions another element of these appearances: Unlike the lower-case appearances by an "angel of the Lord," the "Angel of the Lord" is often a visitor who, within the same passage, is often also referred to as simply "the Lord." In addition, this being often performs a miracle outside the scope of ordinary angels' power, such as raising the dead or even allowing himself to be worshipped. Since we know that the worship of angels is strictly prohibited, how can this be?

Because Scripture makes it abundantly clear that only God Himself is to be worshipped, we can easily conclude that angels themselves are not referred to as "the Lord." In fact, when referred to with the lower-cased "angel of the Lord," the phrase refers to a being who is exactly as he seems—an angel *sent by the Lord*. However, when the being is called the "Angel of the Lord," with a capital *A*, and he is within the same passage referred to as simply "the Lord," these are what biblical scholars refer to as a "theophany" or a "Christophany."

What Is a Theophany/Christophany?

The word "theophany" is derived from the Greek words *theos* ("god") and *phainein* ("show" or "reveal"). A theophany within the context of the Holy Bible, therefore, is a visible appearance of God, Himself, to mankind (not to be confused with a visible appearance of one of the members of the Celestial Order as *sent* by God). A "Christophany" is essentially the same thing, but specific to an appearance of Christ, much like the Apostle Paul's "Road to Damascus" experience. Most theophanies describe God in human form, but some are more mysterious and complicated, such as when He appeared to Moses in the form of a burning bush (Exodus 3:2 and 4:17), or as a cloud or pillar of fire for the fleeing Israelites (Exodus 13:21).

In the King James Version of the Bible, a theophany can *sometimes* be identified by a capitalization of the word "Angel," and even more definitely by the phrases "an Angel of the Lord [or "of God"]" or "*the* Angel of the Lord [or "of God"]" (phrases that collectively occur fifty-six times in the Old Testament). In these cases, the "angel" is not simply the "spirit being" we would normally associate with this "messenger" term, but a literal intervention of God, Himself, recognized in these moments as acting on His own behalf instead of sending a member of the Celestial Order. However, the tendency to capitalize these references in the Word is not a failproof factor, as it isn't treated consistently from one Bible to the next, and translations other than the KJV that have adapted this style of capitalization don't apply it the way the KJV does. Overall, the publishers' and editors' conviction behind capitalizing a perceived theophany/Christophany has been too subjective to consider dependable. Also, scholars of Greek and Hebrew don't always agree about which "angel"/"Angel" reference is a regular messenger/spirit being of God's within the Celestial Order versus which might be a theophany. As such, it would take much more space than we have here to exhaustively visit the topic of theophanies and Christophanies, so we'll stick to a short checklist of elements to consider on the subject.

Identifying the Theophany

When might we know for sure that we're reading about a theophany? Two major clues assist us…

1: When Immediate Context Remedies Confusion

Sometimes we needn't look far for the proof that an "Angel" is, in fact, a theophany, since near the verse in question, another passage clarifies it in no uncertain terms. For instance, Genesis 31:11 says, "And the Angel of God spake unto me in a dream, saying, 'Jacob': And I said, 'Here am I.'" Initially, it's not certain that this is God, Himself. But two verses later, this same "Angel of God" says, "I am the God of Bethel, where thou anointedst the pillar, and where thou vowedst a vow unto me." Nobody needs to wonder whether a mere messenger of the Celestial Order is "the *God* of Bethel" (or the "God of" any place, for that matter). Beyond this, pillar anointings and vows would not be made to a spirit-being *servant* of the Almighty instead of the Almighty, Himself.

This immediate-context rule is often the fastest way to identify a theophany when the language of the Word allows for such illumination. Since not every instance of a theophany is as clear, though, there are other clues we can consider.

2: When the "Angel" Does What a Mere "Messenger" Cannot

At times, Scripture distinguishes a theophany when a passage describes the Angel performing an act, service, miracle, or all-powerful character trait that only God, Himself, is capable of. We'll look at a couple of examples.

God is the *only* power in the universe that can create life (Genesis 1; Isaiah 40:28; Acts 17:24), and even more importantly, He is the only power that can create life out of *nothing* by the sheer force of His command (Colossians 1:16). An angel might be able to *deliver the news* that God has already or is planning to create life (i.e., Gabriel delivering the news of Christ's arrival to Mary in Luke 1:26–38), but a messenger in the Celestial Order isn't independently capable of creating life. Yet in Genesis 16:10, we read: "And the Angel of the Lord said unto her, I will multiply thy seed exceedingly, that it shall not be numbered for multitude." Here again, a "messenger" of the Creator wouldn't have the power to multiply offspring.

Elsewhere, Joshua "fell on his face to the earth, and did worship" the Angel; immediately after Joshua's worshipful expression, the Angel told Joshua—in the same flavor as He had told Moses earlier—that Joshua was standing on "holy ground" (Joshua 5:14–15). Within the boundaries of healthy Christian theology, angels are *not* to be worshipped. This kind of error led to the evil/fallen angels in the first place. Any "holy angel" of the Lord's Celestial Order would not accept worship, as is proven by John's account on Patmos:

And I John saw these things, and heard them. And when I had heard and seen, I fell down to worship before the feet of the angel which shewed me these things. Then saith he unto me, "See thou do it not [i.e., "don't worship me"]: for I am thy fellowservant, and of thy brethren the prophets, and of them which keep the sayings of this book: worship God" (Revelation 22:8–9; see also Matthew 4:9–10; Romans 1:25; Colossians 2:18).

Therefore, we know the Angel in the Joshua account was a theophany, as he openly accepted worship and spoke in the same terms as God.

These aren't the only examples of "the Angel" carrying out what only God can (for instance, angels cannot forgive sins, yet the Angel in Exodus 23:21 has the prerogative to forgive, and so on). Therefore, whenever a reader stumbles upon a narrative referring to an "angel" or "Angel" who exhibits authority elsewhere inappropriate for a messenger of the Celestial Order, it could very well be a signal that the scene involves a theophany.

Where Does "Christophany" Come into Play?

By now, you might be wondering why so many scholars are convinced that some of these theophanies are Christophanies, specifically referencing an appearance of Jesus in the Old Testament ages before He would come in human flesh. A couple of factors contribute to this calculation.

First, scholars consider the attributes and characteristics of each member of the Trinity and find Christ the most likely candidate to appear corporeally. The Word is clear that "no man hath seen God at any time" (John 1:18), yet *many* have seen Christ while He walked in the flesh. This conundrum has confused a great number of Bible students throughout the years, because verses like these are scattered throughout

Scripture: "And he said, 'Thou canst not see my face: for there shall no man see me, and live'" (Exodus 33:20).

But wait a second...*Jacob* saw God and lived: "And Jacob was left alone; and there wrestled a man...[and thereafter said:] 'I have seen God face to face, and my life is preserved'" (Genesis 32:24, 30).

On the other hand, *nobody* can see God: "[God] only hath immortality...which no man can approach unto; whom no man hath seen, nor can see" (1 Timothy 6:16).

But on the *other* other hand: "And Manoah said unto his wife, 'We...have seen God'" (Judges 13:22).

Whereas it appears quite clear in Scripture that no man can see God and live, it's quite obvious that Jesus—God in human form—was "seen" by mankind everywhere He went. He was corporeal, touchable, and physical.

Although countless discussions in the scholarly world exist about whether the "see God and live/die" clause referred to physical death or something more spiritual (therefore negating this "corporeality" angle entirely), one of the most popular explanations for why God *can* and *cannot* be seen by man as the "Angel" in the Old Testament is related to the idea that the "Angel" is the corporeal Christ...in the flesh, just as He would be later.

Second, the "Angel of the Lord" mysteriously disappeared after Jesus Christ was born in the flesh. If the Angel was, in fact, the preincarnate Messiah, then it explains why the theophany/Christophany didn't take place during the years He was going about His Father's business in human form. In a time as spiritually and eternally significant as Christ's ministry years, one might find the absence of theophanies a notable oddity, until we allow that the same God behind the theophanies was walking with the disciples, challenging the Pharisees, etc. It is during this time when God's chief messenger was identified as Gabriel, *not* the "Angel of the Lord."

Third, although we know that Christ is "much better than the angels" (Hebrews 1:4) who in turn "worship Him" (Hebrews 1:6–7)—references to the spirit beings of the Celestial Order—Malachi's prophecy (Malachi 3:1) about the future Messiah specifically identifies Christ as God's *mal'ak*, which, as we discussed earlier, is Hebrew for "messenger" and by extension "angel." This is key language that links Christ, Himself, to theophanies.

Furthermore, Colossians 2:8–9 reveals that Jesus is the member of the Godhead who is given physical manifestation:

> Beware lest any man spoil you through philosophy and vain deceit, after the tradition of men, after the rudiments of the world, and not after Christ. For in him dwelleth all the fullness of the Godhead bodily.

Additionally, a passage in John sheds insight on this phenomenon as well:

> No man hath seen God at any time; the only begotten Son, which is in the bosom of the Father, he hath declared him. (John 1:18)

So, whereas it wouldn't completely make sense to assume that the burning bush, cloud, or pillar of fire was a Christophany—especially since they don't resemble the human form Christ eventually took—sound evidence suggests that *some* of our Old Testament theophanies could have been Jesus in the flesh. This is dealt with case by case by expert theologians, and the verdict is nowhere *near* unanimous for all the potential Christophanies. However, if nothing else, we can appreciate the beauty in the concept that Christ's ministry as fully God and fully human simultaneously *might have* extended as far back as Genesis!

What a pretty picture that paints.

Angels' Involvement in Jesus' Mission

The mission of holy angels is a consistent theme throughout the entire Bible: They are creatures devoted to God who do His will; minister to, protect, and intervene on behalf of creation at His command; rejoice at God's success; and praise Him continually. While this assignment remains unchanged, the role of these creatures manifests differently in the New Testament than in the Old. Naturally, this makes perfect sense: The arrival of Christ in the flesh changed everything for everybody, *angels included*. These servants of the Lord had previously, at God's command, ministered to and strengthened the human beings He created. Now, a member of the Trinity had taken on fleshly form and walked among mankind. For the first time, the angels would strengthen and minister to Jesus, Himself, in the *flesh*. It is no secret that Jesus' ministry here on earth and the pathway to salvation that He put into place forever altered everything for mankind, for all of eternity. Those once subject to judgment were now eligible for forgiveness, and Jesus' work here on earth became the new mission that the Celestial Order engaged in.

Imagine what a different era the angels were experiencing! Perhaps it was exciting for them to be able to minister to their Lord in such a way. Certainly, it is an understatement to say it was heartbreaking for them to watch as He was ridiculed, beaten, and crucified. Imagine their elation as they were privileged to announce that He had risen! Recalling that throughout Scripture, angels rejoiced at the Lord's triumphs, it seems obvious that His victory over the grave brought unspeakable joy to the angels. Just as the eyes of Elisha's servant were opened and he could the surrounding angelic army, imagine the unseen host encircling Jesus each moment He walked the earth! As Jesus carried out God's will on this planet, angels awaited His orders each step of the way.

Announcements Regarding Jesus' Birth

Zacharias Is Told of John the Baptist

To outline the role of angels during Jesus' ministry, it's only natural to start at the beginning. Since one of the most prominent roles they fulfill throughout the Bible is that of making announcements, it isn't surprising that the most miraculous work God has done in the history of mankind—His redemptive work of forgiveness—would begin with a series of proclamations given by heralding visitations. An angel began to lay the groundwork for the arrival of Jesus by approaching the priest, Zacharias—husband of the barren Elisabeth. This was a righteous couple who followed God's commandments. The story begins in Luke 1:

> And there appeared unto him an angel of the Lord standing on the right side of the altar of incense. And when Zacharias saw him, he was troubled, and fear fell upon him. But the angel said unto him, Fear not, Zacharias: for thy prayer is heard; and thy wife Elisabeth shall bear thee a son, and thou shalt call his name John. And thou shalt have joy and gladness; and many shall rejoice at his birth. For he shall be great in the side of the Lord, and shall drink neither wine nor strong drink: and he shall be filled with the Holy Ghost, even from his mother's womb. And many of the children of Israel shall be turned to the Lord their God. And he shall go before him in the spirit and power of Elias, to turn the hearts of the fathers to the children, and the disobedient to the wisdom of the just; and to make ready a people prepared for the Lord. (Luke 1:11–17)

This announcement was given to a righteous husband and wife who had followed God in all their ways, but who hadn't been blessed with a child. Not only were their prayers for a child answered, but his arrival was foretold to them personally by holy messenger! Of course, the reader is probably already aware that the subject of this announcement was indeed John the Baptist, Jesus' cousin whose life was dedicated to priming the people for the Messiah to come.

An interesting side note regarding the announcement made to Zacharias: During the reign of King David, the priestly family of Aaron was divided into twenty-four segments.[62] Zacharias was of the division of Abijah (Luke 5). Subsects of the priestly population were then called to serve within the Temple at Jerusalem on a rotating basis, and when each faction's service time arrived, individuals were selected by drawing lots.[63] Any service of this nature recruited from an individual was a once-in-a-lifetime honor and was certainly an opportunity that many might never experience.[64] Thus, we can see that God had placed Zacharias at the Temple strategically before this divine appointment was to take place.

Mary Is Told of Jesus

The next announcement was made to the young girl, Mary, whom God had chosen to be the mother of Jesus.

> And in the sixth month the angel Gabriel was sent from God unto a city of Galilee, named Nazareth, To a virgin espoused to a man whose name was Joseph, of the house of David; and the virgins name was Mary. And the angel came in unto her, and said, Hail, thou that art highly favoured, the Lord is with thee: blessed art thou among women. And when she saw him, she was troubled at his saying, and cast in her mind what manner of salutation this should be. And the angel said unto her, Fear not, Mary: for thou hast found favour with God. And, behold, thou shalt conceive in thy womb, and bring forth a son, and shalt call his name Jesus. He shall be great, and shall be called the Son of the Highest: and the Lord God shall give unto him the throne

of his father David: And he shall reign over the house of Jacob forever; and of his kingdom there shall be no end. Then Mary said unto the angel, How shall this be, seeing I know not a man? And the angel answered and said to her, The Holy Ghost shall come upon thee, and the power of the Highest shall overshadow thee: therefore also that holy thing which shall be born of thee shall be called the Son of God. And, behold, thy cousin Elisabeth, she hath also conceived a son in her old age: and this is the sixth month with her, who was called barren. For nothing with God shall be impossible. And Mary said, Behold the handmaid of the Lord; be it unto me according to thy word. And the angel departed from her. (Luke 1:26–38)

Joseph Is Visited in a Dream

An equally important announcement was made, this time in a dream, to Joseph, Mary's espoused. Scripture tells us in Matthew 1:18–19 that when Joseph learned that Mary was with child, he intended to put her away quietly. (This often-overlooked detail speaks of Joseph's gentle demeanor: A unmarried woman in this culture who was illegitimately pregnant or committed adultery was, at the very least, a terrible disgrace, and she might even be punished for these infractions by death. Joseph *could* have become outraged and insist that Mary be punished publicly, possibly even fatally. But Joseph was a man of mercy. Instead of making a public spectacle of Mary, he intended to deal with the issue quietly, possibly even sparing the young girl's life. She, likewise, had taken a great step of faith by submitting to God's plan for her life as an unmarried woman in this society's culture. These components show the moral fiber and strength of this betrothed duo, both in character and in faith!)

While Joseph pondered about how to go about a merciful separation from Mary, a message delivered by an angel changed his mind:

But while he thought on these things, behold, an angel of the Lord appeared to him in a dream, saying, Joseph, thou son of David, fear not to take unto the Mary thy wife: for that which is conceived in her is of the Holy Ghost. And she shall bring forth a son, and thou shalt call his name Jesus: for he shall save his people from their sins. (Matthew 1:20–21)

Parents Receive Instruction Regarding the Births

As we look at these passages, we see, just as in the Old Testament, angels announcing the upcoming births of important individuals who would change the world. The angel's function had not changed at this point, but the significance of the events to follow is of much greater import. Notice how much detail was given to the child's future parent regarding the unborn baby. In many ways, these proclamations were providing the parents with prophetic instruction about the forthcoming child. Zacharias was told that his son—to be called John—would prepare the way of the Lord, essentially stirring up revival. Mary was told that her son—to be called Jesus—would reign over the house of Jacob, seeing no end to his kingdom. Beyond this, Joseph was told that the child would actually *save people from sin!* Only an angelic messenger would have the authority to say such things.

Another distinction about the angelic birth announcements—making Jesus' unique—is the number of people to whom the messenger *appeared.* Whereas previous announcements of significant births were made primarily to the parents-to-be, Jesus' was proclaimed not only to Mary and Joseph, but had been foretold much earlier in prophecy, and was further confirmed to Elisabeth with no words. Luke 1:41–42 relates that John the Baptist, yet unborn, "leaped in her womb; and Elisabeth was filled with the Holy Ghost: And she spake out with a loud voice, and said, Blessed art thou among women, and blessed is the fruit of thy womb." Elisabeth immediately replied with a question (verse 43): "What has caused the mother of *her Lord* to pay her a visit?" This, though not delivered through angelic message, validates the other pronouncements made regarding Jesus' arrival.

Shepherds Receive a Supernatural Visit

On the night Jesus was born, complete strangers also received news that the Messiah had arrived. A report of His birth was given to local businessmen right after the event had taken place:

> And there were in the same country shepherds abiding in the field, keeping watch over their flock by night. And, lo, the angel of the Lord came upon them, and the glory of the Lord shone round about them: and they were sore afraid. And the angel said to them, Fear not: for, behold, I bring you good tidings of great joy, which shall be to all people. For unto you is born this day in the city of David a Saviour, which is Christ the Lord. And this shall be a sign unto you; Ye shall find the babe wrapped in swaddling clothes, lying in a manger. And suddenly there was with the angel a multitude of the heavenly host praising God, and saying, Glory to God in the highest, and on earth peace, good will toward men. And it came to pass, as the angels were gone away from them into heaven, the shepherds said one to another, Let us now go even unto Bethlehem, and see this thing which has come to pass, which the Lord hath made known unto us. (Luke 2:8–15)

An important sequence about this passage is often overlooked. Verse 8 informs us that the shepherds were "keeping watch over their flock by night," indicating that darkness had probably fallen, and their flocks were likely secured for the night. Next, Scripture states that "the angel of the Lord" made the announcement. Often, movies, books, and even

Christmas programs in our churches depict this scene with a multitude of angels showing up in the sky (all winged, of course), singing "Glory to God in the highest." However, that is not how the series of events took place. *One* angel appeared, with such a radiant light permeating from his being that the shepherds were frightened. That's why the angel's first words were "Fear not" (as is so often the case in angelic appearances). In typical form, the being's first words to the shepherds were ones of peace and comfort. He reassured the men and expressed that he had brought good news—news so good, in fact, that it would bring them "great joy." Once he explained that the Savior has been born and told them how to find the baby, he was then immediately joined by "a multitude of the heavenly host praising God."

The biblical narrative doesn't elaborate on the nature of these additional visitors. Many assume that they were ordinary angels, but the passage doesn't say "more angels appeared." Instead, it refers to a "multitude of the heavenly host," leaving the nature of the beings open-ended. Thus, other members of the Celestial Order, such as cherubim, seraphim, or others, could have been the ones lifting a chorus of praise to God for this spectacular event. One thing is certain: The shepherds witnessed *something* that night so dynamic and undeniable that they immediately left to find the newborn: "Let us go *now* even unto Bethlehem."

Reading on, we discover that the shepherds "came with haste, and found Mary, and Joseph, and the babe lying in a manger" (verse 16). Note that the shepherds found Jesus while He was *still in the manger*. This indicates that they likely arrived at Bethlehem the same night or in the wee hours of the following morning, because Mary and Joseph wouldn't have tarried for longer than necessary in the stable belonging to the innkeeper. The shepherds experienced something so powerful that they had been moved to travel immediately—despite the risks involved in leaving their flocks unattended, the fact that night had fallen, and even the distance and perils of late-night travel. Imagine what it would have taken to prompt someone to engage in such dramatic action.

Let's consider a modern-day scenario. Somebody knocks on the door of your house late at night and tells you that a really important baby has been born—to a complete stranger, no less—and is now in a distant barn. How would you respond? It is highly doubtful that you or I would immediately trek out into the night to find the babe.

That is, unless...

Something about the celestial announcement that night was *so profound* that these individuals were motivated to act right away. With this in mind, it's extremely unlikely that our modern version of the event even begins to touch on the fierce, powerful reality that the shepherds certainly witnessed on the night of Jesus' birth.

The Wisemen Follow a... Star?

Many people assume that the wisemen arrived at the innkeeper's stable on the night Jesus was born. However, this isn't correct. Matthew 2:1–2 states:

> Now when Jesus was born in Bethlehem of Judaea in the days of Herod the king, behold, there came wisemen from the east to Jerusalem, Saying, Where is he that is born King of the Jews? for we have seen his star in the East, and are come to worship him.

We've learned that angels can manipulate the natural elements of the earth; for example, they can move objects, appear as light, and even cause occurrences such as earthquakes. Is it possible that the "star" referred in this passage might be an angel stationed over our Lord Jesus, illuminating the path for these travelers or keeping guard over the Babe? Surely He was surrounded by these beings. Not only that, but when the heralding angel initially appeared to the shepherds to announce the birth, remember, the light was so bright that the shepherds were afraid. We could speculate that from a distance, such a being could have appeared as a star in the sky.

In Matthew 2:2, the word "star" is a transliteration of the word Greek *astēr*, a masculine noun that means "star…strewn over the sky."[65] Some translators have even interpreted this term to refer to a comet in space. This original word is the same used to describe the seven stars referred to in the book of Revelation, chapters 1 and 2, wherein the "stars" are believed by many scholars to represent angels. In addition, the brilliant light that appeared to the wisemen, according to Scripture, moved about in the sky, *leading them to baby Jesus:*

> When they had heard the king, they departed; and, lo, the star, which they saw in the east, went before them, till it came and stood over where the young child was. (Matthew 2:9)

Because angels are repeatedly reported throughout Scripture as carrying great light within their beings, a case can be made for the possibility that this was no mere, everyday cosmic body of hydrogen and helium, but rather a dazzling, radiant, angelic being who accompanied Jesus, remained stationed overhead and keeping watch during His early days when some sought to kill the seemingly helpless infant (Matthew 2).

The Babe Is Threatened

Regardless of how one chooses to interpret this possibility, without doubt there was soon intervention in the life of young Jesus that resulted from the wisemen's pursuit. We know that Herod was immediately troubled when he was approached by the magi, who asked him the following outrageous question (restated in modern terms): "Where is this Baby, born of your subordinate kingdom, who will rule them all? We are looking for Him (not you, Herod), so that we can worship *Him*" (see Matthew 2:2).

Reading on, Herod launched into damage-control mode, summoning chief priests and scribes to interpret prophetic Scripture in an effort to pinpoint Jesus' location. He then instructed the travelers to find the newborn and return to Him with the location, saying that he, too, wanted to worship Jesus. However, Matthew 2:12 says that the wisemen were "warned of God in a dream that they should not return to Herod, [and] they departed into their own country another way."

In the next verse, Matthew 2:13, Joseph was warned by an angel in a dream:

> Arise, and take the young child and his mother, and flee into Egypt, and be thou there until I bring the word: for Herod will seek the young child to destroy him.

This escape, on behalf of Joseph, Mary, and Jesus, enraged (and threatened) Herod to the point that he sent out a decree ordering the murder of all boys throughout Bethlehem who were two years and younger. The refugees—Joseph, Mary, and Jesus—remained in Egypt until the death of this brutal ruler. Finally, Joseph was given word, once again through angelic visitation in a dream, to return to Israel:

> But when Herod was dead, behold, an angel of the Lord appeareth in a dream to Joseph in Egypt, Saying, Arise, and take the young child and his mother, and go into the land of Israel: for they are dead which sought the young child's life. (Matthew 2:19–20)

At this point, the dynamic work that Jesus did here on earth had barely begun, yet angelic visitation and manifestation had already thoroughly encompassed His existence on earth. As Jesus grew up and began His ministry, the angels' love and devotion for Him is readily apparent.

Angels Prove Jesus Had Heaven's Support

Some theorize that Jesus acted on His own—independently from other members of the Trinity—when He came to earth to complete the plan of salvation. This suggests that heaven was divided regarding whether Jesus should come and give Himself as the Supreme Sacrifice, thus making a way for salvation. For many, this debate was put to rest when Jesus said in Mark 3:24 that a kingdom divided against itself cannot stand. Further fortifying the position that all of the Triune Members acted in unity on this matter is shown through the scene that unfolded when Jesus approached John the Baptist to be baptized:

> Then cometh Jesus from Galilee to Jordan unto John, to be baptized of him. But John forbad him, saying, I have need to be baptized of thee, and comest thou to me? And Jesus answering said unto him, Suffer it to be so now: for thus it becometh us to fulfil all righteousness. Then he suffered him. And Jesus, when he was baptized, went up straightway out of the water: and, lo, the heavens were opened unto him, and he saw the Spirit of God descending like a dove, and lighting up on him: And lo a voice from heaven, saying, This is my beloved Son, in whom I am well pleased. (Matthew 3:13–17)

For anyone with doubts about whether the full Trinity operated in one accord regarding Jesus' arrival on this earth, His ministry, and the salvation plan that He came here to complete, this verse should put that question to rest. After all, the entire Trinity manifested in this scene in harmony. Furthermore, as John attempted to decline performing the baptizing of Jesus, Jesus said, "it becometh us to fulfil all righteousness." In other words, "This is what God has determined is good for us to do."

The Trinity's Impact on Angels

The reason it is important point to note the unity of the Trinity regarding Jesus' ministry here on earth is that it is reflected in the angelic activity in the New Testament, which cyclically fortifies the argument for the Three acting as One throughout Jesus' earthly life. Consider two connecting factors: First, we know that holy angels are loyal to God the Trinity. Second, we have previously established that angels are agents of free will. Thus, if the members of the Trinity were divided—were that *even possible*—there would be division within the Celestial Order as well, yet we see oneness in the holy servants' involvement in Christ's ministry. The collective effort we see within the supernatural realm surrounding Christ's time as a Man illustrates that the Three-in-One acted in harmony.

In addition, on the evening of Jesus' crucifixion—at the very climax of His purpose for coming to earth—He made it clear that He had the full authority of all of heaven behind Him:

> Thinkest thou that I cannot now pray to my Father, and he shall presently give me more than twelve legions of angels? (Matthew 26:53)

Since a Roman legion equals six thousand men, Jesus was stating that He could summon (at least) seventy-two thousand angels to His side immediately, should he choose to call in such an army.

The reason for diverting from our topic of angelic activity into the subject of the Trinity's union throughout Jesus' ministry is necessary because, if there had existed any division between the Three over such matters, there likewise would have been diversity amongst the angels. These celestial beings serving in such a cohesive, active role surrounding the work of Jesus here on earth further illustrates that *all of heaven* was joined in this mission. In fact, the role angels played in Jesus' earthly life is as strong and equally as solid as any other circumstance of angelic involvement found in the Bible up to this point. There can be no doubt regarding the harmony of heaven—and the enthusiasm of angels—concerning Christ's mission and His redemptive work in bringing about the salvation plan.

Angelic Support in Jesus' Ministry

We know that angels engage in spiritual warfare. But when Jesus lived among humankind, He, likewise engaged in spiritual warfare. The most critical account we have of this is found in Matthew chapter 4, the temptation of Jesus. This happened right after He had been baptized and the Holy Spirit had descended upon him as a dove. Filled with the Holy Spirit, Jesus went—in fact, Scripture tells us he was *led by the Spirit*—into the wilderness. Since Jesus knew He would be tried ruthlessly, He fasted for forty days and forty nights in preparation for this test:

> Then was Jesus lead up of the Spirit into the wilderness to be tempted of the devil. And when he had fasted forty days and forty nights, he was afterward an hungred. And when the tempter came to him, he said, If thou be the Son of God, command that these stones be made bread. But he answered and said, It is written, Man shall not live by bread alone, but by every word that proceedeth out of the mouth of God. Then the devil taketh him up into the holy city, and setteth him on a pinnacle of the temple, And saith unto him, If thou be the Son of God, cast thyself down: for it is written, He shall give his angels charge concerning thee: and in their hands they shall bear thee up, lest at any time thou dash thy foot against a stone. Jesus said unto him, It is written again, Thou shalt not tempt the Lord thy God.

Again, the devil taketh him up into an exceeding high mountain and sheweth him all the kingdoms of the world, and the glory of them; And saith unto him, All these things will I give thee, if thou wilt fall down and worship me. Then saith Jesus unto him, Get thee hence, Satan: for it is written, Thou shalt worship the Lord thy God, and him only shalt thou serve. Then the devil leaveth him, and, behold, angels came and ministered unto him. (Matthew 4:1–11)

The passage doesn't elaborate on *exactly how* the angels ministered to Jesus—for example, whether they gave Him food and drink or miraculously healed the agony of fasting for forty days and nights, etc. We can, however, refer to Daniel's account of angelic ministry for a hint at what likely took place for Jesus:

And said, O man greatly beloved, fear not: peace be unto thee, be strong, yea, be strong. And when he had spoken unto me, I was strengthened. (Daniel 10:19)

The angels' ministry to Jesus likely involved similar elements, such as words of comfort and peace along with physical strengthening.

Jesus' Power in Contrast to That of the Angels

There were times during Jesus' ministry when His power was showcased as supremely effective because of the manner in which it stood out in contrast to other supernatural forces, both holy and evil. One example of this is in John 5. In Jerusalem, there was a pool near which the sick and injured would gather and await healing. During a certain season, the angel (a being that Scripture is somewhat vague about) would stir the water of this pool, after which the first person to enter the water would be "made whole of whatsoever disease he had" (John 5:4). Essentially, once the water began to move, a race was on among all of those who were crippled, diseased, or otherwise infirm, and healing was only obtained by the first individual to immerse. One man, whom Scripture notes had been sick for thirty-eight years, lay nearby until questioned by Jesus. When the Son asked the man why he didn't submerge himself in the water for healing, the man explained that he had been unable to reach it before anyone else.

Jesus, in turn, issued the simple command: "Rise, take up thy bed, and walk" (John 5:8). Scripture says the man was immediately made whole. Despite his lack of contact with the healing pool and his thirty-eight years of illness, he merely obeyed Jesus' words. There had been previous angelic involvement in the healing that regularly (once a year) took place at this locale, but Jesus healed whomever He saw fit to heal, whenever He saw fit to do so.

Jesus' Power in Contrast to That of Evil Forces

When interacting with a man possessed by an evil spirit to the extent that he had become both blind and dumb, Jesus' authority over the evil spirit was evident immediately. Not only did the healing Jesus administered demonstrate His power over all creation, including opposing spiritual forces, but it also confirmed that He was indeed an ambassador from the kingdom of heaven:

> But when the Pharisees heard it, they said, This fellow doth not cast out devils, but by Beelzebub the prince of the devils. And Jesus knew their thoughts, and said unto them, Every kingdom divided against itself is brought to desolation; and every city or house divided against itself shall not stand: And if Satan cast out Satan, he is divided against himself; how shall that his kingdom

stand? And if I by Beelzebub cast out devils, by whom do your children cast them out? therefore they shall be your judges. But if I cast out devils by the Spirit of God, then the kingdom of God is come unto you. (Matthew 12:24–28)

Jesus' victory over evil spirits gave Him the opportunity to state to onlookers who He was and where He had come from. Similarly, in Luke 10, Jesus not only said precisely who He is, but identified Satan and indicated His imminent victory over the enemy, explaining to His followers their placement within the supernatural realm of authority:

He that heareth you heareth me; and he that despiseth you despiseth me; and he that despiseth me despiseth him that sent me. And the seventy returned with joy, saying, Lord, even the devils are subject unto us through thy name. And he said unto them, I beheld Satan as lightning fall from heaven. Behold, I give unto you power to tread on serpents and scorpions, and over all the power of the enemy: and nothing shall by any means hurt you. Notwithstanding in this rejoice not, that the spirits are subject unto you; but rather rejoice, because your names are written in heaven. (Luke 10:16–20)

An Angel Helps Jesus Prepare for Crucifixion

Jesus was facing the worst night of His life here on earth: He would be betrayed by a friend; He would be arrested, tried, and convicted despite being innocent; His Father would have to stand aside and allow Him to be tortured, crucified, and sent to engage in a good-versus-evil spiritual battle on His own. Before the evening's horrible events began to unfold, Jesus prayed. It was a prayer more intense any other recorded in the entire Bible; in fact, it was a petition riddled with such agony that Matthew 22:44 tells us that "his sweat was as it were great drops of blood falling down to the ground." While His disciples were sleeping only a stone's throw away, the Savior prayed these words:

> Father, if thou be willing, remove this cup from me: nevertheless not my will, but thine, be done. (Luke 22:42)

While God the Father didn't answer the prayer by removing the cup from Jesus, He *did* send an angel from heaven to strengthen Him.

During the Crucifixion

While Jesus was being crucified, Scripture indicates (Matthew 26:53) that He could have called upon His Father to dispatch legions of angels to end the torment He was enduring. However, He made no such request, and thus completed the work He set out to do on the cross. Many overlook the importance of angels' obedience during this moment. If ever there was a time when any division among the forces of heaven might have been apparent, this was it. If angels within the holy realms had any disunity or any question about their mission, this would have been their opportunity to demonstrate their true loyalties. For the crucifixion to be carried out uninterrupted, every angel within the holy realms had to stand by and allow Jesus' agony to take place without intervening. The work that God the Son had to do, in that moment, was His alone to complete. The heavenly servants' true commitment to God's mission shows in their willingness to obey every one of His orders—even when the command is to stand by silently while their Lord is tortured, crucified, and killed by humans who are confirmed in Scripture as a part of a lower-ranked order of beings (Psalm 8:5).

After the Crucifixion

It had been three days since Jesus had asked the Father to allow this cup to pass from Him. He had since been crucified, and the disciples had been hiding together, in fear. Mary Magdalene arose early and went to the tomb, only to find it open. The stone that had been placed at the doorway of the sepulchre had been moved! Mary ran to two of Jesus' disciples, reporting that the stone was gone and the Lord's body had been moved. The men she reported this to immediately went to the tomb to see for themselves, then returned home. Mary stood there, weeping, alone. What she saw next changed the course of history:

> In the end of the sabbath, as it began to dawn toward the first day of the week, came Mary Magdalene and the other Mary to see the sepulchre. And, behold, there was a great earthquake: for the angel of the Lord descended from heaven, and came and rolled back the stone from the door, and sat upon it. His countenance was like lightning, and his raiment white as snow: And for fear of him the keepers did shake, and became as dead men. And the angel answered and said unto the women, Fear not ye: for I know that ye seek Jesus, which was crucified. He is not here: for he is risen, as he said. Come, see the place where the Lord lay. And go quickly, and tell his disciples that he is risen from the dead; and, behold, he goeth before you into Galilee; there shall ye see him: lo, I have told you. (Matthew 28:1–7)

This explains that when the angel of the Lord descended from heaven, the being caused an earthquake, dislodging the massive stone from the entrance of the tomb. Note that the angel's "countenance was like lightning... And for fear of him keepers did shake, and became as dead men." When this angel descended, it must've been quite a scene.

Jesus had risen! And in His tomb were angels: One was stationed near where His head had lain, and one was near where His feet had been (John 20:12). Even during death, Jesus had been surrounded by these loyal beings. And now, in light of His resurrection, they had remained to help spread the news of His triumph to His followers.

Angels' Involvement in the Early Church

After Jesus' crucifixion and resurrection, His disciples and other followers had an entirely new path to follow. Where previously, favor with God had been sought after by devoutly following levitical law and offering sacrifices, Jesus had paid the ultimate price and offered Himself as the Supreme Sacrifice for all of mankind's sins. This opened the door of salvation to all people from every walk of life, but it also left many reeling. Confusion about being eligible for redemption as it pertained to race, deeds, individual sinful history, economic status, gender, and even cultural and religious background was rampant.

A new day was dawning for the followers of the Almighty God, and the earliest members of the Church were trying to support myriad newcomers to the faith with letters and scriptural direction. It was a crucial time for these believers, and angels played a key role in bringing vital people together to help conduct this new movement in the direction that God intended. We'll briefly look at a few examples of angels directing divine appointments during this period.

In Acts chapter 8, we read about an instance where an angel of the Lord spoke to Philip, telling him to travel south to Gaza. When Philip obeyed, he saw a eunuch from Ethiopia, who sat in his chariot reading the prophetic writings of Esaias. As the angel prompted Philip, the man obediently approached the Ethiopian. During the conversation, Philip had the opportunity to tell the man about Jesus, and even to subsequently baptize him.

In Acts 10, a man named Cornelius saw a vision of an angel of God who told him to send men to Joppa for Simon, surnamed Peter. Peter, in the meantime, had been told by the Lord in a vision that "what God hath cleansed, that call not thou common" (Acts 10:15). In the same vision, Peter was told that the three men who were looking for him had been sent by God, so he wasn't to question their motives when they arrived; he was to go with them. When Peter did so, he recalled the instruction he had been given in his vision, so he cast aside traditional racial tensions that would have otherwise kept the people divided. Unity that transcended racial barriers was thus cemented into the foundation of the early Church via divine appointment assisted by angelic intervention.

We've already covered additional intervention that occurred when angels ministered to—and even rescued—saints of the early Church who were imprisoned. One of the most important occasions, however, was the announcement of hope that they left the apostles as Jesus ascended into heaven:

> They [the apostles] were looking intently up into the sky as he [Jesus] was going, when suddenly two men dressed in white stood beside them. "Men of Galilee," they said, "why do you stand here looking into the sky? This same Jesus, who has been taken from you into heaven, will come back in the same way you have seen him go into heaven." (Acts 1:10)

Surely these were words of hope for those who had seen their Lord persecuted, crucified, arisen, and subsequently ascended into the sky. In the days, months, and years ahead, as these same followers were severely persecuted (and even put to death) as they led Christians after Jesus' departure, certainly they recalled these words with a heart of longing. The blessed hope of the announcement made by the angels ensured them of the promise that Jesus would return. What a comfort, to know that they had not seen the last of their Beloved Lord!

All of the holy angels and the rest of the Celestial Order will play a vital role in the future return of Jesus. What will this look like for those of us here on earth when that long-awaited moment finally arrives? We'll discuss this exciting topic in the next chapter.

6

Angels in the Prophetic Future

What's the Buzz?

*M*odern-day accounts of supernatural and unexplained phenomena seem to be on the rise. Reports of angelic visitations, UFO sightings, and even instances such as hauntings lend to the concept that activity within the spirit realm is heating up around us. Even some churches that claim to be biblically based are introducing new practices and paraphernalia, such as "angel boards" and "angel cards," among other items mentioned earlier in the book. In the meantime, the Internet continues to make available such items as angel color wheels—cards displaying a color spectrum accompanied by lists of angel feather colors and their meanings—and other such gear, along with accompanying false teachings, at the click of a mouse. There is no doubt that supernatural, angelic activity and visitation are increasing as time passes, whether they be holy angels sent by the Almighty God or encounters with malevolent spirits invited through ill-advised or dubious means.

Sadly, claims of encounters with spiritual beings are often embraced by many of us with encouragement to be openminded and open-hearted. Many of us rarely offer those claiming to have been be visited by an angel advice that suggests discernment. Those who *do* urge caution regarding the visitor are often regarded as negative, narrow-minded, or overly skeptical. Open-ended reassurance tends to be the response, with advisors, magazines, and websites encouraging individuals to embrace the phenomena without question. A recent news article online entitled "6 Signs You're Being Visited by Your Guardian Angel" begins by quoting Matthew 18:10, but quickly skews completely away from Scripture, offering such haphazard advice as the following:

> If you are wondering about whether or not you are receiving messages from your angels, one way to determine it is to have faith and trust your intuition…if you feel strongly in your heart that something is guidance from your guardian angel, than [as in original article] it likely is.[66]

The piece goes on to assert that feathers we find are efforts at communications from an angel. Furthermore, the color of the feather indicates the nature of the message:

> A white feather is a major sign that you are being visited by a guardian angel. It is also the most common of all the angel signs.… The cool thing about finding feathers is the angels will align them on your path at just the right time to offer validation, comfort or clue…as in to the answer of a question you've asked or to encourage you on the right path.[67]

As frightening—and as *completely* theologically flawed—as this advice is (nowhere in Scripture is a white feather associated with an angel!), seekers are buying this type of advice hook, line, and sinker for a few reasons. One is that the world is filled with people who are hurting and desperately seeking something to believe in. Another is that supernatural phenomena are so rampant these days, those who aren't careful (or scripturally educated) can find themselves lost amongst all the deception. Beyond this, truth regarding these matters is found in Scripture, but unfortunately Bible reading is at an all-time low (approximately 25 percent of self-professed Christians claim to read the Bible regularly each week), even among believers.[68] Many so-called Scripture-based books and media, and musicians claiming to write God-glorifying songs are misleading when it comes to truth about these heavenly servants, while some even border on advocating the worship of such beings. Consider the lyrics to the song "Gabriela" recorded by the Christian band White-heart and included on their album, *Tales of Wonder*, released in 1992:

> All those empty streets I wandered down,
> Restless nights and lonely dawns,
> Seems like forever I've looked for you,
> Now the dream that I've been waiting for is coming true,
> The dream is you.
> Gabriela, angel of mercy,
> She comes to my night, on wings full of light,
> Gabriela, my love and my friend,
> Come take hand, may the dance never end,
> Gabriela.[69]

A later verse further escalates this dynamic of angel worship and even hints at romantic involvement with the being. Beyond this, it also insinuates that it is *God who leads us to angels* and that angels are the givers of grace, rather than acknowledging angels as God's subordinates and stating that grace comes from God Himself. This is problematic theology in many ways:

> Gabriela, if we were born to some other time and place
> somehow my Lord would lead me to the love and grace
> of my Gabriela,
> Oh, I love you Gabriella.[70]

While this song never glorifies God, the lyrics suggest that the singer continues to profess his love (which strangely alludes to the tangling of worship with romantic love) for this mysterious, female angel who comes to him by night. This is only one example of this type of revered, elevated status of angels that so dangerously lingers in both our secular and ministerial world, and as interest in the subject is piqued, discernment seems to plummet. What does this heightened interest in angelic activity mean for us today? With increased deception regarding what and who angels are, and the convolution involved in discerning the nature of these entities, how do we assess professed angelic activity? Could the surplus of spiritual phenomena in the modern world indicate something even greater—that, perhaps, we are getting close to the end times?

The increased evil in the world around us, UFO sightings, claims of alien abductions, supernatural warfare, and New Age invasion of our churches all indicate that the battle between good and evil is approaching a climax. Many Christians find this idea overwhelming, but they forget the element of comfort for the believer in Scripture's indication that God's coming will be when the earth is "as it was in the days of Noah" (Matthew 24:37). This means that just as the earth was filled with irreversible evil before God poured out His wrath in the form of the Flood, *he likewise intervened and saved the righteous* by placing them in an ark to preserve their lives. Thus, for the redeemed, amplified immorality should—in addition to spurring individuals to action as urged in the Great Commission (Matthew 28:19)—also indicate that the time of the kingdom of God is drawing near, and Satan knows his time is short (Revelation 12:12).

What's That Sound in the Air?

For the last few years, over the entire world, there have been increasing reports of strange, unexplainable, trumpet-like sounds blaring across the air, many of which have been caught on camera or audio device (a simple YouTube search will reveal hours' worth of videos documenting the phenomenon). People from all countries and walks of life are reporting such occurrences, while others try to explain what the cause could be. Some theories suggest that the sounds are a result of technology such as nearby industrial facilities, airplanes, or other airborne technology. Others point to natural sources, such as wind channels or seismic shifts under the earth's surface. Yet others speculate more dramatic causes, such as alien activity, government conspiracy, and even pre-Rapture, angelic bustle.

Some witnesses to these sounds have reported one long, sustained note continuing for a period of time, while others say they've heard a melodic pattern. The unidentified noise has occurred in urban and remote locations at night and during the day. It seems that anyone, anywhere could hear this strange occurence at any time, and thousands have heard them at the same time, over a range spanning many miles. The reactions of those who have heard the noise varies: Some are excited, others are curious or wary, while still others are afraid, describing the sound as "creepy."

The enigma surrounding these manifestations is quickly shaping up to be one of the most confounding mysteries of our day. While some people believe this is new evidence of extraterrestrial activity, others earnestly surmise that it is something angelic in the air. Could this sweeping, widespread phenomenon be indicative of spiritual activity? Will this be explained away by some sort of industry or technology, or is there a more prophetic undertone to these manifestations? Are these events symptoms indicating that the time of Christ's arrival is nearing?

Increased Angelic Activity

Author Josh Peck describes the similarity to the state of the world before the Flood of Noah as having a hopeful significance to us today:

[In]…chapter 6 of the book of Genesis… We read the account of the sons of God mating with human women to produce their evil Nephilim offspring. After that, the Nephilim take control of the world and God sends the Flood. The chronology of this account is what is most important to us today. The angels physically manifested themselves to humanity *prior* to the worldwide Flood… Many, as well as I, believe the global Flood of Genesis can be looked at as an example, or shadow, of the coming rapture of the church. Just prior to God's judgment on the inhabitants of the earth, he made sure Noah and his family were safe in the ark…[thus, today's believers can rest assured that] before God's future judgment on the world, the Church will be removed. If the Flood can be viewed as a shadow of the Rapture, we should expect other details to coincide as well. It would stand to reason, since the world saw angelic manifestations prior to the Flood, we should expect to see them before the Rapture.[71]

Peck acknowledges that in this instance, the angelic manifestation was *malevolent* beings, but he reminds us that during times of God's impending wrath, He likewise sends *holy* angels to intervene on our behalf before destruction manifests.

These angels warned Lot about the coming destruction and instructed him to leave with his family. Once again, parallels can be drawn between God's judgment against Sodom and Gomorrah and the coming judgment against the world. As we can see, angels were sent to ensure the safety of Lot and his family… Benevolent angels manifested themselves physically just prior to God's judgment against Sodom and Gomorrah; thus, it stands to reason we will see the same thing prior to the Rapture of the Church.[72]

The authors of this book agree with Peck's conclusion: If we indeed are living in the end times, it stands to reason that there is increased angelic activity—both holy *and* malevolent—manifesting in the world around us at increasing rates. Our guard should be up as we anticipate these experiences. The Bible repeatedly reminds us not to be deceived. Thus, it is vital in a world where supernatural activity is increasing that we remain vigilant in our discernment regarding the physical *and* the spirit realms.

About Misconceptions

The fact that increased angelic activity indicates that the kingdom of God is at hand also means that time is short for making sure people aren't led astray. Scripture tells us that there will be many deceptions and that arguments for these false teachings will be compelling in the final days:

> For there shall arise false Christ's, and false prophets, and shall shew great signs and wonders; insomuch that, if it were possible, they shall deceive the very elect. (Matthew 24:24)

The understanding that deception will reach an all-time high at the most crucial forthcoming era in history means that misconceptions regarding anything theological—including (possibly *especially*) angels— will be increasingly numerous and dangerous as time progresses. I say this because of the rate at which New Age philosophy is invading the Church (a topic for another book), while those searching outside the Body of Christ for truth call to spirit guides, angel guides, angel boards, angel tarot cards, and other fraudulences on their quest for answers to spiritual questions.

These paths of trickery are more blatant, rampant, and hazardous than ever, while the remaining time to eradicate these treacheries grows shorter with each passing day.

A Case for the Book of Revelation

The book of Revelation is often skimmed over quickly, without lengthy study—even within the Church—because of its apocalyptic themes, varied and controversial (and even political) interpretations, and metaphorical abstractness. If you want to silence a room quickly, ask if anyone understands the book of Revelation! Reasons many people holding this particular book at arm's length range from fear of its implications and heedlessness born from a lack of understanding to the apathetic stance that the contents are so futuristic they have nothing to do with those of us who are living today. Many who attempt to teach the book of Revelation in *any* capacity often limit the study to the first three chapters, which deal with the seven churches of Asia: Ephesus, Smyrna, Pergamos, Thyatira, Sardis, Philadelphia, and Laodicea. After studying the letters written to these churches, most teachings on Revelation often skim the book's remaining storyline briefly, accelerating quickly to a theme that can be nutshelled in the words "God wins!" as the study concludes.

(Note: Within the first three chapters of Revelation, the word "angel" refers to the pastors of the seven churches who are acting as the church's *human messengers*. In this case, the term "angel" does not refer to a celestial being.)

However, consider the implications of people—even Christians—going about their lives without knowing what God says will happen tomorrow. I recently explained this concept in this way:

Imagine talking to your college-aged son about the importance of attending school and trying hard. You tell him that if he is caught skipping classes, he'll be given consequences. These penalties will start small, you explain, adding that they'll intensify the more often he skips. The penalties for repeating this practice in fact will escalate to the point that your son will need to move out of your home (remember, we're talking about your *college-aged* child), forcing him to be his own financial provider. On the other hand, you say there is a reward for him if he works hard, applies himself with his best effort, maintains good attendance, and studies intently. The incentive for doing well, you tell him, is that when he graduates from college, you'll pay off his student debt.

In this scenario, the consequences and rewards that you chart are very important details pertaining *to the future* that should affect how your son conducts himself *in the present*. Assuming that he listened to each detail you outlined, he will fully understand the penalty of disobedience, making him much less likely to defy your requests and motivating him to work toward the full benefits you offer as a reward for continued diligence.

With this information in mind, the moment your son's friend calls him suggesting that they "blow off math class" to attend a rock music concert or see a movie, the fullness of the outcome you've impressed upon him will now hopefully cross his mind and influence his decision. Beyond his understanding that you, as a parent, expect him to do his best in school and attend regularly, his additional knowledge of how his own actions *today* will impact *tomorrow's circumstances* will fortify his determination to do, today, what he *already knows is right*.

The same is true of our relationship with God. If we have a clear understanding of both His wrath and His love and the role each plays in our own lives and the future of the world, the criteria we use to make decisions *today* would be much different. This may seem obvious, but a brief study on the lifestyle of many self-proclaimed Christians quickly reveals that many folks, sadly, confess that they knowingly, daily live in a way that contradicts God's commands. This may not be the case if they had a greater understanding of how their actions today impact the penalties and rewards they'll face tomorrow. Perhaps this is why God warns us not to turn away from the knowledge we have available to us:

> Hear the word of the Lord, ye children of Israel: for the Lord hath a controversy with the inhabitants of the land, because there is no truth, nor mercy, nor knowledge of God in the land.… My people are destroyed for lack of knowledge: because thou hast rejected knowledge, I will also reject thee. (Hosea 4:1, 6)

The truth of this passage applies to many situations in life, and the matter of studying prophecy is no exception. Just as ignorance is dangerous in other, more obvious applications of lives, avoiding study of the book of Revelation stunts our spiritual growth. Furthermore, again, it's in our nature to use a "working-backward heuristic" as a type of theological "fill in the blanks." It is vital that when we try to reason our way through issues, we make it a point to study and pull truth from all of Scripture, not forsaking any of the information God has placed at our fingertips.

Furthermore, as we navigate our lives, each decision we make feeds into a path that leads to yet another. Even a slightly skewed direction from the starting point can make it easy to find ourselves far from our initial destination. This happens every day in simple ways, such as with maxed-out credit card debt, a schedule that is spread too thin, or a "to-do" list that never seems to get completed. These are only a few examples of how we can easily find ourselves off track.

Pointing a Laser

Many modern contractors use a tool called an automatic, self-leveling, laser-pointing tool that allows its user to plan a perfectly straight line over great distances. Manually, such a task would be challenging, if not at times impossible. This valuable device makes many jobs requiring straight linear planning—such as tile, cabinetry, or other construction or architectural work—much simpler and contributes to a beautiful end product. One of the popular models on the market today indicates its level of precision with the slogan: "Measure with a scalpel, not a hatchet."[73]

Similarly, the Word of the Lord will act as our laser if we allow it to: "Lead me, O Lord, in thy righteousness…make thy way straight before my face" (Psalm 5:8). Consider this: The projection of a laser pointer just six inches ahead can adjust the trajectory of our course to the left or the right by a mere degree, and the difference between the two positions, at this distance, may be invisible to the naked eye. However, if we were to extend that laser line ten feet, twenty feet, or even fifty miles, we'll quickly find ourselves standing in a completely *different location* than the one we had originally charted. The point is that carelessness about the direction in which we are heading can carry us to a completely different destination than the one we originally planned. For a Christian to devoutly study the rest of the Bible yet neglect the book of Revelation is similar to a contractor who meticulously sets his laser to a certain location, subsequently bumps it, knocking it out of its position, and then quickly "guesstimates" the resetting of the tool before continuing with his work.

Angels Are Most Active in Revelation

Beyond all of this, those who miss the storyline of Revelation miss out on a plethora of magnificent insight about angels, their mission, their role in prophetic history, and their relationship with God. Additionally, any information regarding angels that can be gleaned from Scripture further arms believers against the misconceptions that surround these mysterious beings.

Unless we roll up our sleeves, lean in, and commit to immerse ourselves in trying to understand the messages and lessons in the book of
Revelation, we can't fully understand the true nature of angels, since so
much of their activity plays out in this book. After all, Revelation mentions these beings more than any other book in the Bible, and—apart
from their role in the redemptive work of Christ—their contribution is
more present and defined in the book of Revelation than in perhaps any
other biblical narrative.

A Beautiful Love Story

Many who, for whatever reason, shy away from studying the book of
Revelation miss out on the fact that it is a beautiful love story of victory and peace. Like so many stories that are filled with conflict at the
midpoint of the plot, but culminate in a beautiful ending, Revelation's
account climaxes (and sadly, here often loses its readers) describing a
world filled with struggle, apocalyptic doom, murder, war, plague, execu-
tions, and injustice. The beauty—if we will only *see* it—is found in realizing that, throughout the story, God is *continually* calling for mankind's
repentance. Furthermore, He uses these disastrous events to cleanse the
world of the evil and sin that mankind allowed to invade with that first
act of disobedience in the Garden of Eden.

Regrettably, the end-time prophecy related in Revelation likewise
foretells that, regardless of the wrath poured out on the earth, large-scale
repentance will not be found, and mankind's response to the Maker will
be increased rebellion and blasphemy. This resembles the state of the
world as it is described in the days of Noah, when "the wickedness of
man was great in the earth, and…every imagination of the thoughts of
his heart was only evil continually" (Genesis 6:5). Although this forthcoming mutiny against God is unfortunate, it is believable, when considering Matthew 24:37, which says, "as the days of Noah were, so shall

also the coming of the Son of man be." The Revelation story's pinnacle, filled with gruesome events, outlines the purging of the evil upon the earth, and this doom is followed by a glorious account of restoration, acceptance, reinstatement, and love from the Almighty. Additionally, the heavenly peace restored to mankind is the result of an effort in which all of heaven participates. What manner of love the Father has given unto us, indeed, that we will be called the sons of God! (See 1 John 3:1.)

The last two chapters of Revelation are filled with a beautiful description of heaven, where only love, joy, peace, and harmony with the Almighty are known, and where we're continually in the presence of God, praising and worshiping Him. The Bible assures us that sadness, tears, death, and pain will all become things of the past (Revelation 21:4)—literally part of a world that no longer exists! The most beautiful and wonderful gift—the salvation plan initiated by Jesus Christ—culminates in a beautiful ending in which the Bride of Christ is finally united in that Great City with Him, and all is glorious. Revelation is the final chapter, in which the fruit of Jesus' sacrificial work of the salvation plan, completed on the cross, is brought into harvest. Those who are unable to appreciate Revelation are missing out on an important part of the love story God has written to all of mankind.

On that note, we'll delve into Revelation's storyline as it pertains to the role angels play. While it isn't possible to entirely isolate the events carried out by these beings without including some aspects of the overall scenario, prophetic events not directly related to functions of the Celestial Order won't be covered extensively in this book. The angels' role within these end-time events, however, are fascinating, and will help us to gain more understanding about the nature of these amazing, holy, celestial creatures. These servants of the Most High have been on standby since the beginning of time, ready to carry out orders given to them by God, and they now await His orders that will usher in end-time events and the judgment of the world, preparing the way for that final Kingdom that brings into recognition the full glory and victory of the Almighty.

A Comforting Thought

The heavy theme of death carried throughout the book of Revelation, as has been stated, can be disconcerting. This is understandable, but another perspective on the role of angels can be considered in a story such as this. An account in Luke tells us that when a beggar named Lazarus died, he "was carried by the angels into Abraham's bosom" (Luke 16:22). Some believe this Scripture indicates that, upon the death, those who remain in Christ are carried into the presence of God by angels. This concept is corroborated by myriad people who have near-death experiences and claim to have seen such beings waiting for them. Some consider 1 Corinthians 15:25–26 to further confirm this possibility:

> For he must reign, till he has put all enemies under his feet. The last enemy that shall be destroyed is death.

Many assert that we live during the time when God's enemies still roam the earth. Hence, the death of a saint marks the last time that they would face a spiritual enemy. God dispatches angels to carry the saints to their final destination. If this is so, then the martyrdom of Christ's followers noted in the book of Revelation is soothed as the soul is carried into the presence of God by angels.

Angels' Role in Prophetic Events

The book of Revelation begins as a series of messages from the Lord to the early Church to help direct and guide new believers into their role here on earth as the Body of Christ. Before we read the details of end-time events and how the world will be judged by God for its sin, we see letters to seven churches to be used as guidelines for what was expected of them and how they were to conduct themselves, including a look at the areas of needed improvement. The message from Jesus Himself was delivered to John, and was sent and signified by an angel (Revelation 1:1). Through John, the Lord gave His instruction to the Church, readying them for worldwide events that that the Church was to be a part of and endure, and in which they held a destiny.

For the early Church coming together after the death of Christ, this was confirmation that their convictions weren't just a momentary trend following the death of a radical. Instead, they represented a true and eternal calling, based on the following of the Living God whose blood had purchased their salvation. In fact, it was so important to God for the early Church to understand their significance that He explained to them that the saints would judge the world—and even angels:

> Do ye not know that the saints shall judge the world? and if the world shall be judged by you, are ye unworthy to judge the smallest matters? Know ye not that we shall judge angels? how much more things that pertain to this life? (1 Corinthians 6:2–3)

God's Throne Room: Where Angels Dwell

After writing letters to the seven churches in Asia, John is taken into the spirit realm where he is shown the throne room in heaven. The throne itself is described as being at the center of a ring, and its materials are compared to emerald, jasper, and sardine. Around this are twenty-four seated elders clothed in white, wearing golden crowns on their heads. From the throne comes lightning, thunder, and a voice that intermittently speaks and praises the Lord. The seven spirits of God are present in the form of seven lamps of fire. Nearby is a sea of glass that appears as crystal, and four beasts covered in eyes are found here: one looks like a lion, another like a calf, a third looks like a man, and a fourth resembles an eagle. Each of these beasts has six wings, the underside of which are likewise covered in eyes. These beasts worship continually, night and day:

> Holy, holy, holy, Lord God Almighty, which was, and is, and is to come. Thou art worthy, O Lord, to receive glory and honor and power: for thou hast created all things, and for thy pleasure they are and were created. (Revelation 4:8, 11)

They are joined by the elders in praising the Lord. (See Revelation 4:1–11.)

Revelation chapter 4 illustrates that multiple types of celestial beings dwell in the throne room, continually instigating and perpetuating the praise of the Lord God Almighty. In Revelation chapter 5, however, we see a slight shift in heaven' ambience. The end is nearing, and something referred to as the Book will be opened by the Lamb; thus, the seals will be loosed.

But who will initiate this call for action? An angel.

> And I saw in the right hand of him that sat on the throne a book written within and on the backside, sealed with seven seals. And I saw a strong angel proclaiming with a loud voice, Who is worthy to open the book, and to lose the seals thereof? (Revelation 5:1–2)

After being moved to tears over the fact that there is not one—in heaven, on earth, or under the earth—worthy to open the Book, John is told that the "Lion of the tribe of Judah, the Root of David" (Revelation 5:5), the Lamb who was slain, is able to open the Book and loose the seals.

Let think about this: The time for opening the Book and breaking the seals has come, but seemingly no individual worthy of performing such an act is available. At the loud invitation voiced by an angel, the Lamb who was slain appears, and end-time prophetic events are launched. This announcement is met by more praise from the beasts and the elders, who utilize harps and golden vials containing the fragrance of the prayers of saints. These are now accompanied by angels, who number "ten thousand times ten thousand, and thousands of thousands" (Revelation 5:11). The praises of the Celestial Order are escalating as the atmosphere in heaven intensifies, as if the entire spirit realm is beginning to surge with the dynamism of what's coming.

The Lamb and the First Four Seals

When the Lamb Himself opens the seals on the Book (chapter 6), we read:

- The first seal: The white horse is released. Its rider carries a bow and wears a crown, and is given the power to conquer.
- The second seal: The red horse is released. Its rider carries a sword and is given the power to take peace from the earth and create war.
- The third seal: The black horse is released. Its rider carries a pair of balances and is given the power to create famine.
- The fourth seal: The pale horse is released. Its rider is named Death, and is followed by Hell. To him was given the power to kill one-fourth of the population of the earth with the sword, hunger, death, and the beasts of the earth.

Who Are the Four Horsemen?

Some believe the four horsemen associated with the first four seals are the angels mentioned in Revelation chapter 7 stationed at the four corners of the earth (more on this in a bit). These often assert that the four beings are archangels or cherubim who hold their position continually, night and day, until the time when they're ordered to relinquish this post, thus allowing destruction to come upon the earth. This is a reasonable argument, since we've already established that God has agents who work destruction at His command to punish mankind for evildoing. Under this theory, these beings are sometimes referred to as the angels of earth, water, air, and fire. Others believe they are "destroying angels," similar to the one sent to judge the Egyptians in Exodus 12.

On the other hand, some maintain the position that the four horsemen are malevolent, based on the notion that the rider of the fourth horse is named "Death" and he is accompanied "by Hell, who follows behind him" (Revelation 6:8). Since Jesus announced in Revelation 1:18 that He held the key to both hell and death, this is plausible. By His own statement, Jesus indicated that a kingdom divided against itself cannot stand (Mark 3:23–24). Announcing possession of the keys to death and hell indicates victory over an enemy during battle, so naming these two entities specifically—with capitalization—strengthens the argument that, unlike other instances in the Bible where God dispatched one of His holy angels to administer judgment, this could be similar to the events of Revelation chapter 9, where Satan's agents of evil are unleashed upon mankind.

Seals Five, Six, and Seven

- The fifth seal: The souls of those who were martyred for the word of God and for their testimony are revealed beneath the altar. These martyrs cry out to God to avenge them. They are given white robes, and told to be patient a little longer.
- The sixth seal: A great earthquake occurs that blackens the sun and makes the moon look like blood, causing stars to fall from the heavens and crash to the earth below. Every mountain and island shifts from its place, and the sky seems to swing like a

"scroll when it is rolled together" (Revelation 6:14). The hand of the Lord is so evident in this event that those who survive—people of every position, race, social status, and economic standing—attempt to hide from His wrath, begging the earth to fall on them.

Angels Seal the Servants of God and Gather the Elect

And after these things I saw four angels standing on the four corners of the earth, holding the four winds of the earth, that the wind should not blow on the earth, nor on the sea, nor on any tree. And I saw another angel ascending from the east, having the seal of the living God: and he cried with a loud voice to the four angels, to whom it was given to hurt the earth and the sea, Saying, Hurt not the earth, neither the sea, nor the trees, until we have sealed the servants of our God in their foreheads. And I heard the number of them which were sealed: and there were sealed an hundred and forty and four thousand of all the tribes of the children of Israel. (Revelation 7:1–4)

God has promised that when we see certain signs (those related in Revelation), Jesus will return, bringing angels with Him.

Immediately after the tribulation of those days shall the sun be darkened, and the moon shall not give her light, and the stars shall fall from heaven, and the powers of the heavens shall be shaken: And then shall appear the sign of the Son of man in heaven: and then shall all the tribes of the earth mourn, and they shall see the Son of man coming in the clouds of heaven with power and great glory. And he shall send his angels with a great sound of a trumpet, and they shall gather together his elect from the four winds, from one end of heaven to the other. (Matthew 24:29–31)

For some people, the word "elect" spurs the debate that God has preselected certain people for salvation. This, however, is not the case at all. In this passage, the word "elect" is taken from the Greek root *eklektos*, which translates to "picked out, chosen by God, or to obtain salvation through Christ,"[74] indicating that we become "elect" when we accept Christ as Savior. Another passage sheds further light on this matter, explaining that the elect will be caught up from across the earth, suggesting a broadened parameter of nationality, culture, and tongues:

And then shall they see the Son of man coming in the clouds with great power and glory. And then shall he send his angels, and shall gather together his elect from the four winds, from the uttermost part of the earth to the uttermost part of heaven. (Mark 13:26–27)

In addition to the promise made in this passage, Matthew chapter 13 tells us that the angels will also separate the good from evil, casting the evil into a furnace of fire:

So shall it be at the end of the world: the angels shall come forth, and sever the wicked from among the just, And shall cast them into the furnace of fire: there shall be wailing and gnashing of teeth. (Matthew 13:49–50)

To put it plainly, Jesus will bring His angels with Him, and they are going to clean house.

Beyond this, Jesus is taking His own back to heaven with Him:

For the Lord himself shall descend from heaven with a shout, with the voice of the archangel, and with the trump of God: and the dead in Christ shall rise first: Then we which are alive and remain shall be caught up together with him in the clouds, to meet the Lord in the air: and so shall we ever be with the Lord. (1 Thessalonians 4:16–17)

Many debate the exact moment when the elect will be "gathered," as it is spoken in Matthew 24:31. Some believe it is at the moment they're sealed (Revelation 7:4), because in the following passages (Revelation 7:9), John refers to a multitude that appears in the presence of God. Immediately after John witnesses the sealing of God's servants, the throne room is filled with countless numbers of people from all nations, families, and languages who are clothed in white robes and carrying palms, praising the Lord with the elders and the four beasts in the throne room, saying, "Salvation to our God, which sits the upon the throne, and unto the Lamb." The angels, likewise, praise the Almighty, and when John asks about the multitude before him, he is told that they are the people who came out of the Great Tribulation. Now, they will remain in the throne room with God, and they will never again hunger, thirst, or feel pain, because the Lamb will provide all that they need and will personally wipe the tears from their eyes (Revelation 7:9–17).

Some scholars, on the other hand, believe that the elect will remain on earth for a time, because subsequent passages point out that they aren't subjected to all the judgments poured out due to God's wrath, and there are also passages that clarify that the elect "will not be deceived." Others believe that time can't be estimated in heaven in the way our mortal measurements would calculate, thus events that seem to be instantaneous in heaven may actually take place over a longer duration for those of us observing from the earth. Passages such as Psalm 90:4, "For a thousand years in thy sight are but as yesterday when it is passed, and as a watch in the night," and 2 Peter 3:8, "But, beloved, be not ignorant of this one thing, that one day is with the Lord as a thousand years, and a thousand years as one day," offer credibility to this position.

Although the exact timing is the subject of much debate (and certainly are a core issue for an altogether *different* book), this passage assures us that at this moment in heaven, God will pause the destruction taking place on earth in order to send a fifth angel, who carries the message to the four angels stationed at the four corners of the earth. After the disasters that have already been poured out onto the earth, God doesn't want further destruction to occur until the beings have carried out the mission of marking His own with His seal upon their foreheads. This task is completed, and its confirmation is later found in Revelation 22:3-4:

> And there shall be no more curse: but the throne of God and of the Lamb shall be in it; and his servants shall serve him: And they shall see his face; and his name shall be in their foreheads.

When the seventh seal is opened, there is silence in heaven for about a half an hour.

The Angels Appear with Trumpets

Following the loosing of the seventh seal, a hush falls over heaven, after which seven angels, each holding trumpets, appear before God. An eighth angel appears and is given a censer (a metal instrument that holds burning embers in a spherical compartment at the end of a chain) and incense, which he is told to offer with the prayers of the saints upon the golden altar that sits before the throne. Explained in detail in Revelation 8:7–21, here what happens next:

> As the smoke of the incense, which came with the prayers of the saints, ascended up before God out of the angel's hand. And the angel took the censer, and filled it with fire of the altar, and cast it into the earth: and there were voices, and thunderings, and lightnings, and an earthquake. As the seven angels which had the seven trumpets prepared themselves to sound. (Revelation 8:4–6)

What a somber moment. Imagine what the earth will look like when this ball of fire is hurled toward it, causing earthquakes, thunder, and lightning! Thousands of years after the destruction of cities like Sodom and Gomorrah, we're still speculating on how horrific the scene of their annihilation must have been, and even with modern technologies and the assistance of recreation and research, we're only beginning to understand what such "fire and brimstone" must have looked like. Yet, this passage assures us that the earth will see this type of devastation again throughout the coming days of prophetic judgment. When that destruction heads our way, it will be launched by the powerful, prevailing hand of an angel.

The Angels Blow Their Trumpets

When the angels blow their trumpets at God's command, a continuing onslaught of God's wrath will pelt the earth in stages. These are God's warnings and the outpouring of His wrath in an attempt to show His supreme indignation, power, and authority to a prideful and fallen mankind, who continually refuses to repent:

> Neither repented they of their murders, nor of their sorceries, nor of their fornication, nor of their thefts. (Revelation 9:21)

When the first angel sounds his trumpet, hail and fire mingled with blood will be thrown toward the earth, burning one-third of the vegetation.

When the second angel sounds his trumpet, it will be as though a "great mountain burning with fire was cast into the sea" (Revelation 8:8). A third of the sea will become blood, killing a third of the creatures in the sea and destroying a third of the ships in the sea.

At the sound of the third angel's trumpet, a great star called Wormwood, burning "as though it is a lamp" will fall from heaven, landing upon one-third of the rivers and waterways, making the water bitter, thus causing it to kill many people.

The fourth angel's trumpet sound will cause one-third of the sun to be "smitten," while a third of the moon and stars will be darkened, rendering a third of both the day and night completely dark.

As foreboding as these judgments will be, God, at this point, will send an angel throughout heaven, who makes an ominous announcement:

> Woe, woe, woe, to the inhabiters of the earth by reason of the other voices of the trumpet of the three angels, which are yet to sound! (Revelation 8:13)

An Angel Opens the Bottomless Pit

> And the fifth angel sounded, and I saw a star fall from heaven unto the earth: and to him was given the key of the bottomless pit. And he opened the bottomless pit; and there arose a smoke out of the pit, as the smoke of a great furnace; and the sun and the air were darkened by reason of the smoke of the pit. (Revelation 9:1–2)

The fifth angel will sound his trumpet and a personified star will fall from heaven to earth, to whom will be given the key to the bottomless pit. Important to note about this reference to the word "star" is that, similar to the one that appeared on the night of Jesus' birth, the original Greek word used in this passage was *astēr*, which many scholars say denotes personage—likely angelic—assigned to this "star." As the bottomless pit opens, smoke will begin to rise, releasing the evil upon mankind from within. The quantity of smoke is compared to that which would emerge from a great furnace, and it will darken the sun and the air on earth. Some scholars believe this is one of the "pillars of smoke" described in Joel 2:30. Out of this smoke will materialize a new enemy for mankind: locusts, which are given the power to torment—but not kill—anyone who doesn't have the seal of God on their foreheads (the seal previously set in place by an angel). These tormentors will resemble horses bearing ironclad armor, and their heads will look like they're wearing crowns made of gold. The sound of their wings in flight will be like chariot horses rushing toward battle. They will have masculine faces, feminine-looking hair, and teeth like a lion. Their stingers—similar to those of a scorpion—will administer a wound so brutal that the locusts' victims will suffer for five months in a way so agonizing that they will wish they were dead, but Scripture tells us that they will not be so fortunate. These creatures, which *emerge out of the bottomless pit,* are subsidiaries of their king, who is named Abaddon (Hebrew) and Apollyon (Greek). The locusts are literally otherworldly creatures, servants of darkness, members of an evil kingdom. Many scholars believe them to be demons. They will be allowed upon the earth only for this time to torment people in ways that earthly creatures are unable to.

An Angel Releases the Angels Bound in Euphrates

Next, the sixth angel will sound his trumpet, and from the four horns on the golden altar that sits before the throne, a voice will speak, commanding the angel of the sixth trumpet to release the four angels who are bound in the great river Euphrates—angels that have been prepared for this very moment. When this is done, an army of two hundred thousand horsemen will be unleashed, each bearing breastplates of fire and brimstone. Their horses will have heads similar to those of lions, and they will spew fire and brimstone out of their mouths. The tails of these horses will be like serpents with heads, which have the power to do harm, presumably with a venomous bite. These forces will kill a third of the population on earth.

Scripture indicates that throughout this outpouring of God's wrath, there is, sadly, still no repentance on the earth for the sin and rebellion of mankind. Instead, humanity will continue to worship false gods and live in sorcery, fornication, and murderous idolatry.

An Angel Announces That Time Has Run Out

In Revelation chapter 10, John reports seeing perhaps the most ominous holy angelic being yet reported throughout these prophetic events (we discussed the fearsome indications of this angel's description earlier, so we'll not linger here):

> Another mighty angel come down from heaven, clothed with a cloud: and a rainbow was upon his head, and his face was as it were the sun, and his feet as pillars of fire: And he had in his hand a little book open: and he set his right foot upon the sea, and his left foot on the earth, And cried with a loud voice, as when a lion roareth: and when he had cried, seven thunders uttered their voices. (Revelation 10:1–4)

The angel immediately instructed John not to write what he heard those voices say. The world will one day know, but for now, this remains one of the mysteries for which we must await the answer. Instead, John explained that the angel will stand over the sea and the earth and lift his hand toward heaven, swearing by the Almighty Creator who lives forever and ever that there is no more time. Imagine what kind of society will be living on earth when, after the onslaught of judgment poured out by God via His angels, there will *still* be no repentance for sin. The day is coming when the most frightening angel described in the Bible will stand, with one foot on sea and the other on land, and shout with the voice of a roaring lion that *there is no more time.*

Between the sixth and seventh's angels' trumpet blasts, two witnesses will prophesy for 1,260 days. They will have supernatural powers and will testify on behalf of God. After their allotted time, the beast that arises out of the bottomless pit will kill them, and their dead bodies will lie in the street for three and a half days while onlookers celebrate their death by exchanging presents. After that, however, the Spirit of life from God will enter them, and they will resurrect and ascend into heaven for all to see. When this happens, a great earthquake will cause one-tenth of the city to fall and seven thousand people to be killed.

Next, the seventh angel will sound his trumpet. This will be met with worship and praise in the throne room, and the heavens will proclaim that the kingdoms of this world are the Lord's. The temple of God will open in heaven, releasing "lightnings, and voices, and thunderings, and an earthquake, and great hail" (Revelation 11:19).

An Angel Preaching in the Heavens

In Revelation 14:6, we're told that after the beast has arisen and deceived the world, an angel will be released, sent with the everlasting gospel to preach to all those on the earth a message of warning in light of the judgment to come. The angel will say in a booming voice:

> Fear God, and give glory to him; for the hour of his judgment
> is come: and worship him that made heaven, and earth, and the
> sea, and the fountains of waters. (Revelation 14:7)

This angel's mission is significant: It shows that despite man's fallen state, his ongoing rebellion and blasphemy toward God, and the condition of the crumbled earth below, God is *still* issuing warnings to persuade people to turn from their wicked ways. After everything that will have happened to this point, God is still a God of love, reaching out to humanity—if only the stubborn people would reciprocate.

In this Scripture, the phrase "the midst of heaven" is taken from the Greek word *mesouranēma*, meaning either "mid heaven" or, more literally, "the highest point in the heavens, which the sun occupies at noon, where what is done can be seen and heard by all."[75] This indicates that this angel will be positioned at the highest place in the sky, where he can be seen and heard by everybody on earth, preaching the "gospel," a word meaning "good news." Despite the ensuing destruction, there is still good news for any person who will turn from his or her rebellious ways. People of all nations, kindreds, and tongues are invited, if they will only follow the order that this angel gives: Fear God, give Him glory, and worship Him.

This angel is followed by another who will announce that Babylon is fallen. A third angel will follow the first two with this warning from God:

If any man worship the beast and his image, and receive his mark in his forehead, or in his hand, The same shall drink of the wine of the wrath of God, which is poured out without mixture into the cup of his indignation; and he shall be tormented with fire and brimstone in the presence of the holy angels, and in the presence of the Lamb: And the smoke of their torment ascended up forever and ever: and they have no rest day nor night, who worship the beast and his image, and whosoever receive if the mark of his name. (Revelation 14:9–11)

This is a very clear message. Three angels, mighty in power, fearsome to observe in the high places over the earth, will be commanding the attention of the everyone on the planet, announcing these three messages in succession. In modern terms, the messages might sound something like this:

Angel number 1: "Everyone on earth, listen to me! You have experienced the wrath of the Almighty God, but it is not too late! There is hope for all of you, if you will only turn from your wicked ways, repent, and worship the one true God! Any and all are invited to escape this wrath, if you will only end your rebelliousness toward Him and serve the Almighty God!"

Angel number 2: "The great city has fallen! Your earthly wealth is crumbling! Life as you know it is coming to an end! Hear my words, people of earth! The great city is fallen, because all the nations of the world have been brought to demise by the city's influence of fornication and immorality!"

Angel number 3: "People of earth, listen to me! *Do not* worship the beast or his image! *Do not* allow him to put his mark in your forehead or your hand! If you do, not only will you continue to suffer the wrath of God as you have been, but you will receive an undiluted version of this wrath, and—*even worse*—it will be mixed with His indignation! You will be tormented, in front of God Himself and all His holy angels, with fire and brimstone forever and ever without so much as a moment of relief! *Do not* worship the beast or his image! *Do not* take his mark!"

These angels, sent by God, stand at the highest point of the earth where all can hear, preaching these messages to—once again—attempt to persuade fallen mankind to change his ways. What a formidable sight to behold!

Angels Pour Out Vials of Wrath

Then, "one like unto the Son of man" will appear upon a cloud, wearing a golden crown and holding a sharp sickle, and another angel will emerge from the temple, announcing that the harvest of the earth is ripe and that it is time for him to thrust in his sickle. The first does this, and the harvest of the earth is reaped.

Immediately, another angel will emerge from the temple in heaven, also carrying a sickle. An additional angel will come out of the altar and instruct the first, who carries the sickle, to use the implement to gather the clusters of the vine of the earth, which will be placed by the angel into the winepress of God's wrath. When constrained, it yields blood, making way for the angels to administer the seven last plagues made up of God's wrath.

These plagues are sealed into vials (some translations of the Bible call them bowls), and will be given to the angels by one of the four beasts in the throne room.

A great voice will resonate from the temple, sending the seven angels to pour the vials of wrath out upon the earth. One will notice that, like before, mankind's response is not repentance, but increased blasphemy of the Lord God Almighty. Below is a synopsis of the impact of each of these vials:

When the first vial is poured out upon the earth, a "noisome and grievous sore" will come upon all of those who have the mark of the beast and those who worshipped him.

The second vial will be poured out upon the sea, which will turn to blood, and all life therein will be killed.

The third vial will be poured out upon the rivers and waterways, and all of these will turn to blood. This angel begins to praise the Lord, because this is justification for the blood of the saints that will have been spilled:

> Thou art righteous, O Lord, which art, and wast, and shalt be, because thou hast judged thus. For they have shed the blood of saints and prophets, and thou hast given them blood to drink; for they are worthy. (Revelation 16:5–6)

The outpouring of the fourth vial will impact the sun: Power will be given to this angel to scorch mankind with fire and excessive heat, but man will respond only by blaspheming the name of God.

The fifth vial will be poured out on the seat of the beast, causing his kingdom to be filled with darkness and all inside to be brought under extreme pain accompanied by sores. The response of those in the kingdom of the beast will be to blaspheme God.

When the sixth vial is poured out upon the great river Euphrates, it will become completely dry, creating a pathway that the kings of the east will travel. At this, three unclean spirits will emerge: one from the mouth of the dragon, one from the mouth of the beast, and one from the mouth of the false prophet. These are the spirits of devils who are able to work miracles, and they will join the kings of the earth to help fight them in their battle against the Lord God Almighty at Armageddon.

Vial number seven will be poured out upon the air and a great voice will resound from the temple of heaven, announcing, "It is done" (Revelation 16:17). At this, boundless noises, thunder and lightning, and an earthquake worse than anything the world has ever seen will be unleashed upon the earth. The great city will be divided, the nations will fall, the islands will disappear, and the mountains will be leveled. Hailstones—estimated by modern theologians to weigh between ninety and one hundred pounds apiece—will rain from heaven, and in response, men will, again, continue to blaspheme God. When the whore of Babylon falls, those who are part of her kingdom will make war with God, but Scripture assures us that "the Lamb shall overcome them: for he is Lord of lords, and King of kings" (Revelation 17:14).

An Angel Announces Babylon's Destruction

The destruction of Babylon will be announced by an extremely powerful angel—one so authoritative that the entire world is lit up by his presence. God will call His people out from within the great city so they will be spared when God pours out His wrath on her kingdom. The plagues she will endure—death, mourning, famine—will occur in one day, before her kingdom is subsequently burned to the ground by fire.

This event will be significant on a global level, as Revelation 18:9–19 outlines the fall of an economy—a fall that impacts even the wealthiest people in the world. The description includes merchandise that covers seemingly every category of trade and merchants of every method of commerce and shipment. In contrast to this, however, heaven will rejoice over her destruction, because the saints and martyrs of Jesus will have been avenged.

An angel will pick up a stone like a great millstone and throw it into the sea, declaring that the great city of Babylon, which deceived all the nations with her sorceries, has been destroyed with violence, never to rise again. This will cause a new round of praises to be sung to the Almighty in heaven. (See Revelation 18:21–22.)

Victory!

And I saw heaven opened, and behold a white horse; and he that sat upon him was called Faithful and True, and in righteousness he doth judge and make war. His eyes were as a flame of fire, and on his head were many crowns; and he had a name written, that no man new, but he himself. And he was clothed with a vesture dipped in blood: and his name is called The Word of God. (Revelation 19:11–13)

Out of the mouth of the Word of God comes a sword that will smite nations and He will rule them with a rod of iron, treading on the winepress of the wrath of God. His name is revealed as: "KING OF KINGS, AND LORD OF LORDS."

At his appearance, an angel will call the fowls of the air to feast on the flesh of those who will have stood against the Lord God. The beast and the false prophet who will have deceived the nation will be taken captive and cast into a lake of fire burning with brimstone, and their remaining followers will be slain with the sword that proceeds from the mouth of the Word of God.

An Angel Banishes Satan to the Bottomless Pit

An angel will then appear from heaven, holding a powerful chain and the key to the bottomless pit, and with that he will capture the dragon (Revelation 20:2 calls this dragon the devil, and names him Satan). The dragon will remain there for a thousand years, while those martyrs beheaded for the witness of Jesus (who won't have taken the mark of the beast) will live and reign with Him. After this period, Satan will be released for a brief time, during which he will attempt one more challenge against God. But Revelation 21:10 assures us that the devil will be "cast into the lake of fire and brimstone, where the beast and the false prophet are, and shall be tormented day and night forever and ever."

Right after this, the Lamb's Book of Life will be examined, and the dead will be judged. The angels will bear witness as Jesus claims us as His own:

> Whosoever shall confess me before men, him shall the Son of man also confess before the angels of God: But he that denieth me before men shall be denied before the angels of God. (Luke 12:8–9)

God will then recreate heaven and earth, describing a beautiful place, one where:

> God shall wipe away all tears from their eyes; and there shall be no more death, neither sorrow, nor crying, neither shall there be any more pain: for the former things are passed away.... Behold, I make all things new. (Revelation 21:4–5)

The story continues when God gives one of the most beautiful promises He has ever given to man:

> It is done. I am Alpha and Omega, the beginning and the end. I will give unto him that is athirst of the fountain of the water of life freely. He that overcometh shall inherit all things; and I will be his God, and he shall be my son. (Revelation 21:6–7)

The Almighty will reign in this new city, made with jasper walls, and the foundation of which is decorated with every kind of precious stone. The gates are made of pearls, and the street of the city is pure gold—gold so pure, in fact, that it looks like glass. There is no temple in this city, because the Lord God Almighty and the Lamb *are* the temple. There is no need for a sun or a moon, because the glory of God is the source of light continually, and there is no night. All whose names are written in the Lamb's Book of Life will dwell here and share in the glory and honor of the Lord. A crystal-clear river, flowing with the water of life, proceeds out of God's throne. This river runs beside the tree of life, which bears healing fruit continually. Sin, sadness, and curse will be forever removed.

This beautiful city is open for any and all who will remain true and faithful to God until the end:

> And the Spirit and the bride say, Come. And let him that heareth say, Come. And let him that is athirst come. And whosoever will, let him take the water of life freely. (Revelation 22:17)

The Lord wants to share this city with us, and this story shows us the lengths to which He is willing to go to bring us into this peaceful, beautiful, eternal setting with Him. He has truly opened up salvation to "whosoever will," and His Celestial Order awaits His command, ready and willing to diligently serve Him through every event that carries us to this peace with our Savior.

It is true that prophecy outlines some events that incite fear (understandably so), but our kind and loving Creator has promised:

I will never leave thee, nor forsake thee. So that we may boldly say, The Lord is my helper, and I will not fear what man shall do unto me. (Hebrews 13:5–6)

In this tranquil scene at the end of time, in that Great City, basking in the glory of our Maker, we can see that this passage is accurate. After all that will have happened from the events falling between Genesis 1:1 and Revelation 22:21, consider everything that has transpired between mankind and our Creator, and remember all that *we* have needed forgiveness for. Yet, the final passages in the Bible still place us as children of the King, adopted into His kingdom and ruling with Him in peace and love.

The grace of our Lord Jesus Christ be with you all. Amen. (Revelation 22:21)

Appendix

Key Terms

Following is a brief glossary of terminology associated with angels in Scripture. While the secular and New Age vocabulary (and definitions thereof) regarding angels and spiritual beings will be much broader than what is offered here, we will adhere to terminology associated with biblical study and definitions offered from a scriptural point of view.

Angel – From Hebrew, *mal'ak*,[76] this is a masculine noun meaning "messenger" or "ambassador." In the heavenly realm, these celestial beings were created by God for His own service, but when Lucifer fell from heaven, many angels followed him, joining evil forces. The term "angel," in reference to human beings, describes one who acts as a messenger.

Archangels – From the Greek *archaggelos*,[77] this is a masculine noun meaning "chief angel." While the Bible only specifically names Michael as an archangel (Jude 9), many scholars believe that extrabiblical or apocryphal texts such as the Book of Enoch and the Book of Tobit name seven archangels of God: Gabriel, Michael, Raguel, Raphael, Remiel, Saraqael, and Uriel. Many of these scholars assign one angel to each day of the week. The term "archangel" identifies the entitled being as holding extremely high or even top-rank status—in strength and power, authority, and import of message—within the celestial order. The archangel's high status of strength is established in Daniel 10:13, when Michael's power is defined as being great reinforcement to other members of the Celestial Order:

> But the prince of the kingdom of Persia withstood me one and 20 days: but, lo, Michael, one of the chief princes, came to help me; and I remained there with the kings of Persia.

While some argue that Michael is the only archangel, it is likely that this is untrue. Despite him being the only archangel whose name is revealed in the Bible, the aforementioned passage calls him "one of the chief princes," indicating that there are others like him. Although many refer to the angel Gabriel as an archangel, the Bible doesn't actually name him as such, despite the importance of the announcements entrusted to him, such as the birth of Jesus (Luke 1:26–38).

Cherubim – From Hebrew *kĕruwb*,[78] this is a masculine noun referring to the spiritual creature described as having four faces, each of which gazes toward a different direction. One face is that of a man, one is that of a lion, one is that of an eagle, and one is like an ox. They have four wings, which are covered with eyes, and these beings have hands similar to that of a man's beneath their wings. These powerful creatures guard the entrance to the Garden of Eden with "a flaming sword that...[turns] every way" (Genesis 3:24), indicating that these powerful creatures can guard in all four directions without rotating. These beings are described in Ezekiel chapters 1 and 10 in greater detail, while 2 Kings 19:15 states that cherubim dwell in the presence of God:

> O Lord God of Israel, which dwellest between the cherubims, thou art the God, even thou alone, of all the kingdoms of the earth.

Many scholars believe that the cherubim are the guardians of the throne room of God. While Scripture is sometimes vague regarding the full nature of these beings, their image appears with significance upon the structures that God commissioned during the Old Testament. By God's order, these holy creatures were symbolized on the mercy seat of the Ark of the Covenant (Exodus 25), on the ten curtains of the tabernacle (Exodus 26:1), upon the walls of the Temple (1 Kings 6:29), in carvings on the doors of the Temple (1 Kings 6:32), and within the inner sanctuary of the Temple, which were overlaid with gold (1 Kings 6:23–28). Some scholars say that Ezekiel 28 describes Lucifer as a cherub.

Christophany – This term is used to describe instances in which a theophany is believed to be an appearance made by Christ Himself. This refers specifically to events occurring before His birth or after His ascension into heaven. Many believe that instances found in the Old Testament wherein an "Angel of the Lord" visited the earth were preincarnate visits by Christ. Examples of these are found in Judges 6:1–23 and Exodus 3:2–6. The theory that theophanies are appearances made specifically by Christ (rendering Christophanies) is reinforced by Colossians 2:5–9, wherein Christ alone is referred to as the bodily manifestation of God upon the earth. Further supporting this concept is John 1:18:

No man hath seen God at any time; the only begotten Son, which is in the bosom of the Father, he hath declared *him*.

Dominions – From Greek *kyriotēs,*[79] a feminine noun meaning "mastery," "concrete and collective rulers," and "holder of dominion and government." This term appears on a list of authorities said in Scripture (Colossians 1:16) to have been created both by God and for God. The term within this context is believed by many scholars to indicate that members of the Celestial Order are assigned to specific regions or territories. Further reinforcing this concept is Ephesians 1:20–21, which states that Christ is the final authority over "all principality, and power, and might, and dominion, and every name that is named, not only in this world, but also in that which is to come." Supplemental arguments for this theory appear in Job 1:7 and Job 2:2, where the Lord asks Satan, "From whence comest thou?" On both occasions, Satan answers: "From going to and fro in the earth, and from walking up and down in it." Having been cast out of heaven at this point, Satan's confession to roaming the earth indicates the pent-up, destructive energy he attempts to expel as he roams about the earth.

Fallen angels – This term refers to angels who joined Lucifer's evil forces. These unholy angels cannot be redeemed (2 Peter 2:4), and were cast out of heaven and alongside Satan (the dragon, the devil, Lucifer). These beings are likewise said in Scripture to be, like Satan, condemned forever:

Depart from me, ye cursed, into everlasting fire, prepared for the devil and his angels. (Matthew 25:41)

Guardian Angels – These are angelic beings whom many believe are assigned to protect and guard specific human beings for either a portion of or the duration of the individual's life on earth. While the concept of personal guardian angels isn't confirmed in Scripture, many believe that passages such as Psalm 91:11 lend credibility to the concept: "For he shall give his angels charge over thee, to keep thee in all thy ways." Many scholars—even those who are unwilling to concede that humans are assigned a guardian angel for their lifetime—believe that *children* are given personal guardian angels, based on Matthew 18:10:

Take heed that ye despise not one of these little ones me: for I say unto you, That in heaven their angels do always behold the face of my Father which is in heaven.

Heaven – From the Greek *ouranos*,[80] this is a masculine noun meaning "the sky," by extension, or heaven as the abode of God. The term is possibly from the same root as the Greek *oros,*[81] a gender-neutral noun meaning "to rise," or a "mountain," as an elevated above the plains or earth. From Hebrew *shamayim,*[82] a masculine noun from a root meaning "to be lofty," "the sky," "the realm in which the clouds hover," or "the area above where celestial bodies exist." While many believe there are three regions of heaven—the sky above the earth, the zone around the earth wherein spiritual warfare occurs, and the heaven that contains the throne room of God—not all three of these zones are directly referenced in Scripture. However, the Bible does use the word "heaven" to describe a high location upon the earth (Revelation 14:6), to describe the spiritual realm (Ephesians 2:2), and additionally to cite the location of the throne room of God (Revelation 4:1).

Heavenly spheres – This term is used to explain the realms of the heavens, which many scholars believe are divided into a first, second, and third, although not all agree on the placement of these realms. Some place the first heaven directly over the earth and the third in heaven where God dwells, while others believe the opposite: The first heaven is the throne room of God, while the third heaven is the realm directly located around the earth. Within these jurisdictions, many likewise believe that the angels have been dispersed across the three zones within a hierarchy of territory and rank. According to this theory, angels within one sphere are the direct servants of God the Trinity: These are the angels who await His order and those who dwell in the throne room praising: "Worthy is the Lamb that was slain to receive power, and riches, and wisdom, and strength, and honor, and glory, and blessing" (Revelation 5:12). While some view this as the first heaven and others refer to it as the third, it is regardless the outermost layer in proximity to the earth.

Within the middle realm is the region referred to as the second heaven, where spiritual battles take place. Some believe this is a type of barrier around the realm of heaven where God dwells, creating a boundary that Satan and his army aren't allowed to cross without permission from God. The second sphere is also where territorial angels and principalities are believed to do warfare. Many believe this region to be the one referenced in Ephesians 2:2:

> Wherein in the time past ye walked according to the course of this world, according to the prince of the power of the air, the spirit that now worketh in the children of disobedience.

The sphere located directly over the earth is referred to by some as the first and by others as the third heaven. This is the region wherein clouds hover and birds fly, and where anything else that is of the earth, but not directly attached to it, dwells.

The concept of multiple heavens is referred to in Nehemiah 9:6, wherein God is praised as the one who made "heaven, the heaven of heavens, with all their host, the earth, and all things that are therein, the seas, and all that is therein, and…preservest them all." The third heaven is likewise mentioned in Scripture:

> I will come to visions and revelations of the Lord. I knew a man in Christ about 14 years ago, (whether in the body, I cannot tell; or whether out of the body, I cannot tell: God knoweth;) such an one caught up to the third heaven. (2 Corinthians 12:1–2)

Utilizing this passage as a reference, one would place the third heaven as being the throne room of God.

Holy ones – From Aramaic *qaddiysh,*[83] an adjective meaning "saint," or used as one being sacred or hallowed. In Luke 9:26, Jesus referred to His angels as the "holy angels." Likewise, Scripture establishes that holy angels will bear witness to the day of judgment:

> Whosoever shall confess me before men, him shall the Son of man also confess before the angels of God: But he that denieth me before men shall be denied before the angels of God. (Luke 12:8–9)

Hosts – From Hebrew *tsaba*,[84] this is a masculine noun indicating a "mass of people," "an army," or a "company prepared for warfare." The Greek *stratia*,[85] is a feminine noun meaning a "heavenly army" or "troop of celestial luminaries." In Luke 2:13–14, a heavenly host appeared to announce the birth of Jesus by singing, "Glory to God in the highest, and on earth peace, good will toward men."

Living Creatures – This phrase refers to the four beasts mentioned in Revelation that exist in the throne room of God amidst the sea of glass (Revelation 4:6). Each creature is described as slightly different: The first is like a lion, the second is like a calf, the third is like a man, and the fourth is like an eagle (Revelation 4:7). Each has six wings that are full of eyes (Revelation 4:8), and they give glory to God by singing "Holy, holy, holy, Lord God Almighty, which was, and is, and is to come" (Revelation 4:8). The word "beast" in Scripture is from the Greek *zōon*,[86] a gender-neutral noun meaning a "live being" or an "animal." Many scholars explain that several of the original translated synonyms for the term *zōon* emphasize the powerful or spiritual element of a creature, and thereby assert that the translation of *zōon* should likewise highlight the spiritual presence. This argument is further supported by Revelation 4:6–9, 6:1–6, and 15:7, where these beings are clearly seen to be more than mere animals, as they continually worship around the throne and even play certain roles in the passing of prophetic judgments. Acknowledging the spiritual element to the word *zōon* provides that the bestial element of these creatures is diminished, and their status as spiritual, heavenly creatures is confirmed, often rendering the preferred phrase "living creatures" over "four beasts."

Lordship – From Greek *katakyrieuō*, this is a derivative of *kata* (preposition meaning "in relations," "concerning," "or to the charge of") and *kyrieuō* (verb meaning "to have dominion over").[87] See also: *dominions* and *territory*.

Minister – From Greek *diakoneō*,[88] this is a verb meaning "to attend," "wait upon," "teach," "serve," or "act as a deacon." As a noun, the word "minister" refers to one who fills the office of performing these actions in a specific setting. While often a term used to describe a person's role within the early Church, Scripture also states that angels minister (Matthew 4:11, Hebrews 1:14).

Powers – From Greek *exousia,*[89] this is a feminine noun meaning "force," "capacity," or "token of control having delegated influence, authority, or jurisdiction." This term is found in Colossians 1:16 amongst the list of authorities created by God and for God. Ephesians 6:12 lists this as one of the forms of spiritual wickedness found in high places.

Principalities – From Greek *archē,*[90] this is a feminine noun meaning "commencement" or "chief at the first estate, magistrate, power, or rule." This term is on the list in Colossians 1:16 of powers created by God and for God, and is also mentioned in Ephesians 6:12 as one of the forms of spiritual wickedness found in high places.

Prince – From Hebrew *sar,*[91] this is a masculine noun meaning "chief," "ruler," or "governor," "steward," or "taskmaster." This term is usually associated with governmental rule or authority over geographical territory. Daniel 10 refers to the prince of the kingdom of Persia as having detained the angel sent to Daniel in a vision, and against whom Michael the archangel had to do warfare. In Daniel 10:13, Michael is referred to as "one of the chief princes," indicating the use of the term within heavenly realms as well as upon earth, and reinforcing the argument for angels having territorial assignments.

Rulers – See *Principalities.*

Seraphim – From Hebrew *saraph,*[92] this is a masculine noun meaning "fiery or poisonous serpent." The only place these creatures are described in Scripture is in Isaiah 6:1–3, where they're defined as standing above the throne of God, over which they cry "Holy, holy, holy, is the Lord of hosts: the whole earth is full of his glory" (verse 3). This powerful being is described as having six wings, two of which cover his face, two of which cover his feet, and two with which he flies. The creature described in Isaiah 6, being of fiery nature, is described as carrying live coal in his hand that he had taken off the altar of God (Isaiah 6:6), and while knowledge of their nature is limited, the ministerial function of these creatures can be seen in Isaiah 6:7, where the seraphim comforts the prophet Isaiah, assuring that his sin has been cleansed. Because of the fiery, serpentine nature of these creatures, some speculate that Lucifer was originally a member of the order of seraphim within heaven before his fall. These scholars associate his appearance as a serpent in the Garden of Eden (the serpent in Genesis chapter 3 is from the Hebrew *nachash*,[93] a masculine noun meaning "serpent" or "snake"). This possibility is reinforced by the fact that seraphim proclaim praise in the throne room of God, and Scripture states that Lucifer was once a special creature, adorned with precious stones and filled with music (Ezekiel 28:13). Additionally, a position of such leadership might explain why Lucifer was able to convert one-third of God's holy angelic forces (Revelation 12:4).

Sons of God – This phrase is made up of the Hebrew *ben* (a masculine noun meaning "nation," "subject," "appointed," "servant of"[94]) and *'elohiym* (a masculine noun meaning "of the supreme God"[95]). The phrase "sons of God" occurs in Scripture referring to both fallen and holy angels. Genesis 6:2 refers to fallen, or unholy angels: "the sons of God saw the daughters of men that they were fair; and they took them wives all of which they chose." Job 38:7 refers to the sons of God who stood in the presence of God and "shouted for joy" during God's divine act of creation.

Stronghold – From Greek *ochyrōma*,[96] (derivative of the Greek verb *echō*, meaning "to fortify" or "hold safely"[97]), this is a noun meaning "fortress" or "castle." Some believe that strongholds as referred to in Scripture are not merely physical locations, but are territories where spiritual battles occur, as 2 Corinthians 10:3–4 indicates:

> For we walk in the flesh, we do not war after the flesh: For the weapons of our warfare are not carnal, but mighty through God to the pulling down of strongholds.

Territory – This is a noun referring to a geographic zone or designated region. Many biblical scholars believe that angels—both holy and evil—are assigned custodial or protective duties over specific territories. Revelation 12:7–9 reinforces this theory by describing the war in heaven wherein Michael and his angels fought against the dragon (named as the devil, and Satan), after which Satan, along with his unholy angels, was cast out of heaven down to the earth. See also: *dominion*.

Theophany – This term refers to an instance within the Bible where the "Angel of the Lord" appears upon the earth, but whose presence manifests parameters, authority, or ability outside the scope of typical biblical angelic visitation. Many times, these instances can be identified by the being's willingness to be worshiped, the angel's proclamation of being God (or within the same instance being referred to as "the Lord," as seen in Exodus 3:2–6), or in some instances, the capitalization of the letter "A," appearing as the "Angel of the Lord." See also: *Christophany.*

Thrones – Taken from the Greek *thronos,*[98] this is a masculine noun meaning "seat" or "having a footstool." Colossians 1:16 lists thrones as part of a series of assets created by God and for God. Some believe that the term "thrones," appearing as it does in the series in Colossians 1:16, between entities such as principalities and dominions, indicates that thrones are more than a physical seat. This is fortified by other instances in Scripture where a voice emanates from the throne, as though it were an independent creature:

And a voice came out of the throne, saying, Praise our God,
all ye his servants, and ye that fear him, both small and great.
(Revelation 19:5)

While many people maintain that the word "thrones" refers to the seat of authority within a region or territory and *not* to a living entity, others believe this to be another term for Ezekiel's wheels (see also *wheels*).

Virtues – This term occurs in Scripture in more than one way. From

Greek *dynamis*,[99] it is a feminine noun meaning "a literal or figurative force providing miraculous power" or a "worker of miracles." This form of the word "virtue" is found in Mark 5:30, where the woman who had been afflicted with an issue of blood for twelve years touched Jesus' garment for healing. The passage states:

> Straightway the fountain of her blood was dried up; and she felt in her body that she was healed of that plague. And Jesus, immediately knowing in himself that virtue had gone out of him, turned him about in the press, and said, Who touched my clothes?

Some believe that virtue is a living member of the Celestial Order—the source of power behind many miracles—and therefore consider this form of the word to represent an angelic entity. (See also *strongholds, dominions,* and *powers.*)

Another form of the word "virtue" found in Scripture, however, is found in Philippians 4:8:

> If there be any virtue, and if there be any praise, think on these things.

This form of the word "virtue" is taken from the Greek *aretē*,[100] and is a feminine noun meaning "intrinsic or attributed valor, excellence, or praise."

Watcher – From Aramaic `iyr (a masculine noun meaning an "angelic observer"[101]), this is a derivative of Hebrew `uwr (verb meaning "opening of the eyes," "to awaken," or "to raise up").[102] This term is often used to refer to fallen angels who copulated with women in Genesis 6.

Wheels – From Hebrew, `owphan[103] this is a masculine noun referring to "revolve" or "material that revolves." Many believe that Ezekiel chapter 1 outlines a holy, celestial being whose title is "wheel." This being is described in Ezekiel 1:15 as having four faces, and in Ezekiel 1:16 as being "a wheel in the middle of a wheel." While many assert that the wheels presented in Ezekiel are material structures, their status as a spiritual being is detailed in Ezekiel 1:20, where it is said "the spirit of the living creature was in the wheels."

Notes

1. Van Natta, Bruce. *A Miraculous Life: True Stories of Supernatural Encounters with God.* (Lake Mary, FL: Charisma House, 2013) 53.

2. Ibid., 55.

3. Ibid., 56.

4. *A Strange Encounter: A Real Life Angelic Visitation,* CBN, http://www1.cbn.com/video/a-strange-encounter-a-real-life-angelic-visitation (accessed June 12, June 2018).

5. Ibid.

6. Ibid.

7. Ibid.

8. Ibid.

9. Horn, Thomas R. *Spiritual Warfare: The Invisible Invasion.* (Lafayette, Louisiana, 1998).

10. Brinkmann, Sue. "Angels Boards Are Ouija Boards in Disguise." *Women of Grace,* 4 Dec. 2015, http://www.womenofgrace.com/blog/?p=45367 (accessed June 12, 2018).

11. Jules Michelet and Orlando Williams Wight, *Joan of Arc: Or, the Maiden of Orleans—from Michelet's History of France* (Boston, New York: Houghton Mifflin, 1858) 218.

12. Ibid., 220–221.
13. Ibid., 221–222.
14. Ibid., 223–224.
15. Ibid., 228–229.
16. Note that the original trial transcript recorded mostly indirect discourse, not direct exchange of dialogue, which is common. To avoid confusion, the reflection of Joan's trial included herein has been converted only to direct dialogue so the readers of this book may find her account easier to follow, as well as more personal. All dialogue taken from W. P. Barrett et. al., *The Trial of Jeanne D'Arc*.
17. Ibid., 43–45.
18. *Chronique de Charles VII*, as quoted by: "Joan of Arc & Charles VII: First Meeting," *Maid of Heaven*, http://www.maidofheaven.com/joanofarc_charlesvii_firstmeet.asp (last accessed June 21, 2018).
19. W. P. Barrett et. al., *The Trial…*, 46.
20. Ibid., 51–53.
21. Ibid., 60.
22. Ibid., 75.
23. Ibid., 77.
24. Ibid., 125.
25. Ibid., 209.
26. "Text of the Seventh Ecumenical Council," *History and Apologetics*, http://www.historyandapologetics.com/2015/02/text-of-seventh-ecumenical-council.html (last accessed July 2, 2018).
27. Ibid.
28. Ibid.
29. Ibid.
30. Ibid.
31. Ibid.
32. Ibid.

33. Ibid.

34. Ibid., emphasis added.

35. Stephen Rhea and James Hawes, *Angels: Messengers of the Gods* (Alexandria, VA: Non Fiction Films, Café Productions, Little Bird Productions, 1995) 33:47–34:35.

36. *History of Angels* (History Channel: 2015) 33:16–34:01. View this documentary online here: "History of Angels; History Channel 2015 Documentary," uploaded by ShiningStone Documentaries, *Daily Motion* https://www.dailymotion.com/video/x36mggh (last accessed July 18, 2018).

37. Ibid., 35:03–35:15.

38. Dr. Helen Castor, *Joan of Arc: God's Warrior* (BBC, Matchlight: May 26, 2015; originally aired in the UK) 41:58–42:25.

39. *Angels: Messengers of the Gods*, 38:14–40:43; emphasis added.

40. Michelet and Wight, *Joan of Arc*, 230.

41. Ibid., 231.

42. Rachel Gibbons, in an interview toward the beginning of the "Joan of Arc" episode of *Mystery Files* (Parthenon Entertainment Ltd; broadcast on the National Geographic Channel within the UK, 2010; season 1, episode 13) 1:43–1:51.

43. Many biographies of Jonathan Edwards' life reflect this as a fact. Merely as one example: George M. Marsden, *Jonathan Edwards: A Life* (New Haven and London, Yale University Press: 2003; Kindle Edition) Kindle Locations 1913–1917.

44. Griggs, R. A. (2009). *Psychology: A Concise Introduction* (New York, NY: Worth Publishers) 250.

45. Strong's G5613, *Blue Letter Bible Online*, https://www.blueletterbible.org/lang/lexicon/lexicon.cfm?Strongs=G5613&t=KJV (last accessed July 20, 2018).

46. Strong's G2470, *Blue Letter Bible Online*, https://www.blueletterbible.org/lang/lexicon/lexicon.cfm?strongs=G2470&t=KJV (last accessed July 20, 2018).

47. Heiser, Michael S., *Angels: What the Bible Really Says About God's Heavenly Host* (Bellingham, WA: Lexham Press, 2018) 165.

48. Ibid., 164–165.

49. "Did Archaeologists Discover the Biblical City of Sodom?" *Huffington Post*, October 13, 2015. Retrieved from https://www. huffingtonpost.com/entry/did-archaeologists-discover-the-biblical-city-of-sodom_us_561d3810e4b028dd7ea544c5 (accessed October 11, 2018).

50. "Have Sodom and Gomorrah Been Found?" *WND Online*, March 4, 2018. Retrieved from https://www.wnd.com/2018/03/have-sodom-and-gomorrah-been-found/ (accessed August15, 2018).

51. "Strong's H7843," as cited on *Blue Letter Bible*, https://www.blueletterbible.org/lang/lexicon/lexicon. cfm?Strongs=H7843&t=KJV (last accessed October 12, 2018).

52. "Strong's H7200," as cited on *Blue Letter Bible*, https://www.blueletterbible.org/lang/lexicon/lexicon. cfm?Strongs=H7200&t=KJV (last accessed October 12, 2018).

53. "Strong's H1818," as cited on *Blue Letter Bible*, https://www.blueletterbible.org/lang/lexicon/lexicon. cfm?Strongs=H1818&t=KJV (last accessed October 12, 2018).

54. "Strong's H6452," as cited on *Blue Letter Bible*, https://www.blueletterbible.org/lang/lexicon/lexicon. cfm?Strongs=H6452&t=KJV (last accessed October 12, 2018).

55. "Strong's H5063," as cited on *Blue Letter Bible*, https://www.blueletterbible.org/lang/lexicon/lexicon. cfm?Strongs=H5063&t=KJV (last accessed October 12, 2018).

56. "Strong's H4889," as cited on *Blue Letter Bible*, https://www.blueletterbible.org/lang/lexicon/lexicon. cfm?Strongs=H4889&t=KJV (last accessed October 12, 2018).

57. "Strong's H5221," as cited on *Blue Letter Bible*, https://www.blueletterbible.org/lang/lexicon/lexicon. cfm?Strongs=H5221&t=KJV (last accessed October 12, 2018).

58. "Strong's H776," as cited on *Blue Letter Bible*, https://www.blueletterbible.org/lang/lexicon/lexicon.cfm?Strongs=H776&t=KJV (last accessed October 12, 2018).

59. "Strong's H4714," as cited on *Blue Letter Bible*, https://www.blueletterbible.org/lang/lexicon/lexicon.cfm?Strongs=H4714&t=KJV (last accessed October 12, 2018).

60. "Strong's H4397," as cited on *Blue Letter Bible*, https://www.blueletterbible.org/lang/lexicon/lexicon.cfm?Strongs=H4397&t=KJV (last accessed October 12, 2018).

61. "Strong's H3068," as cited on *Blue Letter Bible*, https://www.blueletterbible.org/lang/lexicon/lexicon.cfm?Strongs=H3068&t=KJV (last accessed October 12, 2018).

62. McClaflin, Mike. *The Life of Christ in the Synoptic Gospels* (Springfield, MO: Global University, 2017) 69.

63. Ibid.

64. Ibid.

65. Blue Letter Bible (2018) Retrieved from: https://www.blueletterbible.org/lang/lexicon/lexicon.cfm?Strongs=G792&t=KJV (accessed August 16, 2018).

66. White, Leslie. *6 Signs You're Being Visited by Your Guardian Angel.* 2018. Beliefnet.com. Retrieved from http://www.beliefnet.com/inspiration/angels/6-signs-youre-being-visited-by-your-guardian-angel.aspx?p=2 (accessed September 20, 2018).

67. Ibid.

68. Bell, Caleb. *Poll: Americans Love the Bible but Don't Read It Much,* April 4, 2013, ReligionNews.com. Retrieved from https://religionnews.com/2013/04/04/poll-americans-love-the-bible-but-dont-read-it-much/ (accessed September 20, 2018).

69. Whiteheart. "Gabriela." Recorded 1992. Track 9 on *Tales of Wonder.* Star Song Music. Compact Disc.

70. Ibid.

71. Josh Peck, *I Predict!* (Crane, MO: Defender Publishing, 2016) 158.

72. Ibid, 159.

73. "D810 Touch Pro Pack," Leica Geosystems, 2018. Retrieved from https://lasers.leica-geosystems.com/disto-pro-packs/d810-touch-pro-pack?c1=GAW_SE_NW&source=PLA_USA&cr2=USA__-__Leica__-__ PLA&kw=806648&cr6=pla&cr7=c&gclid=EAIaIQobChMIvbWWpNrH3QIVHLbACh1r6QcpEAQYASABEgKsHfD_BwE (accessed September 19, 2018).

74. Eklektos. In *Blue Letter Bible Online Edition.* Retrieved from https://www.blueletterbible.org/lang/lexicon/lexicon.cfm?Strongs=G1588&t=KJV (accessed September 20, 2018).

75. Mesouranēma. In *Blue Letter Bible Online Edition.* Retrieved from https://www.blueletterbible.org/lang/lexicon/lexicon.cfm?Strongs=G3321&t=KJV (accessed September 20, 2018).

76. "Strong's H4397," as cited on *Blue Letter Bible*, https://www.blueletterbible.org/lang/lexicon/lexicon.cfm?Strongs=H4397&t=KJV (last accessed September 21, 2018).

77. "Strong's G743," as cited on *Blue Letter Bible*, https://www.blueletterbible.org/lang/lexicon/lexicon.cfm?Strongs=G743&t=KJV (last accessed September 28, 2018).

78. "Strong's H3742," as cited on *Blue Letter Bible*, https://www.blueletterbible.org/lang/lexicon/lexicon.cfm?Strongs=H3742&t=KJV (last accessed on September 28, 2018).

79. "Strong's G2963," as cited on *Blue Letter Bible*, https://www.blueletterbible.org/lang/lexicon/lexicon.cfm?Strongs=G2963&t=KJV (last accessed September 28, 2018).

80. "Strong's G3772," as cited on *Blue Letter Bible*, https://www.blueletterbible.org/lang/lexicon/lexicon.cfm?Strongs=G3772&t=KJV (last accessed September 29, 2018).

81. "Strong's G3735," as cited on *Blue Letter Bible*, https://www.blueletterbible.org/lang/lexicon/lexicon.cfm?strongs=G3735&t=KJV (last accessed September 29, 2018).

82. "Strong's H8064," as cited on *Blue Letter Bible*, https://www.blueletterbible.org/lang/lexicon/lexicon.cfm?Strongs=H8064&t=KJV (last accessed September 29, 2018).

83. "Strong's H6922," as cited on *Blue Letter Bible*, https://www.blueletterbible.org/lang/lexicon/lexicon.cfm?Strongs=H6922&t=KJV (last accessed September 28, 2018).

84. "Strong's H6635," as cited on *Blue Letter Bible*, https://www.blueletterbible.org/lang/lexicon/lexicon.cfm?Strongs=H6635&t=KJV (last accessed September 28, 2018).

85. "Strong's G4756," as cited on *Blue Letter Bible*, https://www.blueletterbible.org/lang/lexicon/lexicon.cfm?Strongs=G4756&t=KJV (last accessed September 28, 2018).

86. "Strong's G2226," as cited on *Blue Letter Bible*, https://www.blueletterbible.org/lang/lexicon/lexicon.cfm?Strongs=G2226&t=KJV (last accessed September 29, 2018).

87. "Strong's G2634," as cited on *Blue Letter Bible*, https://www.blueletterbible.org/lang/lexicon/lexicon.cfm?Strongs=G2634&t=KJV (last accessed September 28, 2018).

88. "Strong's G1247," as cited on *Blue Letter Bible*, https://www.blueletterbible.org/lang/lexicon/lexicon.cfm?Strongs=G1247&t=KJV (last accessed September 28, 2018).

89. "Strong's G1849," as cited on *Blue Letter Bible*, https://www.blueletterbible.org/lang/lexicon/lexicon.cfm?Strongs=G1849&t=KJV (last accessed September 28, 2018).

90. "Strong's G746," as cited on *Blue Letter Bible*, https://www.blueletterbible.org/lang/lexicon/lexicon.cfm?Strongs=G746&t=KJV (last accessed September 28, 2018).

91. "Strong's H8269," as cited on *Blue Letter Bible*, https://www.blueletterbible.org/lang/lexicon/lexicon.cfm?Strongs=H8269&t=KJV (last accessed September 28, 2018).

92. "Strong's H8314," as cited on *Blue Letter Bible*, (https://www.blueletterbible.org/lang/lexicon/lexicon.cfm?Strongs=H8314&t=KJV (last accessed September 29, 2018).

93. "Strong's H5175," as cited on *Blue Letter Bible*, https://www.blueletterbible.org/lang/lexicon/lexicon. cfm?Strongs=H5175&t=KJV (last accessed September 29, 2018).

94. "Strong's H1121," as cited on *Blue Letter Bible*, https://www.blueletterbible.org/lang/lexicon/lexicon. cfm?Strongs=H1121&t=KJV (last accessed September 28, 2018).

95. "Strong's H430," as cited on *Blue Letter Bible*, https://www.blueletterbible.org/lang/lexicon/lexicon. cfm?Strongs=H430&t=KJV (last accessed September 28, 2018).

96. "Strong's G3794," as cited on *Blue Letter Bible*, https://www.blueletterbible.org/lang/lexicon/lexicon. cfm?Strongs=G3794&t=KJV (last accessed September 28, 2018).

97. "Strong's G2192," as cited on *Blue Letter Bible*, https://www. blueletterbible.org/lang/lexicon/lexicon.cfm?Strongs=G2192 (last accessed on September 28, 2018).

98. "Strong's G2362," as cited on *Blue Letter Bible*, https://www.blueletterbible.org/lang/lexicon/lexicon. cfm?Strongs=G2362&t=KJV (last accessed September 21, 2018.)

99. "Strong's G1411," as cited on *Blue Letter Bible*, https://www.blueletterbible.org/lang/lexicon/lexicon. cfm?Strongs=G1411&t=KJV (last accessed September 28, 2018).

100. "Strong's G703," as cited on *Blue Letter Bible*, https://www.blueletterbible.org/lang/lexicon/lexicon. cfm?Strongs=G703&t=KJV (last accessed September 28, 2018).

101. "Strong's H5894," as cited on *Blue Letter Bible*, https://www.blueletterbible.org/lang/lexicon/lexicon. cfm?Strongs=H5894&t=KJV (last accessed September 28, 2018).

102. "Strong's H5782," as cited on *Blue Letter Bible*, https://www.blueletterbible.org/lang/lexicon/lexicon. cfm?strongs=H5782&t=KJV (last accessed September 28, 2018).

103. "Strong's H212," as cited on *Blue Letter Bible*, https://www.blueletterbible.org/lang/lexicon/lexicon. cfm?Strongs=H212&t=KJV (last accessed September 21, 2018).